Praise for *Melting Point*

'Ingenious . . . wonderfully vital and idiosyncratic,
a model of how history writing can be made fresh . . .
an innovative and immediate account of a story that
has world-historical significance.' – *Guardian*

'Cockerell tells the entire story through extracts from
newspaper reports, letters, memoirs, documents and
interviews. This is an ambitious and high-risk venture.
Yet she pulls it off with verve. She handles her material
with a maestro's touch.' – *The Times*

'Truly ground-breaking . . . I have not enjoyed a book so
much for years.' – **Antony Beevor**

'Eclectic, fascinating . . . Cockerell shows, doesn't tell,
and the reader is left to consider how no family's story
can be disentangled from history's complex web.'
– *New Statesman*

'Nothing less than an alternative history of the twentieth
century . . . the radical implications of Cockerell's
narrative sneak up on you. But they are likely to linger
long after the last page has been read.' – *TLS*

'A work of history that reads like a novel . . . bristles into
vivid, bustling life.' – **Robert Macfarlane**

'So fascinating, so enjoyable, and beautifully told.'
– **Simon Sebag Montefiore**

'A fabulous family history . . . Cockerell has an unerring eye for selecting, editing and juxtaposing the most revealing quotations. So the result feels deeply immersive and dramatic. One gets a thrilling sense of history unfolding in real time, of people confused and flailing about in response to immediate events without any sense of what we know now. Exceptionally vivid and compelling.' – *Observer*

'Cockerell's approach, drawing together a vast range of original source material, brings her cast of characters to life with vivacity, their idiosyncrasies and foibles intact.' – *Telegraph*

'Spectacularly successful, a joy to be immersed in. Spellbinding' – **Simon Schama**

'A bold and provocative book' – *Literary Review*

'A truly radical book; radical in subject, radical in form. For the most tragic Reasons, it could not feel more immediate; and yet it's a fluid, fast-paced, hugely enjoyable and engaging read.' – **Andrew Marr**

'Meticulously researched, elegantly constructed, unforgettable.' – **Jonathan Freedland**

'This is an extraordinarily original way of writing memoir, history and truth. An enthralling book and a wonderful new writer.' – **Laura Cumming**

'Utterly compelling, at times amusing, at times heartbreaking. The characters of *Melting Point* will live with you long after the final page.' – **Antonia Fraser**

'Electric . . . I can scarcely think of a book I've read in years that will stay with me as this has.' – *Jewish Chronicle*

'A fascinating saga, full of unexpected twists and encounters ranging across continents, compellingly told through contemporary snippets and insights. A bold and surprisingly successful formula.' – **Adam Zamoyski**

'Rachel Cockerell has crafted a superbly original work of narrative history – an epic tale of memory and migration. It would be difficult to read this book and remain unmoved.' – **Francisco Garcia**

'Strikingly original . . . Cockerell succeeds admirably in her stated intention to tell this little-known story in a way that is more like a novel than a work of history.' – *The Bookseller*

'A captivating exploration of identity and a search for belonging, a quest that reverberates into the present.' – *Financial Times*

Rachel Cockerell was born and raised in London, the sixth of seven children. She did her BA at the Courtauld Institute and her MA at City University. *Melting Point* is her first non-fiction book. Her research has taken her to Texas, Ohio, New York, Tel Aviv and Jerusalem.

Rachel Cockerell

Melting Point

WILDFIRE

First published in 2024 by WILDFIRE
an imprint of Headline Publishing Group Limited

This paperback edition published in 2025

3

The quotations on page 51 and 71 are reproduced with permission of
Curtis Brown Ltd., London, on behalf of The Estate of Sir Winston Churchill.
Copyright Winston S. Churchill.

The image on page 60 is from the Herzl and Zionism Collection of
David Matlow, Toronto, Canada (www.herzlcollection.com)

The originals of the images on page 31, 33, 38 and 93 are held at the
Central Zionist Archives, Jerusalem.

Cataloguing in Publication Data is available from the British Library.

Paperback ISBN 978 1 0354 0893 1

Designed and typeset by EM&EN
Printed and bound in Great Britain by Clays Ltd, Elcograf S.p.A.

Headline's policy is to use papers that are natural, renewable and recyclable
products and made from wood grown in well-managed forests and other
controlled sources. The logging and manufacturing processes are expected
to conform to the environmental regulations of the country of origin.

Headline Publishing Group Limited
An Hachette UK Company
Carmelite House
50 Victoria Embankment
London EC4Y 0DZ

The authorized representative in the EEA is Hachette Ireland,
8 Castlecourt Centre, Dublin 15, D15 XTP3, Ireland (email: info@hbgi.ie)

www.headline.co.uk
www.hachette.co.uk

For Jo

Author's Note

Spellings, especially the names of far-flung places and people, were more open to interpretation at the beginning of the twentieth century. I have left them unchanged, in part to illustrate (as one character says in the book) that 'the distance between countries was greater than it is now, mentally.'

I have also left grammar and punctuation as it originally appeared.

Some sources have been edited down for clarity, but never added to.

Contents

If we cannot get the Holy Land,
we can make another land holy.

- *Israel Zangwill, 1906*

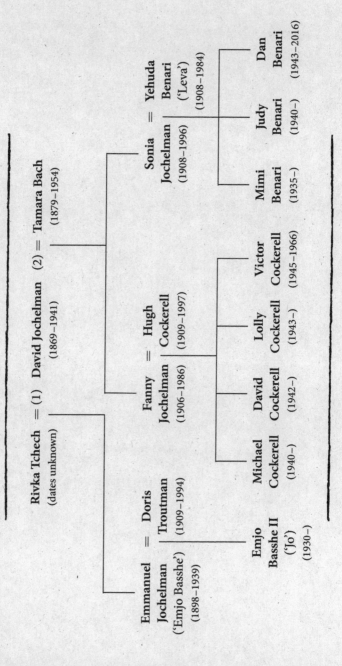

Preface

This book consists entirely of memories – taken from diaries, letters, memoirs, articles and recordings. They reinforce each other, bristle against each other, converse with each other, and come together to build a story which, I hope, has a memory-like quality: elastic, shifting, filled with small details. The book explores a line said by one of the characters: 'You can't trust witnesses.'

I have always instinctively recoiled from books that claim to be 'experimental', but I hope in this case the form serves the function. My first draft was written conventionally, with my own narrative woven through primary sources. As I revised, I began to notice my irritation at my own interjections, and found myself reaching to delete them.

Everything I said fell into three categories: a twenty-first-century-tinged observation, a paraphrase of a primary source, or a description of a character's feelings. All of them felt useless. The first took the reader out of the story, the second could be substituted with the original quotation, and the third could be shown, not told. At the time I was listening to a lot of interviews with George Saunders, whose 2017 Booker-winning *Lincoln in the Bardo* had lodged in my brain. The novel is set in the American Civil War, and contains real nineteenth-century accounts. 'The question was,' Saunders said in one interview, 'how do you get all this historical backstory in? I turned to myself and said, "Put it into the reader's head the way it got into your head."'

I gradually began to delete more and more of my own 'voiceover'. At a certain point I realised it might be possible to tell the entire story through the eyes of those who were there, and create something that felt more like a novel than a history.

A line from Robert Macfarlane's *The Old Ways* has been with me constantly for the last three years. 'The past felt fissile, its recovery only partially possible at best. There is dust on the phonograph needle: voices, if heard at all, reach us through a burr of distortion, or are snatched briefly from the static as we twist the tuning wheel.' Above all this book is an attempt to transport myself back in time, to see things as they really were. Sometimes, after finding one evocative sentence in an otherwise dull and lengthy hundred-year-old newspaper article, smudged with ink and almost illegible, I knew I had only caught a glimpse of the past, heard the faintest, most distant voice. Other times, I would stumble out of a day of research feeling like I had been transported to the cobbled streets of Vienna in 1897, the oleander-lined boulevards of Galveston in 1911, the cacophonous alleys of the Lower East Side of New York in 1926, the bomb-ravaged terraces of London in 1944, or the unpaved tracks of Jerusalem in 1951.

***

The book began as the story of my grandmother and her sister, who raised their children together in a giant, Edwardian North London house in the 1940s. Their father, David Jochelmann, had bought 22 Mapesbury Road soon after the family arrived in England from Kyiv at the outbreak of the First World War. I thought perhaps at the start of the book I should mention how and why they came to England – in a sentence or two, a paragraph at most. My dad, his siblings and his cousins had always maintained that David Jochelmann was a businessman, involved somehow in stocks and shares. The only other fact they knew about him was that as soon as he landed on British shores he removed the extra 'n' from the family surname, for fear of sounding German. I imagined he had a banking job in Kyiv, and he was transferred to London. However, being an assiduous researcher, I decided I might as well double-check, so I googled him – just to see what, if anything, came up.

A surprising number of search results appeared, and none of them mentioned stocks or shares. Instead, his name always appeared in the same sentence as the word Galveston. What, or who, was Galveston, I wondered, vaguely annoyed that my neat summation of my great-grandfather was threatening to become more complicated. (Unfortunately I was not taught much Texan geography at school.) Eventually I discovered that Galveston was not a person but a place, and the destination for 10,000 Jews in the years leading up to the First World War – sent there from Russia by my great-grandfather. None of my family knew about this: at some point the story of the Galveston Plan, and my great-grandfather's role in it, was lost down the generations. Perhaps David Jochelmann told his daughters about his work in Russia, or perhaps, as a new arrival in England in the 1910s and '20s, his pre-war existence belonged to a lost world. 'I think how little we can hold in mind,' wrote W. G. Sebald, 'how everything is constantly lapsing into oblivion with every extinguished life, how the world is, as it were, draining itself.'

The Galveston Plan was part of the search for a temporary Jewish homeland that took place in the early twentieth century, a search that looked beyond Palestine to Kenya (mistakenly identified at the time as Uganda), Australia, Canada, Mexico and many other places. In hindsight, the idea of establishing a Jewish state in any of these countries seems slightly surreal, but they were all

3

seriously considered. A Jewish homeland in Palestine was only one of several possibilities: as one character in the book says, 'It's never inevitable at the time.'

My family's arrival in England had roots that seemed to go deeper and deeper. I learnt that the Galveston Plan was a direct result of the early Zionist movement, another subject I knew nothing about. There was a vague link in my mind between Zionism and the name Theodor Herzl, but I imagined him as a wizened, solemn figure with a white beard, stranded in a bygone era. I soon realised my mistake: Herzl was a charismatic Viennese journalist who founded the Zionist movement aged thirty-five, and half thought he would soon return to his articles and columns. I had certainly never heard of Israel Zangwill, the most famous Jewish figure in the English-speaking world at the turn of the century, and an early adopter of Zionism, but I soon began to understand his significance – both to the early twentieth century and to my family. The Canadian novelist Emily St. John Mandel has written about 'the pieces of a pattern drifting closer together': Zionism is an unlikely place for this story to begin, but it set the trajectory for all that followed.

A few months into my research, I discovered that David Jochelmann had been married before he met my great-grandmother. He and his first wife lived in Vilna, Lithuania, and had three children. Their youngest son, Emmanuel, born in 1898, was sent to America aged fourteen. David accompanied him across the Atlantic on the *Kaiser Wilhelm II*, which docked in New York in October 1912, six months after the sinking of the *Titanic*. As a young man Emmanuel became a playwright, founding a theatre which aimed to reflect life in 1920s New York and 'the rush and roar of things as they are'. In 1929 he married Doris Elisa Troutman, an actress from North Carolina, and in 1930 they had a daughter, half a Southerner and half a Russian-Jewish New Yorker.

I wondered for a while how to structure the story, until I realised it naturally fell into three parts. The first part is about Zionism, Galveston, the scouring of the globe for a homeland outside Palestine, and my great-grandfather's role in some of this. Part Two takes place after Emmanuel's arrival in New York. Part Three begins with David's arrival in England with his second wife and their two daughters: my grandmother, Fanny, and her sister, Sonia. And, eventually, it is the story of Sonia and Fanny's children – including my dad, Michael.

Unlike the other figures in the book, my great-grandfather wrote nothing about himself. He was, as one character puts it, 'a mysteriously (and deliberately) unpublicized personage'. He does not appear until a quarter of the way through, although he witnessed the earlier events. He is the almost silent figure at the heart of *Melting Point*. My only image of him growing up took the form of a huge, sombre portrait, probably painted in the 1920s, which hangs in the living room at Mapesbury Road, where my dad grew up. He has dark hair and dark clothes, and seems about to be enveloped by the surrounding gloom – a perfect metaphor for the obscurity

he has fallen into, even for his family, since he died. My three-year attempt to grapple with this evasive figure is encapsulated in a line from Laura Cumming's *On Chapel Sands*: 'And though he is my grandfather, and I have his blood, he is like all long-distant ancestors to me – these people of the past who elude us, no matter how hard we try to drag them back out of time's tide.' I hope if he were somehow alive today and read this book, he would be amazed at how much of his life, and the world he lived in, has been dragged back from time's tide.

Part One

Vienna, Basel, Galveston

Chapter 1

London Star, 1901 A year ago, while I was drinking afternoon tea in a London drawing room, there entered a tall, lithe man, with coal black hair, beard and mustaches, restless visionary eyes, and a nervous mouth, twitching with half sad humour. I did not know him, but he magnetised me immediately.

At that time Herzl could not speak a word of English. After a few commonplaces he drifted away again, leaving me profoundly interested in his romantic genius. He had done nothing, said nothing, but he had been himself. Now, the man who can be himself in a drawing room is rare. And this man's self was so bizarre, so disturbing, so strange, that I caught myself wondering at its persistence in my mind. Why should I keep in my memory so clear a picture of Herzl when so many other men and women fade out of it like shadows of shadows?

In appearance, Herzl is not only handsome, but royal – tall, broad-shouldered, with finely shaped head and features.

Ray Frank, *American Hebrew*, 1898

Those who see him for the first time are at once both attracted and repelled. He has the face and bearing of a king, with a reserve which at first keeps the stranger at a distance, but he quickly fascinates by the dignity of his bearing and by the classic beauty of his face and figure.

William Durban, *Pall Mall Gazette*

An artist might paint him, and without the slightest idealization, make an ideal picture. Tall, handsome, black-bearded, clear-eyed, erect in bearing, suave in manner, he looks like kings ought to look.

Cyrus L. Sulzberger

He was graceful in every movement. Without posing, he assumed a royal air, and even those to whom nothing of him was a mystery, could never rid themselves of a certain awe and reverence which his presence compelled. His individuality was striking, and he was fully conscious of it; he liked to be surrounded by friends. In society he would flash a hundred phrases of polished thought. He had a wonderful capacity for detail, and would throw an odd phrase back at one, years after its utterance.

Jacob de Haas

I still remember the first time I saw you. You were making a speech, and being 'sharp' – so sharp! You were smiling ironically. And I began to envy you. If only I could speak and smile in that way, I thought to myself. I remember a meeting with you at some ball or other one night. I was in a particularly happy mood that evening and, as I thought, inexpressibly elegant. Then you appeared. With a steady haughty glance you examined my tie and crushed me. It was clear that I must learn how to make up my ties better, or at least to do something distinguished in some other field.

Arthur Schnitzler to Theodor Herzl

Leon Kellner

I regard him as the most successful man I know. When I meet him in the street in Vienna I always join him even if he is going north while I intended going south, for invariably Herzl is going right.

Vladimir Jabotinsky

Theodor Herzl made a colossal impression on me. This is no exaggeration. There is no other word for it: colossal. Altogether, in my life's experience, I do not remember anybody who 'made an impression' on me, either before Herzl or after him.

Pall Mall Gazette,
1897

Dr. Herzl has practised law and written plays, and is now one of the best known journalists and literary men in Austria.

Stefan Zweig

He had become the darling of the Vienna public. His readers were fascinated by his essays, now faintly tinged with melancholy, now brilliantly sparkling, full of profound pathos, and yet as lucid as crystal. None was more beloved, better known or more celebrated than he among the entire bourgeoisie – and also the aristocracy – of old Austria. To me his authority was the highest, his judgment fundamental and absolute. And thus, when I wrote my first short story – I was then nineteen years old – it never occurred to me to submit it to any one but him. As I did not know him personally, and had no means of meeting him, I chose, with the happy naïveté and now irretrievably lost courage of youth, the simplest way of all: to look him up in the editorial office of his paper.

I had made inquiry as to his office hours, which, I believe, were from two to three o'clock in the afternoon; and one fine day I simply went to see him. To my surprise, I was admitted at once; to my even greater amazement, into a very narrow little room with but one window, a room reeking with dust and printer's ink. And suddenly, before I had collected my thoughts, I stood before him;

and he had risen politely and offered me a chair beside his desk.

His natural, charming courtesy cast its spell upon me at that first moment and at every one of our later meetings. The character of that courtesy was French, but his majestic appearance unquestionably gave it something of the dignity of kings or great diplomats. His very physical appearance was sufficient to cause everyone to defer to him involuntarily.

He welcomed me in friendly fashion, and asked me what I had brought him. Wasting no time with introductions, I stammered words to the effect that I wanted to submit a story to him. He took it from me, counted the pages of the manuscript, regarded the first page with great interest, leaned back in his chair. It was with a certain feeling of terror that I watched him begin to read in my presence. The minutes seemed to pass slowly; but this first view of his face, seen from one side, made a deep impression upon me. It was a faultlessly handsome face. The soft, well-kept black beard gave it a clear, almost rectangular outline, into which the clean-cut nose, set exactly in the middle, fitted well, as did also the high, slightly rounded forehead. But this beauty – perhaps almost too regular, too much like a work of art – was deepened by the almond-shaped eyes with their heavy black, melancholy lashes – ancient Oriental eyes in this somewhat French face, in this face which would have seemed slightly artificial or effeminate, or suggestive of the beau, had not the thousand-year-old melancholy of his soul shone through it. He seemed to notice that I was observing him, for once, as he turned a page, he looked at me keenly, but not severely. He was used to being regarded; perhaps he even liked it.

Finally he turned over the last page, and went through a remarkable performance: shaking the pages into place, he put them together, wrote something on them with a blue pencil, and put them into a drawer on his left. Only then, after these curious actions, evidently intended for effect (for he was never free from a strange theatrical pose), did he turn to me and say, conscious of making a great announcement: 'Your story is accepted.'

***

Theodor Herzl,
June 1895

For some time past, I have been occupied with a work of infinite grandeur. At the moment I do not know if I shall complete it. It has the appearance of a dream, but for days and weeks it has possessed me beyond the limits of consciousness. It accompanies me wherever I go, it hovers over my ordinary conversation, looks over my shoulder at my comically trivial journalistic work, haunts me and intoxicates me.

It is still too early to surmise what will come of it. But my experience tells me that even as a dream it is something remarkable, and that I ought to write it down – if not as a reminder to mankind, then at least for my own delight or reflection in later years. And if my conception is not translated into reality, at least out of my activity can come a novel. Title: The Promised Land.

I wrote walking, standing, lying down, on the street, at the table, at night when it roused me out of my sleep. I cannot remember ever having written anything in such a mood of exaltation. Heine tells us that he heard the flapping of eagles' wings above his head when he wrote certain verses. I too seemed to hear the flutter of wings above my head while I wrote this book. I worked on it every day until I was quite exhausted. When I had finished it, I offered the manuscript to one of my oldest friends to read. While he was reading it he suddenly began to weep. This I found quite natural, because he was a Jew; while writing it I had often wept myself. But to my consternation he gave quite other grounds for his tears. He thought I had gone out of my mind, and because he was my friend, my misfortune made him most unhappy.

As the century approached its close, there gradually penetrated a rumour (for no one ever dreamed of reading his pamphlet) that this graceful, aristocratic, masterly causeur had, without warning, written an abstruse treatise which demanded nothing less than that the Jews should leave their Ringstrasse homes and their villas, their businesses and their offices – in short, that they should emigrate, bag and baggage, to Palestine, there establish a nation.

I can still remember the general astonishment and annoyance of the bourgeois Jewish circles of Vienna. What had happened, they said angrily, to this otherwise intelligent, witty, and cultivated writer? What foolishness is this that he has thought up and writes about? Why should we go to Palestine? Our language is German and not Hebrew, and Austria is our homeland. Why does he attempt to separate us, when every day brings us more closely and intimately into the German world?

Stefan Zweig

In Vienna, he caught looks and hints: 'A very gifted man, indeed a man of genius, but unfortunately something is not quite right – you know, the business with the Jewish state.' Many had supposed that Herzl would abandon the Jewish theme after that peculiar aberration, and return to writing beautiful, innocuous, completely non-political feuilletons.

Erwin Rosenberger

When he entered the theatre, a sibilation arose on all sides: 'His Majesty has arrived.' This ironic title peered at him through every conversation, every glance.

Stefan Zweig

Dr. Beck, my parents' old family physician, has examined me and diagnosed a heart ailment caused by excitement. He cannot understand why I concern myself with the Jewish cause, and among the Jews he associates with, no one understands it either. Acquaintances ask me:

Theodor Herzl

14

'Is that pamphlet people are talking about by you? Is it a joke or something meant to be serious?'

Stefan Zweig

Vienna, where he thought himself most secure because he had been beloved there for so many years, not only deserted him but even laughed at him. But then the answer roared suddenly back with such force that he was almost frightened to see how mighty a movement he had brought into being with his few dozen pages. True, it did not come from the well-situated, comfortable bourgeois Jews of the West but from the gigantic masses of the East, from the Galicians, the Polish, the Russians of the ghetto.

Shmarya Levin

Theodor Herzl came into the orbit of Jewish life with the unexpectedness and the mysteriousness of a comet. To us, to Russian Jewry, only the fanlike rays of the comet were visible, and the great voice reached us from a distance. Overnight the name Theodor Herzl became a household word. No one had seen the man, but stories were told about him which already bore the character of legends.

Chaim Weizmann

The personality of Herzl grew not only in the eyes of those who came into direct contact with him but also in those of people who never saw him. He became a monumental, mythical Jewish figure – something of a legend. Herzl's brochure did not remain just on paper. The message was soon passed on to every town, great or small, in Poland and Russia in which a Jewish ghetto existed.

Utica Sunday Journal

Recent movements seem to indicate that the wandering Jew is near the end of his wanderings.

Jersey City News

That one watchword, the 'Jewish State,' has been sufficient to rouse the Jews to a state of enthusiasm in the remotest corners of the earth.

Middlesex Gazette

If the project reaches realisation it will have to be considered as one of the world's marvels. Imagine the spectacle of a million or more men and women, scattered all over the face of the earth at present, journeying back to the place of the origination of their race – with all its peculiarities intact – after eighteen centuries of persecution.

Until about thirty years ago old men made pilgrimages in order that their bones might be laid to rest in the sacred soil. When a Jew died in Europe a little of the dust of Palestine was sprinkled over his closed eyes.

Pall Mall Gazette

It has always been the pious Jew's desire 'to die in Jerusalem;' to be buried in the holy ground with his forefathers. Today the young generation joins the old in the wish to go to Palestine not to die, but to live.

Wichita Daily Eagle

We are face to face with a new phenomenon. The astonishing sight is now presented of the revival of the old, and as one imagined dead, ideal of a Jewish nationality. Dr Herzl takes a dark and discouraging view. Anti-Semitism, he holds, changes its dress but not its essence. He foresees coming storms all over the civilised world. From these catastrophes there is, in his view, no possible escape, unless the Jews deliberately determine to remove themselves from the storm-laden atmosphere before the irresistible doom breaks over them. We find it ourselves hard to accept these gloomy prognostications. We hardly anticipate a great future for a scheme which is the outcome of despair. But we do not wish to anticipate our reader's judgment.

Jewish Chronicle

It will be interesting to glance at this country.

Elmira Morning Telegram

The entire country is only 150 miles long and 80 miles wide at the widest part. The area is smaller than the State of New Jersey.

New York Sun

The climate of Palestine is very much like that of southern California. It is claimed that the soil of Palestine,

Elmira Morning Telegram

which is generally considered unproductive, is barren because it has been deserted for centuries. All that Palestine needs to restore it to its pristine fertility is the work of men's hands. Let the trees be restored, the wells dug as of old, and the holy land will again flow with milk and honey. Even now, desolate as it is, burning in the blazing sun, and left to be the home of the Bedouin and the desert dweller, Palestine produces apricots as sweet as any on earth, oranges and lemons, figs and dates; olives, from which oil as clear as water is pressed.

Julius Uprimny,
Maccabaean

Herzl has realized the dream of every man to make for himself a name famous in every clime. His friends marvel at his unceasing activity. He is always at work either receiving people, attending conferences, writing letters or doing his literary work. One task follows the other in quick succession, but everything is executed thoroughly down to the minutest details. The few moments he can spare from his work he is anxious to devote to his private life. Dr. Herzl resides in the suburbs where the cultured classes of Vienna live. His reception room is at the same time his library and study. The walls are hidden by bookcases, with everything in the neatest order. A youthful portrait of the occupant of the room has space on the wall.

The most striking piece of furniture in this study is the desk. The desk appears striking because of an arrangement of pigeon-holes, which contain documents and other papers carefully arranged in a manner liked by Dr. Herzl. Nothing is untidy; even the bunch of cigars and Viennese holders have their fixed place. Herzl is intensely methodical; he opens his letters with care, and the gist of each one is caught in a single glance, and is assigned to its place for immediate answer or reference. This room is the scene of the evening reunion of the whole family. This is the happiest hour that is spent by them. In the

midst of this sits Dr. Herzl and – works. The prattling of his children is to the ears of the loving father music which quickens his thoughts.

To understand Theodor Herzl you need but watch the flash of his magnetic eyes; they are constantly changing; and while you read there the power to dream, you gather in a restful moment an idea of unflinching determination and patience.

***

The campaign's centre of gravity is shifted to London. Visit to Israel Zangwill, the writer. He lives in Kilburn, N.W. A drive in the fog through endless streets. Arrived a bit out of sorts. The house is rather shabby. In his book-lined

Theodor Herzl, 21 November 1895

study Zangwill sits before an enormous writing table with his back to the fireplace. Also close to the fire, his brother, reading.

Israel Zangwill is of the long-nosed Negroid type, with very woolly deep-black hair, parted in the middle. The disorder in his room and on his desk leads me to infer that he is an internalised person. I have not read any of his writings, but I think I know him.

Israel Zangwill

I was the first person that Dr. Herzl came to in London. He had heard of me, but I had never heard of him then.

Louis Zangwill

I have the most vivid recollection of that bitterly freezing afternoon – between two blizzards – of Thursday, November 21, 1895. As Herzl appeared, framed in the doorway, his handsome presence and extraordinarily stately demeanour at once made a deep impression on us. He was obviously 'foreign': you would take him at a glance as a personage of distinction, playing a high part in some one of the European capitals. That sombre face, with its contemplative eyes, framed by the black beard, once seen, was unforgettable. A remarkable contrast, indeed, to the English type of 'gentleman.' His waistcoat was cut low, revealing a long length of shirt front, and his frock-coat with its voluminous skirts was, in its lines, of a turn quite alien to Savile Row. The English 'gentleman' of the day had a bluff breeziness – a free, frank approach. Herzl was neither bluff nor breezy. His gravity of demeanour exercised an immediate charm of its own. He spoke on calmly and earnestly, yet at times rising, and addressing us standing.

Israel Zangwill

He was a man of striking personal beauty, with a long black beard and glowing eyes, and the face of the old Assyrian Kings. His manner was courtly, his conversation fascinating.

Our conversation is laborious. We speak in French, his command of which is inadequate. I don't even know whether he understands me. Still, we agree on major points.

Theodor Herzl

A black-bearded stranger knocked at my study-door, like one dropped from the skies, and said: 'I am Theodor Herzl. Help me to rebuild the Jewish State.'

Israel Zangwill

Chapter 2

Referee, 1891 There is a new writer of the astonishing name of Zangwill.

Vogue, 1896 When, about five years ago, the name I. Zangwill began to appear, many people must, like myself, have believed it to be a pseudonym. Then, as books bearing the name began to be praised for the brilliancy of their wit and style, it was discovered that there really was such a person as I. Zangwill; and that he was a young Hebrew.

G. B. Burgin, Harper's Weekly Walk down Fleet Street some bright spring afternoon, and see Zangwill come slowly along, peering with short-sighted vision into shop windows, with an abstracted air. He generally carries some manuscripts under his arm, is slightly round-shouldered, thin, without a particle of color, stoops a little, and scorns an umbrella in any weather.

Grand Ledge Independent Mr Zangwill possesses a peculiar hawklike cast of countenance.

New York Herald The very archetype of his race – shrewd, witty, wise; spare of form and bent of shoulder, and with a face that suggests nothing so much as one of those sculptured gargoyles in a mediaeval cathedral.

Washington Times The dramatist is not so much of any type as he is a type of himself. He is tall and rather slight, with long arms, long legs, long fingers, and exceedingly long black hair.

He looks as if he had stepped out of an old book. I am half convinced that he did. He is dark – altogether dark. When he sits with the shadows playing across his face, he looks more than ever as if he were a black and white illustration done by a great artist.

New York Press

Zangwill was the very limit of Bohemian carelessness in his dress.

Hayden Church

He was always a little – to express it mildly – negligent of his apparel.

Reuben Brainin

He was probably one of the worst-dressed men in London. He wore a long and ill-cut frock-coat, over which his hair would straggle; with his flashing eyes he looked like a Hebrew prophet.

Alfred Sutro

Walking the streets of London with Zangwill I found him to be one of the best known and most generally recognized men in English public life. To tread a crowd with him is to perceive the faces of people in the street light up with a smile and to hear the whispered words,

Hamlin Garland

Israel Zangwill.

'There's Zangwill.' In a crowd at the International Art Gallery, in the swarming Strand, or in Piccadilly, the large, plain, kindly face, the thick curly hair, the peculiar shuffling walk distinguish him to hundreds. Men and women stop him to say, 'You don't know me, but I know you. I've just read,' etc. For all his keen wit and gift of sarcasm he is of a kindly nature and listens patiently to those laborious compliments, though a sly gleam in his big black eyes betrays his humorous perception of the speaker's folly. It was observable that the brightest and handsomest women are surest of an audience with him.

Boston Budget
When I first met him I thought him the homeliest man I ever saw. He came toward us walking with slightly bent shoulders and a loose gait, his spectacled gaze wandering everywhere, and apparently noting nothing. A cape coat hung loosely about him, its pockets overflowing with manuscripts, proof-sheets, newspaper clippings – in fact, every scrap he had thought worth saving for days past. He has a trick of pulling out a worn bundle of letters and jotting down a stray note or two, more for the sake of memorizing by writing, I think, than as a future reference, since the task of sorting such a mass of hieroglyphics must be herculean. I came back a victim to the charms of this young Englishman, of whom all the English reading world is talking.

New York Times
Mr. Zangwill lives in a little house in a very quiet street in St. John's Wood, London, up two flights of very steep, straight stairs. When I entered he was stirring the fire, his back toward the door, nor did he turn around to receive me. 'Come in,' he said. 'Take a seat. It's foggy out, isn't it?' The beauty of his voice made me forgive the uncompromising, unfriendly back.

Hayden Church
I well remember the first time I called upon him there. For a few moments, Zangwill, who was busy at his desk,

seemed to be wholly unconscious of my presence. Accordingly I had the opportunity to take him in in detail, and told myself that never had I seen so ill groomed a man of genius. An instant later, however, Zangwill had come out of his trance and greeted me courteously, after which his glance wandered to the window. 'Ah, the fogs,' he murmured dreamily, 'the fogs! They come too early.'

His library is barely-furnished and untidy-looking, filled with books that are for use and not for ornament. The only books one misses from the shelves are the author's own works, of which he can never keep a set, they are either begged, borrowed, or stolen. As for papers they litter the whole room, and overflow into an adjoining one. Drawers are stuffed full of letters from all sorts of eminent people. A large battered trunk is crammed with press cuttings.

Isidore Harris, *The Bookman*

Mr. Zangwill is manifestly a genius, for no less gifted sort of person could find anything when he wanted it in that den of his. Open bookshelves line every available inch of the total wall space from floor to ceiling. The desk, the chairs, the window ledge, and even the floor in places are covered with stray manuscripts, old letters, and bits of writing paper.

Billboard

He has a wonderful faculty, most fascinating and also inexplicable to a visitor, of simply extending one of his long arms and bringing in any book or paper that he wants, as if he had known all the time exactly where it was.

New York Press

Of course everyone knows what books Zangwill has written, but it has not been given to everyone to see him after he has just finished a book. His method of work is to start a book and work at it day and night without cessation until it is finished. He emerges from the struggle pale, cavernous-eyed, exhausted – looking more like a corpse than a living man.

G. B. Burgin

Illustrated Buffalo Express

As the well-informed reader knows, Mr. Zangwill's pen is one of the brightest and ablest in the literature of the day.

American Israelite

It may be said that this man, young though he may be, is the foremost writer of the day in England. He has been styled by his admirers 'The Dickens of the Ghetto,' and with much reason, for never, since the death of the author of 'David Copperfield' and 'Pickwick,' has an author arisen who has, by the power of his pen, so thoroughly endeared himself to his readers.

Louisville Courier-Journal

Zangwill is the man who first threw wide open the doors of the Ghetto to the English-speaking world and took the Gentile hand in hand through the crowded, dingy streets of the Jewish quarter.

Gentlewoman

If you have not read the 'Children of the Ghetto' you are, as yet, unacquainted with the East-end of London, and a new and interesting experience lies before you.

Reform Advocate

The 'Children of the Ghetto' is what the title implies, a portrayal of the life of the inmates of the London Ghetto.

It is a vivid presentation, sparing no truth, and picturing the minutest details. His work might be described as a living photograph, if such a thing were possible.

We are glad to have these descriptions of a life quite unknown to us – a life as remote from our experience as if it were 200 years ago and 1000 miles away.

Queen

With the firm strokes of a great artist, the author brings before you the poverty, the squalor, the narrowness of the convictions in which so many of these people live.

Washington Gladden, *American Hebrew*

'Children of the Ghetto' has charmed the public beyond measure.

Derby Daily Telegraph

Few books have within the present half-century created such a sensation.

New York Herald

Zangwill will carve his name deep in English literature. No one who has read 'Children of the Ghetto' will be disposed to doubt it.

South Wales Daily Post

***

After many 'ifs' and 'perhaps,' Israel Zangwill is nearing our shores, and we bid him a hearty welcome.

American Hebrew, 26 August 1898

Israel Zangwill is the most interesting foreigner that has been in this country in a decade.

New York Press

It was an easy task to pick out Mr. Zangwill from among the many passengers upon the ship, the pictures and caricatures of him that have been printed in various publications sufficiently impressing upon the mind his marked features.

American Hebrew

I. Zangwill is not a handsome creature. You have seen his pictures. He looks like them.

Elmira Evening Gazette

The first impression one gains of Israel Zangwill is that he is the ugliest man in the world. Mr. Zangwill's

New York Journal

countenance, as it appeared to reporters on the Luciana yesterday morning, was a thing to scare horses with. His apparel was in line with his visage. His necktie was an affair to make a careful dresser dive to the depths of the ocean. But it took but a few words of conversation with him to make one forget all about his powerfully ugly face and his weakly ugly clothes. He is a 'skimmy' talker, flitting from one subject to another with the agile grace of the man who jumps over a long line of elephants in the circus, touching each elephant with his toe as he sails toward the mattress.

Boston Budget

His conversation is brilliant with those epigrams and pithy remarks that have already added the word 'Zangwillism' to our English vocabulary. His eyes beam with a shy twinkle, in inward appreciation of his own quaint sayings.

Buffalo Press

His mind seems an encyclopaedia of every branch of art and science. He reminds one of the fancy glass worker who, with perfect ease, turns out constantly sparkling, glinting creations of beauty.

New York Recorder

You feel yourself irresistibly drawn toward him.

Theodore Dreiser

If he were ignorant, you would turn him out of doors for his looks. As it is, you draw near and listen.

***

Leon Kellner

It was in the spring when I received an invitation from Herzl. Israel Zangwill was in Vienna. Herzl had invited him to dinner, and fearing that Zangwill knew as little German as he English, he wanted me to be present to act as interpreter. I remember that Frau Herzl, who had been carefully informed by her husband how distinguished a visitor she was about to receive, was visibly disappointed. She had probably expected a tall, well-built man, carefully groomed, dressed in the latest English mode, and displaying perfect society manners. Instead there sat down at her festive table, which had been prepared with such loving care, an average-sized gentleman of grotesquely Jewish appearance and awkward behavior, with ill-fitting and neglected clothes.

In honor of her guest Frau Herzl had prepared crabs for the first course. Zangwill unfolded his napkin, then started back stiffly at the sight of the monster before him, which he apparently did not know how to tackle. Making up his mind swiftly, he seized the crab with an effort at bravado, and put it to his mouth. An outcry from Frau Herzl, a polite smile from the host – and we tried to show the impossible Englishman how to handle the beast on his plate. It was of no avail. There was a signal from Theodor Herzl, the crabs were removed, and Zangwill enjoyed the other dishes in comfort.

His table manners did not contrast too awkwardly with those of good society, and the meal continued under a barrage of intellectual fireworks between Herzl and Zangwill. But Frau Herzl did not wait a minute longer than was compatible with good manners, and when the dessert was being served she left the room without a word.

Chapter 3

Brooklyn Daily
Eagle, 24 July 1897
Since Dr. Theodore Herzl a few months ago published his 'The Jewish State,' the word Zionism has been a favorite term in the press. The great Project of the celebrated Vienna author has attracted universal attention, and the subject will have more amplified discussion at the general conference of Jews from all over the world.

Albany Times-Union
And now an Associated Press dispatch comes from Switzerland, to the effect that a universal congress of Zionists will be held beneath the shadow of the Alps to devise ways and means of establishing a Jewish state. Almost all European countries, America, Asia and Africa, have announced coming delegates.

Theodor Herzl,
23 August 1897
On the train, *en route* to Basel, to the Zionist congress. The amount of work in recent days was enormous.

Yehoshua Thon
It was Herzl alone who organised the congress, all by himself, with his own money and his own labour. He saw to every detail, nothing escaped his attention. There were times when he sat up all night and did all sorts of jobs, even addressing envelopes.

Erwin Rosenberger
He assumed the entire burden of carrying it out. Headquarters of the whole undertaking was his study. Day after day, I saw him sitting quietly writing the innumerable letters to future participants in the congress. Several times, speaking of the Zionist movement, he had said to me: 'If I should stop working today, the whole apparatus would come to a standstill.' And what he said was true.

29

He had invented the apparatus, he had constructed it, and now he serviced it – a master mechanic whom no one could replace. He assumed a burden of work that would have taxed three or four men.

Most of the threads I have spun up to now will converge in Basel. Stage-managing the congress will involve a rare feat. I have to run the show impersonally and yet cannot afford to let go of the reins.

Theodor Herzl

The Zionist congress at Basle, Switzerland, though the name may suggest nothing to most of us, is one of the epoch making gatherings of this century.

Oswego Daily Times

Every train brings Congress members from all sorts of places, caked with coal-dust, sweaty from their journey.

Theodor Herzl

Stirred by earnest thoughts, our hearts filled by joyful expectation, we travel towards Basel. The journey is an excellent introduction to the Congress. It is congress in a railway carriage, one improvised by chance. When we left we were only a small company, but by the time we had arrived we had become a considerable gathering. What joy there was when we found a 'Basler' and made each other's acquaintance. There were hearty, brotherly handshakes and then we got to know each other. What did we speak about? Congress, of course, was the main subject. We did not want to betray how tensely and hopefully we regarded it.

Berthold Feiwel

Writers and journalists, poets and novelists and merchants, professors and men of professions come from many places; from far lands and from near, from unknown villages of Bukowina and the Caucasus, and from the great European capitals; thickliest from the pales of persecution, in rare units from the free realms of England and America – a strange phantasmagoria of faces.

Israel Zangwill

Syracuse Daily Journal This parliament of Jews contains almost every type of the Hebrew race. There are many swarthy Jews with long black unkempt hair and bronzed complexions from Russia, Roumania and Palestine; blonde, fair haired, blue eyed, pale skinned Jews from Galicia. The great majority of the delegates from Russia and the East wear the quaint costume which distinguishes Jews in their countries from their fellow inhabitants. This consists of a round black cap and a long cloak. These delegates also wear little ringlets of hair hanging down on each temple, which is the especial characteristic of the Russian Jews.

Jewish Chronicle Prominent were our Russian coreligionists. Let not the reader think for a moment to identify them with the haggard, wistful looking immigrant one is wont to meet in the neighbourhood of Brick Lane or Whitechapel. Dressed in a thorough European style, with intelligence and nobility marked on almost every face, one could only recognise them by their native tongue (Russian) in which they conversed.

Pall Mall Gazette Every street corner of this strange, old-fashioned yet massive-built town has its little group of Jews gesticulating passionately and talking at a tremendous rate.

The excited throng includes Jews from England, France, Holland, Germany, Austria, Hungary, Galicia, Russia, Bulgaria, Poland, Algeria, New York, Baltimore, and four from Palestine itself. Dr. Herzl, himself a Jew of the thorough Assyrian type, tall, with jet black hair, and eyes of rare lustre, is the hero of the hour.

Everybody came to me for information about everything, important and indifferent. Four or five people were always talking to me at the same time. An enormous mental strain, since everybody had to be given a definite decision. I felt as though I had to play thirty-two games of chess simultaneously.

Theodor Herzl

Good humour and friendly feeling prevails. There is but one Jewish restaurant in Basle, and it is here that the delegates may be found morn, noon, and night, discussing, chatting, raising a clamour of tongues and a clatter of culinary utensils. Hebrew, German, Platt-Deutsch, Russian, Roumanian mix up horribly, and the English delegates are silent in self-defence.

Pall Mall Gazette

Never has such a conglomeration of tongues been exercised in the same place at the same time – and simultaneously.

London Daily News

Perhaps the streets of no city have ever listened to the like.

Jacob de Haas

All possible languages are heard, but we all understand one another, for all the languages contain the same word: Zion.

Berthold Feiwel

With sunset everybody was down at work, a crowd of journalists buzzing round every group, taking notes, writing impressions. It was early into the next morning that a majority of us obtained even a modicum of rest. And still there was no Congress, and no one could say

Jacob de Haas

what the congress would be like. Telegrams were pouring in in loads and mail needed sorting and thousands of details required attention. And yet we were confident, strangely confident that out of this mixed medley order would come.

Theodor Herzl

One of my first practical ideas, months ago, was that people should be made to attend the opening session in tails and white tie. This worked out splendidly. Formal dress makes most people stiff. This stiffness immediately gave rise to a sedate tone – one they might not have had in light-coloured summer suits or travel clothes – and I did not fail to heighten this tone to the point of solemnity.

Joseph Cohen

The first time I saw Herzl was in Basle in 1897, dressed in evening clothes at ten o'clock in the morning. He had given strict orders that all delegates were to appear at this First Zionist Congress in festive attire. This was not snobbery. He wished to impress the world with the fact

that the Jews were coming out of the ghetto and were from then on to be regarded as a normal people. What immediately impressed me about the man was his Jewish and Biblical appearance. He possessed that intangible thing which is nowadays called 'charm' to a greater extent than any person I have ever met before or since. And this appeal was to all classes and races, whether Russian students in the gallery of the Congress, hansom cab drivers in London, old orange-selling women in the streets of any city or Rabbis from the ghetto. All looked up to him with a glint in their eyes as if struck by something of another world.

The entrance ticket to Congress is much coveted. Even the day before Congress people crowded the office, applying for tickets. Many had to be sent away and fed with hopes of tickets for the afternoon, for tomorrow or the day after. There is sometimes even a small fight when someone goes away for a minute and finds upon his return that someone else has stolen his seat in the meantime. The gallery is filled long before the session begins.

Berthold Feiwel

The opening session was announced for nine o'clock this (Sunday) morning. By this time, nearly two hundred gentlemen, most of them in evening dress, and a few ladies, had assembled in the body of the hall, and in the gallery were a considerable number of spectators.

Jewish Chronicle

The great hall of the town casino is full to suffocation. All seats are occupied long before the opening. Everybody is seized with impatience.

Die Welt

Buzz and buzz for half an hour, of delegates being seated, evening dress and black frock coats the order of the day, the audience in the gallery craning their necks, and all expectancy. Then Dr. Herzl came out of the side room and stepped on to the platform. The gathering

Jacob de Haas

leaped to its feet and cheered and cheered, in the acclaiming notes of a dozen nationalities.

Jewish Chronicle To say that he was received with an ovation is to use too mild an expression. Such cheering, such excitement is rarely experienced in England, and it was some minutes before the meeting resumed the calm that had hitherto characterised it. A less strong man than Herzl would have been unnerved by his reception.

Theodor Herzl I was greeted with storms of applause, but I was calm and remained so, and deliberately refrained from bowing, so as to keep things at the outset from turning into a cheap performance.

Jacob de Haas No man perhaps in this generation has been listened to with such spell-bound, tense, ear-straining attention as Dr. Herzl as he delivered his first address.

Israel Zangwill His voice is for the most part subdued; there is a dry undertone, almost harsh. And yet beneath all this statesmanlike prose, lurk the romance of the poet, the dramatic self-consciousness of the literary artist.

Theodor Herzl Fellow Delegates: as one of those who called this Congress into being I have been granted the privilege of welcoming you. This I shall do briefly, for if we wish to serve the cause we should economize the valuable moments of the Congress. We want to lay the cornerstone of the edifice which is one day to house the Jewish nation. The task is so great that we may treat of it in none but the simplest terms.

A summary of the present status of the Jewish question will be submitted within the coming three days. We shall hear reports of the Jewish situation in the various countries. You all know, even if only in a vague way, that with few exceptions the situation is not cheering. Were

it otherwise we should probably not have convened. The scattered fragments of the Jewish people have everywhere undergone similar ills. In these times, so progressive in most respects, we know ourselves to be surrounded by the old, old hatred.

At this moment the hopes of thousands upon thousands of our people depend on our assemblage. In the coming hour the news of our deliberations and decisions will fly to distant lands, over the seven seas. Therefore enlightenment should go forth from this Congress. Let everyone find out what Zionism really is – that it is a moral, lawful, humanitarian movement, directed toward the long-yearned-for goal of our people. Today we are here in the hospitable limits of this free city – where shall we be next year?

Loud cheers greeted Dr. Herzl as he left the tribune, and from all parts of the room men flocked to shake him by the hand.

Jewish Chronicle

For fifteen minutes the hall shook with the shouts of joy, the applause, the cheers and the feet-stomping.

Mordecai Ben-Ami

The two-thousand-year dream of our people seemed to be approaching fulfilment; and I was seized by an overpowering desire, in the midst of this storm of joy, to cry out, loudly, for all to hear: '*Yechi Ha-melech!* Long live the King!'

Bernard Horwich

I shall never forget an incident that occurred at the Congress. On my way to the first session, I stopped a poorly-dressed, unattractive-looking young man, to inquire regarding the building where the session was to take place. Assuming that he did not understand English, I said to him in German: 'Will you please direct me to the hall where the Zionist Congress is to be held?'

Taking my arm, the stranger replied: 'We can talk Yiddish. I am going there, and you can come along with me.' When we entered the hall, there was great cheering and applause on all sides. At first I thought the applause was for me, because I was an American; but I immediately realized this was impossible, as very few knew me. I, therefore, responded with a faint smile, and my young friend and I sat down.

Still speaking to him in German-Yiddish, I introduced myself, saying: 'We might as well get better acquainted with each other. My name is B. Horwich, and I come from Chicago, in America. May I know your name?'

'My name,' he answered, 'is Israel Zangwill, and I come from London, England.' I was greatly embarrassed and confused, but managed to say: 'Well, now I know for whom they applauded. I came pretty near making a darn fool of myself.'

'Oh, no,' he answered, 'the applause was for you. They know you are an American, and they expect to get big money from the Americans.'

Leon Kellner

At the first congress, Zangwill was one of the most striking and most observed personages.

Zangwill began by sitting at the rear. The next morning he had crept up to the journalists' table and was taking notes. Later I saw him still nearer the front.

Jacob de Haas

***

The Congress was from beginning to end characterized by unremitting work. No social features interrupted its earnest proceedings.

Rosa Sonneschein

To understand and appreciate the real Jew it is necessary to follow the Zionists as they walk about Basle with their blue and white decorations, in no sense ostentatious, or with thoughtful faces sit through the long day and the still longer night in committee to debate every point. There always seemed to be a moment when the energy of these delegates must give out. Sittings began at 11 a.m., adjourned for lunch, and then with a slight pause continued to three or four hours after midnight.

London Daily News

Isaac Cohen,
Sunderland Daily Echo

It seems that each day brings in its train more interesting proceedings than its predecessor.

Yorkshire Post

Mostly all address the Congress in German, though some emit a harsh torrent of Russian, while a few stray into French and occasionally English. One thing is certain – not one word of the Yiddish jargon was heard.

Isaac Cohen

One out of every three delegates you meet is either a professor, doctor, rabbi, theologist, jurist, novelist. There is scarcely one amongst them who is not able to converse in at least three or four languages. It is wonderful to see some of the Russian students, who are the most fiery element of the Congress, when once they step into the speakers' tribune, burst forth with glowing oratory, commanding the rapt attention of every one of their hearers. With flashing eye and animated gesture they stand, shooting forth firebolts, but at times degenerate into a turbulent state. Only the cool, commanding voice of Dr Herzl could control those excessive outbursts of rhetoric. Contrasted with them the English and German delegates look cold and matter-of-fact.

Theodor Herzl

Once, while Nordau was presiding, I entered the hall from the rear. The long, green table, with the elevated seat of the president, the platform draped in green, the table for the stenographers and the press, all made such a strong impression on me that I quickly walked out again, so as not to lose my composure. Later I found my own explanation why I was so relaxed while everyone else was excited and dazed. I had no idea how magnificent the Congress looked in this sober concert-hall with its unadorned grey walls. I had had no previous experience of such things, otherwise I, too, would probably have been swept with emotion.

Pall Mall Gazette

An historic and unique congress ended this evening. For the first time in Jewish history the dispersed members of Israel have been momentarily united, and the closing scene illustrated well what this meant.

Amid an impressive silence, Dr. Herzl delivered a short farewell speech. *American Hebrew*

It was a simple, unaffected speech. It was strange to listen to this Jew, with his aristocratic manner, his proud bearing, offering humble excuses for possible presidential mistakes. Then he raised the note slightly: The Congress had been worthy of itself and worthy of Israel, it had been unanimous, it had been enthusiastic, from the ends of the earth they had gathered together, by their efforts they would realise all their desires. Further words were drowned in applause, then came silence again. 'The congress is at an end.' *Pall Mall Gazette*

To describe the fervid enthusiasm which ensued is well-nigh an impossible task. No hero ever received a greater ovation than did Dr. Herzl. Men who by their nature are not usually demonstrative caught the infection and shared with the rest the emotions of the moment. The tremendous cheering and the waving of handkerchiefs were renewed again and again. *American Hebrew*

Israel Zangwill, who had been sitting silently at the reporters' table, sprang up, his face aflame with enthusiasm, cheering, waving his kerchief with energy. It was a scene better seen than imagined. *Pall Mall Gazette*

It was not a question of cheering, but of ventilating hearts full of emotion. I have seen bigger crowds and have heard more vociferous outbursts, but the like of this mass of waving handkerchiefs – I made a mental picture of Zangwill's spare figure on a chair waving a red bandana in the midst of it all – the like of this I have never seen. The simple words of the president, 'The first Congress is at an end,' were heard, but not understood: that is to say, no *Jacob de Haas* one realized and no one could realize that after so many ages of separation there was to be so speedy a parting. The delegates remained standing, cheering. Some one broke out into the Hatikvoh; another began singing the 'Watch on the Jordan.' From side to side of the hall came shouts of 'A year to come in Jerusalem.'

Pall Mall Gazette

The barely united were to be re-dispersed. Herzl shook hands with everyone in turn; men invited each other to homes at the four corners of the globe. Even journalists felt this was no common parting. 'To the next congress,' 'A year to come in Jerusalem;' none dared say more than 'To our next meeting;' farewell was too harsh a term.

Jacob de Haas

The scene continued for an hour, and even then the end was not. The delegates collected their scraps of notes. They walked aimlessly and listlessly about the room. They shook hands with each other. A hundred times they bade each other Godspeed in a dozen corners. But at length even the Congress hall had to empty itself. They went down the wide, white stone steps on to the hilly street, and no sooner were they down but they inconsequently reascended, and being up they came down again.

A friend and myself, observing as journalists while we too felt all this emotion, concluded somewhere about midnight that this was no time to sleep. It was a sultry August night, and all old Basle was at rest. The hundreds of fountains were splashing as usual. We made for our hotel and drew back again at the door. Where to and what for? It was impossible to think of sleeping after such a wave of emotion. We bethought ourselves. There was a stretch of greensward by the side of the Rhine which rushes through the city. We would sit there into the cool of the morning and allow the Congress thus to breathe itself out. So we made for the greensward – and we found all the delegates there. The same thought had apparently

41

struck the majority. They sat there quietly, looking pensively into the gleaming of the waters. Some got up and strolled away, and then came back. The majority sat there till the dawn showed itself over the Jura mountains.

Chapter 4

Michael Davitt,
May 1903

Kishineff is a handsome town. Its leading boulevard, Alexandra Street, would do credit to any American city. It is more than twice the width of Broadway, New York.

The city has the look of a comfortable, fairly wealthy, up-to-date bourgeois centre, a most unlikely place, in the eyes of a visitor, to offer itself as a theatre for one of the most abominable tragedies in modern times.

American Hebrew,
-15 May 1903

The Russian journals now reaching this country bear out the wildest statements that have come over the cable. By now sufficient facts are known to speak of the Kishinev riots with some degree of certainty. The more details brought to our knowledge, the graver the situation appears to be.

The civilized world has read with a thrill of horror this week the revelations of the massacre perpetrated in the Russian town of Kishineff.

Hampshire Telegraph

As fuller information filters through to Western Europe, it becomes evident that the anti-Jewish riots which took place at Easter at Kischineff, in South Russia, were of a singularly brutal and violent description.

St James's Gazette

Reports grow hourly more appalling as details are received here. The immediate cause has not yet been made clear, though for weeks a propaganda of hatred had been preparing the Russians for the outbreak.

New York Evening World

The feeling against the Jews has been intense in that part of Russia for some time. Not long before Easter a Russian boy disappeared mysteriously, and a rumor spread among the people that the child had been killed by the Jews.

Independent

A report was circulated that the boy's blood was to be used in preparing the Passover bread.

Lockport Journal

The Kishinev Jews knew that during Easter disorders would break out. Circulars were found in the saloons and on the street. These circulars declared that during the holidays vengeance would be taken on the Jews. But no one thought that the disorders would end so disastrously.

Der Fraind

The riots began on Easter Sunday, in the afternoon, and on that day were confined to the ordinary acts of a turbulent crowd – *e.g.*, the smashing of windows and door-panels in Jewish houses.

V. H. C. Bosanquet

Street kiosks were overturned and smashed, and signboards torn down and used as battering-rams against shuttered windows and closed doors.

Evening Standard

Bands of half-drunk ruffians began to break into shops and houses in the Jewish quarter of the town.

Sheffield Daily Telegraph

American Israelite

They ripped up the floors, scattered the content of bedding and pillows in the street, tore out and smashed costly mantels and fireplaces. What they could not destroy or carry away they saturated with paraffin and burned.

Joseph Feldman

We all went inside and locked the doors and barricaded the windows. Christians, males and females, battered down our barricades and broke the doors. Then they broke all the furniture, not leaving a piece for our use.

Novosti

The most awful bacchanalia were those in the New Market and Armenia Street which, being almost exclusively inhabited by Jews, had all their shops and houses plundered and ruined. The destroyed goods were piled in the centre of the road, thus stopping all vehicular traffic including the tramcars.

Jewish Chronicle

The noise of the smashing of windows and the cracking of doors mingled with cries of terror – a terrific cacophony that caused consternation among the population in the centre of town.

Isidore Singer

In the meanwhile bands were playing in the city garden. With the sounds of the music were mingled the cries and shouts of the marauders, the dual noise of falling furniture and the crash of broken window-panes in the thoroughfares of the city. In the streets in which the mob was raging the elegant world drove by in carriages, to enjoy the spectacle of wild destruction.

All day the riot raged; and, though it ceased at nightfall, it began again with the next morning's sun.

Jewish Chronicle

Early the next morning it became known that the mob had assembled in strong bodies in the New Market, Nicolai Street, Gostinaja Street, Charlampiew Street, Pushkin Street and several other streets.

Joso Taker

I took refuge in the cellar with my wife and children. About 1 o'clock in the afternoon men with sledges, crowbars and bludgeons commenced breaking in the door. Entering, they smashed everything in the house, throwing some things into the street. They broke into the cellar. Several men attacked and robbed me of eight roubles I had in my pocket. They clubbed me, after which I remembered nothing. I don't know how I was brought to the hospital.

Most of the victims were killed or injured by stones, pieces of wrecked furniture, blocks of wood, and sticks. Many of the bodies were unrecognisable, as the skull and jaws had been shattered, the nose and teeth broken, the eyes driven in.

Sheffield Daily Telegraph

The men in the mob did the killing, with stones, and spikes and bars, while women followed the crowds to rob the dead.

Mendel Schulmeister

Many Jews sought refuge with Christians, but in several cases shelter was denied them. The Jews concealed themselves in all manner of places, whence they were dragged out.

New York Times

At five in the afternoon, a telegraphic despatch arrived from St. Petersburg with the command to put an end to the excesses.

Isidore Singer

The chief of police announced that the rioting must stop, and that we would be safe on the streets. I then went up to the cemetery, where I saw fifty bodies of men and women laid out on the grass, waiting to be buried. I helped to dig the graves for them. The bodies were all badly mutilated. The heads were crushed in, and some of them had large holes through from ear to ear. The people told me these were made by driving spikes through their heads.

Mendel Schulmeister

It is bad enough for those who have been killed, but worse for those who are left to live such lives of misery.

David Snyder

Every day people are dying round about us. May God grant that I may soon be able to turn my back upon this bloody country.

***

Manchester Courier,
12 May 1903 Kishineff has been almost deserted since the anti-Semite disturbances of which it was the scene.

Voskhod Last night the city presented a complete picture of destruction: broken doors and windows, devastated residences, broken furniture, both in residences and streets, broken and torn pieces of goods in the streets, and all of these covered with a white pall of down and feathers from Jewish feather beds and pillows.

Novosti The streets resemble churchyard avenues. One sees the unfortunate Jews wandering about like ghosts, most of them with wounds on their heads and faces.

Der Fraind Gloom and sorrow have fallen upon Kishinev. Unusually sorrowful and gloomy is the city at nightfall. On the streets a dead quiet, no activity.

Evening Standard When I arrived here late last evening, the Bessarabian capital presented all the appearance of a city suddenly evacuated by its inhabitants. At eleven p.m., not a civilian

was to be seen. Just before nightfall I had an opportunity of penetrating, unmolested by the police or Military patrols, more closely into the lanes and alleys of the purely Jewish quarters. Whole streets, throughout their lengths, show nothing but sacked houses, shops, and booths. The open doors and windows gape darkly like those of structures gutted by fire. Whichever way one turns in the lower part of the city, the same scenes meet the eye.

Thousands of pillaged Jews with their wives and children are crowding the railroad depots. The trains can hardly carry one tenth of those who wish to get away from the city.

Voskhod

A dispatch giving the official casualties at Kishineff was received here today. It placed the killed at forty-five, the severely injured at seventy-four, and the slightly injured at 350. Private information, however, gives much higher figures.

Washington Times,
18 May 1903

All of the readers of this paper are aware of the terrible massacre of the Jewish population at Kishineff. The

Pokeepsie Evening
Enterprise

civilized people of the world stand aghast at the results of the religious persecution in that far away Russian town.

Ithaca Daily Journal   The outrages are so horrible as to be almost beyond belief. They are further proof of the semi-oriental barbarity that underlies the thin veneer of Russian civilization.

Shields Daily News   The murderous anti-Semitic riots reported this week warn society that the Jewish problem does not melt away before the advance of modern civilization.

Jewish Exponent   The leopard cannot change its spots, nor can the Russian bear transform his brutal nature. The Jews of Kischeneff have been made to feel the force of this truth.

Belfast Newsletter   The outlook for the Russian Jews is extremely black.

Oscar S. Straus   No one can read without a shudder of horror the reports of the fiendish outrages at Kishinev. This barbaric holocaust appeals for redress not to the Jews throughout the world, but to the civilized world; not to those professing the religion of the slaughtered, but those professing the religion of the slaughterers; it is a crime against civilization and Christianity as well.

Grover Cleveland   Every American humane sentiment has been shocked by the attack on the Jews in Russia. There is something intensely horrible about the wholesale murder of unoffending, defenseless men, women and children. Such things give rise to a distressing fear that even the enlightenment of the twentieth century has neither destroyed nor subdued the barbarity of human nature.

Theodore Roosevelt   I need not dwell upon the fact so patent as the widespread indignation with which the American people heard of the dreadful outrages upon the Jews in Kishineff.

I have never in my experience in this country known of a more immediate or a deeper expression of sympathy for the victims and of horror over the appalling calamity. Nothing that has occurred recently has had my more constant thought, and nothing will have my more constant thought than this subject.

What is the lesson of Kishineff? That is the question burning to-day in the brain of Jews the world over. Kishineff, a slaughter in this dawn of the twentieth century, with its vaunted civilization. What is the lesson of Kishineff? In a dispatch from London, discussing the Kishineff horror, Israel Zangwill says: 'The only solution of the Jewish question is to take the Jews out of Russia, and plant them in a soil of their own.'

Brooklyn Daily Eagle

Such persecution as the Jews are now experiencing in Russia lends color and adds interest to the Zionist movement.

Syracuse Post-Standard

It is possible that the Kishineff massacre may be the starting point for the re-establishment of the Jews as a nation. If so, it will be a blessing most thoroughly disguised.

Batavia Daily News

The news from Kishenev puts back the clock of European time, which already was slow enough in Russia. I have never heeded the glib optimism of those who think human nature evolves by leaps and bounds.

Israel Zangwill

Kishinev is not over. The effects are yet to come.

Theodor Herzl

Chapter 5

Winston Churchill One mark of a great man is the power of making lasting impressions upon people he meets. Another is so to have handled matters during his life that the course of after events is continuously affected by what he did. Mr. Chamberlain was incomparably the most live, sparkling, insurgent, compulsive figure in British affairs. 'Joe' was the one who made the weather.

Theodor Herzl I am thinking of giving the movement a closer territorial goal, preserving Zion as the final goal. The poor masses need immediate help.

Theodor Herzl, 23 October 1902 Talked yesterday with the famous master of England, Joe Chamberlain. One hour. I expounded everything I had intended to bring up, and he was a good listener.

51

Unfortunately my voice trembled at first, which greatly annoyed me while I was speaking. After a few minutes, however, things improved and I talked calmly and incisively, to the extent that my rough-and-ready English permits it. Addressing myself to Joe Chamberlain's motionless mask, I presented the whole Jewish question as I understand it and wish to resolve it.

Chamberlain does not give the impression of being brilliant. Not a man of imagination. A mind devoid of literary or artistic resources, a businessman, but with a clear, unclouded head. The most striking thing about the interview was that he didn't have a very detailed knowledge of the British possessions which undoubtedly are at his command now. It was like a big junk shop whose manager isn't quite sure whether some unusual article is in the stock-room. I need a place for the Jewish people to assemble. He's going to take a look and see if England happens to have something like that in stock.

With Chamberlain yesterday noon. He received me amiably, like an old acquaintance. He struck me as having grown a great deal older and more care-worn, though still mentally alert.

'Since we last met, I have seen quite a bit of the world,' he began. 'In the course of my journey I saw a land for you, and that's Uganda. It's hot on the coast, but farther inland the climate becomes excellent. So I thought to myself: that would be just the country for Dr. Herzl.'

Theodor Herzl, 24 April 1903

The whole country bears considerable resemblance to the Sussex Downs, and, in parts, to an English park. English roses bloom profusely, and all English fruits and vegetables can be cultivated. If Dr. Herzl were at all inclined to transfer his efforts to East Africa, there would be no difficulty in finding land suitable for Jewish settlers. But I assume that this country is too far removed from Palestine to have any attractions for him.

Joseph Chamberlain, December 1902

Theodor Herzl My personal point of view is that we have not the right simply to reject such a proposal, fling it back without even asking the people whether they want it or not. I say only: 'Here is a piece of bread.' I, who perhaps have cake to eat, have no right to reject this piece of bread which is offered to the poor. There are some people who, in the midst of their need and hunger, are strong enough in their idealism to say: 'No, we don't want that bread.' But I am obliged at least to transmit the offer to the people. That is my conviction.

***

Sketch, 26 August 1903 By the time these lines are printed, the Zionists will be holding their annual Congress at Basle.

Isaac Cohen, *Sunderland Daily Echo* Five congresses have already been held, four at Basel in 1897, 1898, 1899, and 1901, and one in London in 1900.

Jewish Chronicle How the movement has progressed since the delegates last separated, we do not know. Rumours there have been in abundance – rumours of negotiations with the British Government. But the leaders jealously guard their secrets and hold their peace. Mr. Zangwill has told us that the coming Congress will be the most important of the series. We suppose this assertion is based upon information now in his possession, but withheld from the rest of the world. One sentence in his speech last Saturday seems to point to a move being made in an area other than Palestine. 'I am certain,' he says, 'that the time has come when a beginning must be made somewhere, even if it is only a step towards Palestine.'

Leeds Mercury The attendance is expected to be the largest in the history of the movement. No fewer than 500 delegates are looked for, of whom 60 will represent Britain.

American Hebrew A conservative estimate places the number of delegates at six hundred; another report places it at eight hundred.

As on past occasions Jews in the most distant parts of the world will be represented. So great is the enthusiasm that one delegate has walked all the way from Bulgaria in order to be present, the journey taking him 62 days.

Manchester Courier

The delegates began to arrive a week before the opening day. In numbers and enthusiasm the Russians exceeded all others.

American Hebrew

Basel was strewn with Zionist delegates, and hotel accommodations were at a premium. One could recognize the Zionists by their solemn appearance, by their animated conversation, by their polyglot articulation, by the bright bronze badges in the shape of six-pointed stars representing the 'shield of David,' set on circular ribbons of white and blue and worn on the lapels of their coats. Hard sounding Russian was interspersed with soft, smoothly flowing French, terse English was seasoned with musical Italian, the choicest German was crossed by lisping 'Yiddish,' and quaint biblical sounds from the lips of oriental Jews talking Hebrew added strange coloring to the mixture. The liveliest spot in Basel was naturally the Stadt Kasino. Zionist flags floated over the entrance, and underneath swarmed the delegates, giving the stately edifice the appearance of a huge beehive. Cabs and carriages brought new delegates and guests in rapid succession, and men and women were coming and going, singly, in pairs, and in groups, talking earnestly, embracing and gesticulating, filling the scene with intense motion and life.

Leon Zolotkoff, *Chicago Tribune*

Three days before the congress began 1000 admission tickets had been issued.

Gotthard Deutsch, *American Israelite*

Those who were present during the first act of the yearly Basle drama will not readily forget the picturesque intensity of the opening scene. The Stadt-Casino was

Manchester Guardian

crowded to its utmost limit on that languorous August morning.

American Hebrew
The Sixth Zionist Congress assembled Sunday morning, August 23, at ten o'clock. Many of the delegates were obliged to stand; the galleries were crowded with visitors.

Gotthard Deutsch
80–100 delegates could not find a seat and some of the reporters had to write holding their notebooks on their knees.

Jewish Chronicle
Basle has grown too small for the Congress, the platform was too crowded, the galleries overflowing. The building was one mass of faces.

Shmarya Levin
It was an impatient horde of delegates, conscious of the fearful emergency, that waited for the Congress to be opened.

Isaac Cohen
A little after ten, the official time of the opening, Dr Herzl stepped on the platform and was received by the whole assembly standing, and cheering over and over again, which lasted two or three minutes.

Manchester Guardian
Wave after wave of applause eddied and swept around the platform to greet him. The year's anxieties have touched Herzl somewhat; he was paler than usual, and grey hairs begin to streak his beard.

American Hebrew
He did not wait for the applause to subside, but began at once to read his opening address.

Theodor Herzl
Fellow delegates: we are assembled for the Sixth Zionist Congress in the good city of Basle, which has earned our gratitude on former occasions. Again we come together in mingled hope and anxiety. In truth, the situation of the Jews throughout the world is no more favourable to-day than it was in the years of the earlier

Congresses. Many of us thought things could not grow worse; but they have grown worse. Misery has swept over Jewry like a tidal wave. Those who lived in the depths have been submerged. It is distasteful to us to turn disasters into political ends and to search for propaganda material in the anguish of the unfortunate. But we must state from this platform how great was our pain and our horror when we learned of the hideous occurrences of Kishinev, and how overwhelming our grief to think that Jews must live under such conditions.

Kishinev exists in all places where the Jew is afflicted in body or in soul; where his honour is assailed; where his possessions are attacked, because he is a Jew. Let us save those who can still be saved. This is a new period into which we have entered.

Last year, I put myself in communication with certain members of the British government. They have made me an offer of a territory for the purposes of Jewish colonisation. This territory has not historic, religious and Zionist significance; but I do not doubt that the Congress, as the representative of the Jewish people as a whole, will receive this new offer with the warmest gratitude. The proposal consists of an autonomous Jewish settlement in East Africa. When this proposal was made I did not feel myself justified, considering the plight of Jewry and the immediate necessity of ameliorating this plight, in taking any other course than to submit it to the Congress.

It goes without saying that the Jewish people can have no other goal than Palestine and that, whatever the fate of the proposition may be, our attitude toward the land of our fathers is and shall remain unchangeable. Nevertheless, I believe that the Congress will be able to find means to make use of this offer. Zion it is not and can never be. It is an emergency measure to prevent the loss of these detached fragments of our people. Its effects are yet to be seen, but with renewed courage and with brighter prospects than ever before, we may continue our efforts to strive for Palestine.

Tablet   The offer took away the breath of the Congress.

Shmarya Levin   I was sitting on the platform, and I was therefore able to watch closely the effect produced by the announcement on the listeners. It was one of almost agonised attention. On their faces was written astonishment and admiration – but not a sign of protest.

Chaim Weizmann   The effect on the Congress was a curious one. The delegates were electrified by the news. But as soon as the substance of the offer sank home, a spirit of disquiet, dejection and anxiety spread through the Congress.

Shmarya Levin   When the map of Palestine was covered by a map of Uganda, the delegates felt as though they were watching a total eclipse of the sun.

Leon Zolotkoff, *Chicago Tribune*   The first word of rebellion against Dr. Herzl was heard – he was the beloved leader because he was leading to Zion, not to East Africa.

Shmarya Levin   The session became tense. Interruptions like 'Suicide!' 'Criminal!' 'Treachery!' began to fly from all sides.

A. H. Reich   When a young Russian student hurled the word 'traitor' at him, I saw Herzl's face blanch to the lips and his entire body quiver.

Chaim Weizmann   No one was mistaken as to the symbolic significance of that proposal. When the first session was suspended, a young woman ran up onto the platform, and with a vehement gesture tore down the map of Uganda.

Martin Buber   After his speech Herzl retired into his conference room. Berthold Feiwel and I soon followed him there. As we walked the short distance to the conference room

I was profoundly perturbed. I had not for a moment lost my faith in the man. Now, for the first time, my soul revolted – so violently that I still have a physical recollection of it. Herzl was pacing the room with long strides exactly like a caged lion. His breast rose and fell quickly; I had never dreamed that he, whose actions always bespoke a masterly self-control, could be thrown into such agitation. Since then I have often thought over that occasion.

***

The congress was re-opened to-day, with Dr Herzl in the chair, the congress hall again being crowded. The debate on the East African scheme, for and against, was carried on for the best part of the day.

Isaac Cohen, 24 August

For days the work of the Congress progressed with unflagging energy, with undiminished zeal. Without, the summer sun blazed relentlessly. The white-faced buildings seemed to vibrate in the intense heat. And when the sun sank in a welter of golden light beneath the distant Vosges, and night fell like a curtain, there was no respite from anxious toil. Day after day was one unceasing round of orations, reports, discussions, resolutions. Demonstrations and counter-demonstrations, innumerable speeches for and against, in five languages at least. The two-thousand-year-old tragedy of the wandering Jew appears to near its climax.

Daily Telegraph

Although England, in comparison with other countries, such as Russia, is poorly represented, they can boast at least one delegate who compares favourably with many of the most prominent members the Congress, and that is our noted novelist, playwright, orator, wit, and, above all, Jewish Nationalist – Mr Israel Zangwill. Yesterday morning, Herzl called upon Mr Zangwill to deliver his address. Mr Zangwill delivered a speech which evoked tremen-

Isaac Cohen

dous applause from the enormous gathering. The eminent novelist addressed the assembly in English, which came as a relaxation from the incessant flow of German, Russian, and French that characterised the various orations.

Israel Zangwill

Israel has been the Ulysses of history! But Homer tells us 'There is nought that makes a people more unhappy than moving from place to place.' We must have a home and a refuge for those of our brethren who are the victims of Kishineffs, and, if we wait much longer, who knows but that there will be none left alive to reach that home?

Isaac Cohen

Dr Herzl called upon Dr Max Nordau as the last speaker on the question.

Leon Zolotkoff

Dr. Nordau stood up and proved himself master of the dialectical art.

Max Nordau

Before attaining the inalterable goal of Palestine there must only be one halting-place on the road. Like a shuttlecock, our unhappy brethen are being tossed to and fro from continent to continent, from ocean to ocean. Before we can give them a permanent home, we must open a night refuge.

Cyrus L. Sulzberger

Max Nordau is the orator of the Congress, silver haired and silver tongued. His speech was superb. Wit, satire, invective, argument and all with an eloquence unmatchable.

Abram Lipsky, American Hebrew

The tide began to turn when Max Nordau was given the floor to close the debate. The venerable presence of Nordau, the authority of his fame, as well as his masterly eloquence, won over many waverers.

Jewish Chronicle

The most important sitting of the Congress began at 4.45, the hall being crowded from floor to roof. The situation was extremely tense. Some of the delegates were trying to raise questions and comments about the vote and its formulation, but Herzl put a stop to this and rejected it all fiercely: 'we are voting.'

Everywhere there was an ominous silence, nothing moved, everything was silent as if before a storm.

Yechiel Tchlenov

At five o'clock, the roll call was begun.

Cyrus L. Sulzberger

Every delegate had to say 'Yes' or 'No'. The replies fell, in a deathly silence, like hammer blows.

Chaim Weizmann

Ja, nein, ja, nein were heard alternately all over the hall. The vote went on for two hours. It is very rare for a roll-call vote to be taken in a parliament with so many delegates. The entire hall followed the course of the voting with concentration. Many jotted down and counted the votes. I admit I was stunned to hear how often the word nein was heard.

Yechiel Tchlenov

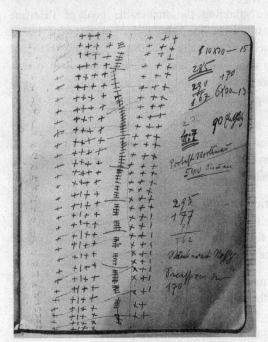

Chaim Weizmann	The names of the two delegates from Kishinev were called, and both said: 'No.'
Abram Lipsky	The resolution passed by a vote of 295 yeas to 178 nays.
Shmarya Levin	The No-Sayers shouted more loudly, but the number of Yes-sayers was greater. It was therefore decided that an expedition be sent to the territory of Uganda, in order that detailed information might be obtained as to its possibilities.
Chaim Weizmann	When the result of the roll call was announced the older statesmen wept openly. There were some delegates who, in the extremity of their distress, sat down on the floor in the traditional ritual mourning which is observed for the dead.
Israel Zangwill	Curiously imagining that they had been robbed of Palestine, which they had never possessed, some of the Russians burst into hysteric tears, wrung their hands, and even rolled on the floor. Women fainted. Men wept and wailed. I was surrounded by a sobbing crowd. Over the sobs of the mourners, I heard the tumultuous applause of the vast assembly ushering in the physical regeneration of our race.
Cyrus L. Sulzberger	Hats, handkerchiefs, arms waved frantically, while from 295 throats came shouts and cheers as though from so many thousands, dying out only to be renewed again and again. Meanwhile there sat silent the 177 who had voted in the negative – some stolidly silent, some silently sobbing, a few crying aloud. Presently, however, the whole picture changed. About 140 delegates, all Russians, left the hall, the whole Congress standing the while in semi-stupefaction.
Manchester Guardian	As a protest, many of the Russian delegates who had voted against the Commission left the hall amid scenes of wild disorder. If anything were needed to show how

deep a root Zionism has taken in the hearts and minds of Russian Jewry, their acute and poignant grief at the temporary overshadowing of their passionate hopes for Palestine was enough to show it.

The scene was suggestive of tragedy. The friends of the East African Commission were made to feel that they had assisted at some assassination, whether of a hope, an ideal, or an illusion, they must decide for themselves. The power of the Russian Jew's mind to hold an ideal fixedly is incomprehensible to other nationalities.

Abram Lipsky

I was one of the minority that voted against Uganda and, together with the rest of the 'neinsagers,' walked out of the hall. I wondered myself at the motive hidden deep within my soul that prompted me to vote against. I had no romantic love for Israel. Yet I still voted against. I do not know why. Simply because.

Vladimir Jabotinsky

It was the Russian delegation that would hear nothing of Uganda. They were in a minority and were outvoted, but Zionism without Russia is a lifeless, senseless wreck.

Jewish Exponent

The very delegates from the blood-reeking Kishineff refused to accept the new land of refuge.

Israel Zangwill

These people have a rope around their necks, but still they refuse.

Theodor Herzl

The last night of the Congress was a wakeful night for all of us. The oppositionists held an all-night session. Late in the night the leader appeared in our midst, and asked to be heard.

Shmarya Levin

As we sat in caucus, our hearts filled with bitterness, a message was brought in that Herzl would like to speak to us. We sent back word that we would be glad to hear him. He came in, looking haggard and exhausted.

Chaim Weizmann

Vladimir Jabotinsky

It was precisely here where he appeared without his formal jacket, without the gavel and the stage and the whole pompous apparatus that separated him from the public, that he appeared simply as a delegate, to explain himself and almost to justify himself. Precisely here, it piqued my curiosity to find out how he would behave, how he would win over his audience, whether he would lose control of his tone, whether he would stumble. Herzl spoke, as always, calmly, expressively, without any rhetorical devices, entirely in control of himself. In each word one could hear self-assurance, and standing before his opponents, he did not hesitate to speak to them sharply, and at the same time with condescension, as one in power, almost as an elder with a child. There were moments when I thought that now the protesting voices would break in, but the voices didn't. Starting from his first words, from the expression that appeared on almost every face, in the extraordinary quiet that had now taken shape, I understood the entire meaning of Lomonosov's historic utterance: 'it would be easier to take the Academy from me than to take me from the Academy.'

Chaim Weizmann

He was received in dead silence. Nobody rose from his seat to greet him, nobody applauded when he ended. He assured us of his unswerving devotion to Palestine, and spoke again of the urgent need for finding an immediate refuge for large masses of homeless Jews. We listened in silence; no one attempted to reply. It was probably the only time that Herzl was thus received at any Zionist gathering; he, the idol of all Zionists. He left as he had entered.

Shmarya Levin

The war against Herzl was conducted with too much bitterness. It was not necessary to be so bitter.

***

American Hebrew

Over two thousand persons were in the Stadt Casino when the Congress came to an end on Friday.

63

The closing of the Sixth Congress was at hand and everybody felt that it was an occasion when a certain degree of solemnity was appropriate. There was a general impression something had been accomplished that, perhaps, the future would show had been one of the most important events in Jewish history. Everybody was standing and the silence was profound when Dr. Herzl began his closing remarks. The sad seriousness of the leader's voice gave his words the effect of a prayer. *Abram Lipsky*

This has been a remarkable Congress. Much has satisfied us, much has been burdensome. It was a difficult, but permit me to say, it was a great Congress. I must repeat, 'this is not Zion and can never be.' After all that has passed, not for a second, not in thought, have we departed from the Basle programme. I thought of providing a place of refuge, and having learnt to know your hearts, I desire to offer you a word of condolence and which is at once a pledge on my part. If I forget thee, O Jerusalem, may my right hand forget its cunning. *Theodor Herzl*

When Herzl said that he reaffirmed his allegiance to Palestine, the cries in Hebrew were extraordinary. *American Hebrew*

It seems to me I can still hear his voice ringing in my ears as he took the oath. *Vladimir Jabotinksy*

He uttered the words as if they were written for him, at this moment. That speech of his was his swan-song. *Shmarya Levin*

Dr. Herzl restored calm for one moment. He said: 'I repeat our thanks to the city of Basle and close the Sixth Congress.' So here, then, was the end. The leader stepped backward, but the whole Congress rushed forward. *Jewish Chronicle*

President Herzl's announcement, 'The sixth Zionist congress is closed,' was the signal for an outburst of pent *Leon Zolotkoff* up feeling, which manifested itself in a long, thunderlike roaring by a couple of thousand throats, in which the Hebrew 'Hedad!' was heard to mingle with the 'bravos,' 'eliens,' 'vivas,' and with the singing of the Hebrews' national song, 'Our Hope Is Not Yet Forlorn.'

Jewish Chronicle

The scene went on, nearing in its intensity the closing scene of the First Congress, for two hours.

Abram Lipsky

Dr. Herzl immediately left the hall at the conclusion of his address. But not so the delegates. They remained in their places and sang the Hatikvah, brokenly at first and then all together. They sang it over and over.

Jewish Chronicle

Theodor Herzl left Basle this evening, every feature and every limb full of spring, motion and determination.

***

Theodor Herzl

The Sixth Congress. The old hurly-burly. My heart is acting up from fatigue. When, completely worn out, I returned after the closing session, with my friends Zangwill, Nordau, and Cowen, and we sat in Cowen's room around a bottle of mineral water, I said to them: I want to tell you now what my speech at the Seventh Congress is to be – if I live till then. By that time I shall either have obtained Palestine or realised the complete futility of all further effort. In the latter case, my speech will be as follows:

It was not possible. The ultimate goal has not been reached and will not be reached within a foreseeable time. But a temporary result is at hand: this land in which we can settle our suffering masses. I do not believe that we have a right to withhold this relief from the unfortunate.

I understand that with this situation a decisive split has entered our movement, and this split passes through my person. In order to heal this split there is only one thing to be done: I must resign from the leadership. I will, if you so desire, conduct the next Congress; after that, you can elect two Committees, one for East Africa and one for Palestine. I shall not stand for election in either.

Chapter 6

Chicago Tribune,
24 August 1903

England Offers Jews a Country.

Birmingham
Daily Gazette

The English Government has decided to let the wandering tribes of Israel make their home in East Africa.

Elsley Zeitlyn,
Daily Mail

The sensational announcement has been made that the British Government has offered to the Zionists a large extent of territory in East Africa. Thus a new light, born of new hope, glints through the chinks of the sombre Ghetto.

Daily Telegraph

It is a noble offer, nobly made; the offer of a humane and generous Government which has come to realise the tragedy of squalid ghettos in Eastern Europe, the hopelessness of Jewish slums in England and America, and the iniquity of shuttle-cocking human beings backwards and forwards across God's earth.

Manchester
Evening News

In no other nation is there a deeper, truer sympathy with the Jewish national movement than exists in ours.

Newcastle
Daily Chronicle

British East Africa is not Palestine, nor can it even be regarded as on the way to that promised land, but the scattered tribes of Israel are not inclined to look a gift horse in the teeth, and prefer even this remote Zion to none.

Roger P. Barnum

It is not too much to say that Dr. Herzl is pleased with the British offer which made such a favorable impression upon the Basel congress. It is believed in diplomatic circles that the gift will ultimately be accepted.

A crowded meeting was held last Saturday evening at the Great Assembly Hall, Mile End Road, for the purpose of welcoming back the delegates to the Zionist Congress, and of receiving their report. Mr. I. Zangwill, whose rising was the signal for an outburst of loud applause, which lasted several minutes, then addressed the gathering as follows; – *Jewish Chronicle,* 11 September 1903

East Africa has suddenly jumped into the middle of our map. What is the total impression that I have carried away from this great Congress? It is this – that never has Palestine stood so near our hopes as it stands to-day. For the first time we are on the road to Zion. We have awakened from empty dreaming. Palestine may remain closed to us for centuries – are we therefore to stand still? Certainly it is a long way round to go by East Africa, but sometimes it is the short cut that proves the longest, and the long way that is the shortest. Nearness is not only geographical. A man in London with a ten-pound note is nearer to New York than a man in Chicago without a dollar. Let them both start tomorrow morning, and see who gets there first.

British east Africa has an area of 280,000 square miles, being larger than the states of Maine, New Hampshire, Vermont, Massachusetts, Rhode Island, Connecticut, New York, New Jersey, and Pennsylvania. *Chicago Tribune*

The proffered territory is part of a great plateau almost 4,000 feet above sea level and is described as well watered, well timbered, fertile and healthy. About it rise lofty mountains, snow capped, a background to a wonderful picture of forest and plain. The region is said to be one of the few sections of Africa where white men may thrive. Roger P. Barnum

This plateau is overflowing with milk and honey, to say nothing of hartebeests and giraffes. *Manchester Guardian*

Jewish Chronicle

Here we have an equatorial land with European features. It is a white man's land set in the heart of the tropics. It is a quaint country, too, where a jam-pot is a favourite form of ear-ring, where a lion calmly lifts a first-class passenger out of his carriage and walks off with him; and where telegraph wires are in danger of being stolen by vain native ladies for purposes of fashionable decorations, or of being injured by monkeys who persist in swinging on the wires and by giraffes, who will cross the line without making allowance for the length of their necks. But these are only minor troubles.

Harry Johnston, 1902

The country is of noble appearance. For the most part the downs, over which one's gaze can stretch fifty or sixty miles, are clothed with soft, silky grass, which takes a pale pink, mauve, grey, or russet sheen as the wind bends the flowering stems before it. Over this roam countless wild animals. Here may be seen large herds of giraffes as one might see cattle peacefully standing about in an English park.

The scenery reminds the homesick traveller over and over again of England, of Wales, of Scotland. This beautiful land has not in it a single ugly or unfriendly spot. Everywhere the landscape is gracious and pleasing in a quiet, homely way, offering few violent forms or startling effects. As it is almost entirely without native inhabitants, it seems to be awaiting the advent of another race which should make it a wonderland of wealth and comfort, a little England, half a Scotland, or a large Wales, lying exactly under the equator.

Edward Julian

The green forest, purple in the distance, the richly colored date palms, the orange of their fruit contrasting with the green of their waving foliage, the brilliant blues and greens of the river, touched with white foam and glimmering through the spray, present a charming picture. On the shores of the lakes, in the magnificent forests, in fact through the whole Uganda territory, are to be found birds of every variety, shape and coloring; storks, pheasants, ostriches, birds of the most cumbersome shape and those of daintiest anatomy fill the air with their cries or songs. The beauty of the forests is said to oppress one traveling through them until the impression of living in a bygone age becomes almost unbearable. Trees with heavy black trunks, with beautiful white stems, with dark, almost impenetrable foliage, with graceful, lightly-waving leaves, with vines of every grotesque or pleasing shape and variety of color climbing over them, the whole inter-mixed with flowering trees of almost incredible brilliancy and enveloped in an atmosphere of over-development and rapid vegetable decay, in time induce a sensation of such awfulness that one finds it necessary to, as soon as possible, seek the open country and bright sunshine.

Although the territory is sparsely inhabited, it is said that there are no less than seven distinct varieties of savage represented. One of these is already in a state of semicivilization, but the others are still typical barbari-ans, although described as well disposed to white men. Perhaps the strangest are the Kiagwe dwarfs, a tribe of nomads. Another unique people are the Kavirondos, at one time cannibals and preserving their cannibalistic tendencies so far as to file their teeth to needlelike points.

Roger P. Barnum

Excursionists will see before them coal-black, hand-somely formed negroes and negresses without a shred of clothing, though with many adornments in the way of hippopotamus teeth, bead necklaces, ear-rings, and leglets of brass.

Harry Johnston

The native trouble would seem to be a very minor matter. Sir Charles Eliot tells us that 'as soon as a tribe have a real knowledge of the Europeans they not only

Jewish Chronicle

A MASI WARRIOR OF THE "PROMISED
LAND."

admit our superiority, but admit it in the friendliest way
and without any sign of a grudge.'

New York
Daily News

The country which has been tendered as a gift to
the Zionists was opened up and made accessible by the
completion of the Uganda railway last year.

Winston Churchill

The two iron streaks of rail wind away among the hills
and foliage. And thus is made a sure, swift road along
which the white man and all that he brings with him, for
good or ill, may penetrate into the heart of Africa as easily
and safely as he may travel from London to Vienna. Every
few miles are little trim stations, with their water-tanks,
signals, ticket-offices, and flower-beds, backed by impenetrable bush. In brief one slender thread of scientific
civilization, of order, authority, and arrangement, drawn
across the primeval chaos.

New York
Daily News

It is not improbable that the new Zion may grow
up in the Uganda country. The children of Israel will

make another journey in the wilderness and found a new nation. But they will not be forced to make weary marches on foot. English and American railway engineers have preceded them to British East Africa, and if they enter that country they will do so in modern railway carriages, crossing ravines and rivers that have been bridged by the skilled workmen of the new world.

Under the stimulus of the Zionist project, British east Africa could easily support a population of several millions. With the wealth of the Jews, the country now a wilderness would spring at a bound into the importance of a nation.

Chicago Tribune

The experiment which seems almost certain to be tried will be watched with the closest interest by all Imperialists.

Western Morning News

Zionism passes, for the time being, into a new phase of its existence.

Daily Telegraph

Manchester
Evening News

Naturally the offer created varied feelings in the Congress. Be the result what it may, there will be no turning back from the point which this unique movement has reached. The heart of the Jewish race has been gripped.

Julius I. Goldstein,
New York Sun

Would it be profitable for the Jews to accept England's offer? That proposed grant in Africa is near the equator, with the burning sun overhead, and disease-breeding swamps below, the air swept by hot winds from all directions, with no civilized country around it. This barren land England expects the Jews to transform into a cultivated and flourishing region. Should the Jews, after 2,000 years of persecution, after being driven from land to land, living under difficulties everywhere, but with the national feeling still warm in their hearts, hoping and waiting, collect all their energies and settle in wild Africa, and begin anew to hope for Zion? The world cannot afford to allow the Jews to be lost among the different nations and cease to exist. What is the remedy? A nation to find itself at home must return to where it was born. The mere feeling that he is in his 'fatherland' will strengthen the Jew. The protest of the Russian delegates at the congress against Uganda is the strongest proof of the feeling of the Russian Jews: 'We are Zionists and want Zion.' The downtrodden Jews of the world cry out with them: 'Give us Zion or we remain in exile.'

Jewish Chronicle

We can understand the repugnance which Zionists must feel at the apparent abandonment of the great dream of a Jewish State in the ancestral home of the race, for the sake of a settlement among half savage tribes, remote from the haunts of civilisation. The first impulse on the part of many must have been to ask impatiently whether the history of Israel was, after all, to end in an African swamp. The future of Jewry does not lie in the tropics. Not thus is to end the grand drama of the Jewish race. It would be the grimmest anti-climax.

It is said that England's offer has not met with the approval of the few British people who live in east Africa.

New York Daily News

· We have received the following telegram from Lord Delamere, dated Nairobi, Uganda, August 28: – Feeling here very strong against the introduction of alien Jews. Is British taxpayer, proprietor of East Africa, content that beautiful and valuable country be handed over to aliens? Have we no colonialists of our own race? Country being settled slowly but surely by desirable British colonial settlers. Englishmen here appeal public opinion, especially those who know this country, against this arbitrary proceeding and consequent swamping bright future of country.

The Times

A white population is the crying need of all our East African territory. Its lofty plateaus are a paradise for the white man, and there is ample room in the broad expanses for all our surplus population. At the same time, it is not a pleasing prospect to picture the foundation of an exclusively Hebrew State in the Protectorate, populated, perhaps, to a large extent by a class of Jews who are by no means desirable colonists.

Northampton Mercury

I think that it would be very unfair to allot to a community of foreigners – i.e., non-British Jews – a large proportion of the very limited area open to European colonisation in British East Africa, an area which has been dearly purchased by the money and blood of British subjects.

Harry Johnston to the *Jewish Chronicle*

A Polish ghetto would establish itself in East Africa free from all necessary restraining influences. The results could not be beneficial to East Africa or creditable to the Jewish race.

Lucien Wolf to *The Times*

Is it to be 'Jewganda?'

Arnold White, *Daily Express*

The aspirations of the Jews do not materially concern us as Englishmen; but, with all respect to the fervour and earnestness of Mr. Zangwill, we may fairly ask whether it would be to the ultimate advantage of his co-religionists to take any step which would accentuate and confirm their separateness as a race. Wherever, as in this country, Jews have enjoyed complete liberty, their tendency has been towards amalgamation with their neighbours, and towards what may be described as a softening down of the salient points of their national character. We believe that these conditions are the most hopeful that can be conceived for the future of the race. That they should be assisted to emigrate en masse, and to set up a little State or community of their own, is, we think, a rather questionable proposition.

Chapter 7

New York Times,
29 October 1903

Israel Zangwill to Marry.

Western Daily Press

The friends of Mr Israel Zangwill have been accustomed to look upon him as a confirmed bachelor. It was, therefore, with surprise that many of them heard he was contemplating matrimony.

Shields Daily
Gazette

A sensation has been created in Jewish circles by the announcement of the engagement of Mr. Zangwill, the novelist, to the daughter of Professor Ayrton, who is not a member of the 'chosen race.'

New York Evening
Telegram

Zangwill's Betrothal to a Gentile.

Aberdeen Press
and Journal

Miss Ayrton's tastes coincide with those of her future husband, who is now taking his task as the leader of Zionism in England even more seriously than his novel-writing.

New-York Daily Tribune The bride has thrown herself with intensity of purpose into Mr. Zangwill's movement.

Washington Post Miss Ayrton also is an author, many of her stories having appeared under the name E. Ayrton in many American and English magazines.

Westminster Gazette, 26 November 1903 Early to-day, very quietly at a registry office in the West End of London, Mr. Israel Zangwill was married to Miss Edith Ayrton. Only the bride and bridegroom, Professor and Mrs. Ayrton, and one or two relations were present.

Daily Mirror After the ceremony a reception was held at Professor Ayrton's house in Norfolk-square, at which a great many guests distinguished in literature, art, and science were present. The bride – looking charmingly pretty and happy – and bridegroom were warmly congratulated by hosts of friends.

Yorkshire Evening Post Professor and Mrs. Ayrton received their guests at the top of the staircase, and Mr. and Mrs. Israel Zangwill greeted them in the drawing-room, standing together against a background of lovely white flowers. Higher up again, at the top of the house, the many beautiful presents were set out, and on the curtains of the rooms were pinned the many telegrams of congratulation that had been received.

Daily Mirror The presents were numerous and interesting, being particularly rich in old Japanese ware, beautifully bound books, and handwrought jewellery.

London Evening Standard The presents could not all be displayed owing to lack of accommodation.

Elgin Courant The clever author of 'The Children of the Ghetto' looked remarkably well and radiantly happy. So did his bride, who looked a perfect poem.

The bride was quite a picture in her lovely gown, made of very rich satin, the colour of old ivory – infinitely more becoming than the dead white affected by so many modern brides.

London Daily News

Miss Ayrton is a dark, sweet-looking girl.

Daily Express

Beautiful, tall and unmistakably English, of the type that Rossetti treated so poetically in the Pre-Raphaelite renascence of his pictures.

Florence Brooks, New York Times

Her soft voice and quiet manner are like Israel's. She has no Jewish blood, but that dark, foreign look of hers is rich and exotic enough to make her seem in harmony with Israel's own personality and atmosphere.

Helen Zangwill Horn

She has black eyes, dark hair of marvellous texture and a complexion which is Oriental in its richness of color. Since a serious illness through which she passed a few years ago, there has been a sad cast to her face, which has set off her charms admirably.

New York Sunday Telegraph

Seeing this delightfully ill-assorted though none the less delightfully congenial couple together, one feels that

Noel Y. Harte

nobody is enjoying the contrast which they present more than Zangwill himself. Beside his fair young wife, the Zangwillian face and the Zangwillian figure are even more Zangwillian than we have known them heretofore.

Truth

The new Mrs. Zangwill is intellectual and a great philanthropist, as you may guess when you hear that the bridegroom's present to her consisted of three cheques, one for each of the three causes to which she devotes her energies, Zionism, Women's Suffrage, and the Charity Organisation Society.

Washington Post

Although Miss Ayrton has little, if any, Jewish blood, she is an ardent believer in the plan to establish a Zion somewhere for the Jews, and Mr. Zangwill tells me that if the present proposal to establish such a colony in East Africa is adopted he and his bride will go there to live.

Manchester Guardian,
22 June 1904

Mr. Zangwill made some comments yesterday as to the scheme for setting up a Jewish colony in British East Africa. 'There seems to be an idea,' he said, 'that if we accept the Government's offer we shall set up a kind of Ghetto on a large scale. That would not be so. It would be a settlement of the most modern kind, and I believe that under the new conditions of freedom and life in the open air we should develop a quite new type of Jew.'

Mr. Zangwill was unable to say when the report might be expected from the Commissioners which the Basle Congress sent to East Africa to spy out the land. A good deal of delay had been caused by the illness of Dr. Herzl, the leader of the Zionist movement.

Chapter 8

Ever since the Zionist movement was started by Dr. Theodor Herzl seven years ago it has severely taxed his energy, and during the last two years the strain has been uninterrupted and intense. Few human beings could withstand such an experience without sooner or later showing its physical effects. The announcement made in Vienna that the condition of Dr. Herzl's health will prevent his active participation in Zionist labors for at least several months will be received by his fellow-Zionists with the greatest concern. No man now living has as strong a hold on millions of Jewish hearts as Dr. Herzl has, and they will fervently pray for his speedy restoration to complete health and strength.

Jewish Exponent, 3 June 1904

My physicians are sending me to Franzensbad on account of my heart trouble. I had been feeling tired for a long time, but kept going. It will probably be a few weeks before I have patched up my heart a bit, since it is in need of repair.

Theodor Herzl, 2 May 1904

I don't know whether I was insufficiently observant, whether I saw only what I wished to see, or whether it was Herzl who deliberately feigned perfect health. Herzl never uttered a word to suggest that he was in failing health or even that he was tired. Once, he said good-humoredly, slowly moving his shoulders as though to test them: 'I can hardly move today; I played tennis too long the day before yesterday.' That was all.

Erwin Rosenberger

Theodor Herzl came to consult me in December 1903. He had long fascinated me as an author. The imagery of

Dr Gustav Singer

his travel pieces, the mastery with which he captured the flavour of the Parisian salons in the German language, the grace and feeling with which he wrote about his children had made me feel very close to him. But now a very different man came to see me, a pale, tired, sick patient. His pulse was irregular, the heart output greatly impaired as manifested by obvious congestive symptoms. In addition, there were circles around his once so fiery eyes. I believe that I succeeded in deceiving him for a while and in calming him down. But in consultation with Ortner, who was also treating him, we were forced to postulate a disease of the heart muscle, which implied rapidly progressive heart failure. He came to see me whenever he felt bad, or whenever Ortner's prescriptions made him suspect a worsening of his condition. Actually, all I did for him was to provide emotional support.

Dr. Siegmund Werner

I was called to Herzl's bedside. Pneumonia had settled on the left lung, with his heart too weak to meet the increasing pressure of circulation. His wife had told him of my arrival and he called for me immediately. I hurried through the dark garden towards the pavilion where my dear friend and leader was lying. At the entrance I was met by his wife. Mrs. Herzl led me through an adjoining room; another door – and I saw him, with outstretched arms, wink to me, and I heard the voice, which was so caressing when he greeted a friend: 'My dear Werner!'

For a moment I became so weak that I had to lean on the foot of the bed, but the next instant I was standing at the bedside shaking his hands. With his usual consideration he asked me to forgive him for giving me trouble. Only when I had assured him that I was envied by many for being near him, he expressed his satisfaction. 'You shall see,' said he, again and again shaking my hands, 'you shall see that I am an obedient patient. Nurse me to health, and then we shall rejoice!' I asked him not to talk so much, as it was a strain for him. He obeyed and lay quietly, after showing me how to hold him during the attacks of coughing. Now I could observe him well. It was clear that he was a very sick man. He breathed with a whistling sound. His forehead was covered with cold perspiration, the eyes half-closed most of the time. His face was yellow. Still, it had not lost the beauty and character of the olden days. This sick, suffering man was Herzl, whom I had seen for so many years full of proud strength.

I sat there and looked at him. I tried to guess what was going on behind that forehead. And I see the Congress Hall at Basle. The thick mass of delegates in their formal dress, the gallery full to the breaking point; the reporters, full of expectation, around the tribune, and in front Herzl, in all his dignity, with a paper in his hand. I hear him read, slowly, loud, stressing with marked strength the more important parts. And then an endless storm of ovation. And he stands upright, in the midst of new outbreaks of applause, and looks earnestly and unmoved at the noisy throng and – suddenly I think my heart will burst.

At five o'clock on Sunday, July 3, 1904, the Jewish people lost its great son. At the bedside stood the stricken family. I, however, slipped into the garden and wept.'

***

In a beautiful spot overlooking the hills surrounding Vienna, Theodor Herzl has just been laid to his eternal rest. I have never witnessed such an enormous concourse of people assembled round a grave.

Jewish Chronicle, 7 July 1904

A strange day it was, a day in July, unforgettable to all who were there to see it. At every railroad station in the city, with every train, night and day, from every country and corner of the world, masses of people kept arriving. Western and Eastern Jews, Russian and Turkish Jews,

Stefan Zweig

from every province and every little town they came streaming in, the shock of the news still written on their faces.

Jewish Chronicle   The library at Herzl's residence had been converted into a mortuary.

Erwin Rosenberger   The coffin lay in Herzl's study, with six unlit candles in tall silver candle-sticks on either side. The walls and windows of the room were hung with black drapery. An oil lamp at the head of the coffin provided only feeble illumination. From outside came the sound of a vast multitude of persons – thousands who had come from near and far to escort Herzl's body to its final resting place.

Die Welt   In front of the house and in the surrounding streets, a crowd of several thousands had gathered. The body was conveyed to the hearse, which was followed by the grief-stricken mother, widow and family.

Jewish Chronicle   The vast gathering fell into marching line and walked from the house to the cemetery.

Erwin Rosenberger   I walked, almost somnambulistically, a short distance behind the plain black hearse.

Die Welt   The bulk of the procession, numbering over 5,000 persons, marched on foot. Among those present were L. J. Greenberg, Jassinwoski, Jochelmann.

Stefan Zweig   The procession was endless.

Jewish Chronicle   Cheek by jowl with the correctly-attired Western Jew one noticed the caftaned heavy-bearded Jew from Galicia, and side by side with the dark-eyed Roumanian was the fair-skinned North German.

Hermann Bahr   The dark mass of people silently whispered sounds I could not comprehend; it rolled through the streets of Vienna.

The greatest procession I have yet seen. In my imagi- *Shmarya Levin*
nation, I saw the unresting chain of events that had led to
this moment: Kishineff–Uganda, Uganda–Herzl.

We were now at the grave. Not a whisper was heard. *American Hebrew*
Never were five thousand people more orderly.

Herzl's body was borne into the vault in which his *Jewish Chronicle*
father was interred, and lowered to its resting-place, there
to remain till Herzl's wish to be carried to the Holy Land
shall be fulfilled. Looking from the stone steps around
the grave, one could see nothing but a sea of faces. It was
a Zionist Congress, and for the last time Herzl was the
central figure. From the dumb stillness of his silent grave
he was almost as eloquent as he had been in the rostrum
at Basle.

For him it was, to be sure, the best possible time to *Martin Buber*
die, before all the unavoidable events, disappointments,
and decline, and at the height. What shape the movement

will take cannot yet be foreseen. But one can barely think about that, so deeply is one shattered.

Ahad Ha'am

He died at the right moment. His career and activities during the last seven years had the character of a romantic tale, and if some great writer had written such a tale, he, too, would have made his hero die after the Sixth Congress.

Israel Zangwill

We sat at midnight on the veranda of the 'Three Kings,' Herzl and I, after the first Basle Congress, looking down on the sombre rushing Rhine, and I was ironically touching off the humours of the Jewish exile – the middle classes prattling of their glorious fatherlands, the rabbis praying for Zion and panic-stricken at the idea of getting there, the masses divided against themselves in mutual superiorities of Sephardim and Ashkenazim, Lithuanians and Dutchmen. Herzl turned upon me: 'It is not comedy, it is high-tragedy.'

High-tragedy it has, indeed, proved for him. Had he known more, he would have dared less. One walks fearlessly over a narrow plank, so long as one is ignorant that it bridges an abyss.

Chapter 9

Zionist Movement Without a Leader. All now is sad confusion.

Syracuse Daily Journal, 2 December 1904

One wonders whether the movement can continue, for Herzl is dead, and Zionism without him seems almost impossible.

Daily Telegraph

The future of the movement is in the lap of the gods.

Leeds Mercury

It is, of course, too soon yet to speak of a successor.

American Hebrew

Some favor the election of Max Nordau to be their future leader. Other groups demand the election of noted Jewish author, Israel Zangwill.

Syracuse Daily Journal

Since the death of Theodor Herzl, Zangwill is probably the strongest personal force in the Zionist movement. If the new Zion is established, he will be its laureate and philosopher – perhaps its greatest statesman.

William Thorp, Washington Evening Star

There has been a great deal of foolish talk as to the choice of leaders. I have never wavered from the idea that Max Nordau is the natural successor of Dr. Herzl. He was our Vice-President, and naturally steps up into the Presidency.

Israel Zangwill to the Jewish Chronicle

***

Mr. Zangwill sails for New York.

New York Times, 13 October 1904

Israel Zangwill, author, writer of plays and stage manager, appeared in New York on Thursday evening in a new part.

New-York Daily Tribune

On previous visits he made his bow as the literary artist, the witty critic of life, the epigrammatic lecturer on paradoxical subjects, and the playwright. Now we are to see him as the Zionist advocate who comes to expound the merits of the East African project.

Israel Zangwill, with his bride, arrived in New York this evening from Liverpool to interest Jews of America in the possibility of establishing a Jewish colony in British East Africa on a tract of land 400 miles square, at present unfortunately the lair of wild animals only. 'I am here,' Mr. Zangwill said, 'only to stir up interest in the project. Some colonization scheme is necessary for the welfare of the Jews. England has got all the Jews she wants, and America is apparently approaching the same way of thinking. It is true the Jews have done well here, but America has reached the point of saturation.'

We have in sight a country of our own. If we do not accomplish something now, we never will. East Africa is our only hope.

Mr. Zangwill has come here from London to push forward this project, and at the same time to watch the progress of several plays he has on the American stage. His 'Children of the Ghetto' is now being acted in Yiddish in Brooklyn, and Cecelia Loftus is starring in his new comedy, entitled 'The Serio-comic Governess.' He is well satisfied with his success in these respects. He tells me, however, that he hopes one day to write a drama of a higher nature than anything he has yet produced. The novelist has his serious as well as his humorous side, and this is especially shown in his work for his people in forwarding the interests of the Jewish East African state.

Walking to and fro in the large spaces of the studio apartment where Israel Zangwill and his young wife are staying, the Jewish novelist, playwright, and Zionist spoke with an anxious deliberation. Mr Zangwill's appearance is that of a man of intense seriousness. He is slight, nervous, and grave; his countenance pale, with deep shadows. He wears black, and is literally without color, as an old etching. 'As Mr Chamberlain said, this is the very spot for the Zionists. This is not merely a dream in the air,' he explained, rather restlessly; 'it is an actual offer of the Government. The striking thing is that the Jews have not possessed an inch of land for nineteen centuries. This tract is the first thing that has ever been offered. In Russia they say that America is as big a Zion as could be desired. But I have elsewhere pointed out that New York cannot absorb any more Jews. Of course,' he admitted, 'Zionism may not touch the people in America at all. The needy are cared for, those already flourishing do not need help. In the second generation those who have struggled here will merge, will melt away, amalgamate, and become Americans by losing pronounced Hebraic traits and gaining those of the young race of this country.'

Any territory which was Jewish, under a Jewish flag, would save the Jews' body and the Jews' soul. Perhaps in our days the blue and white flag of Zion shall float, if not over Palestine proper, at least over a provisional Palestine, over a land where our oppressed masses shall draw free breath, where soul and body shall grow straight again; where we shall know again what it is to love mountains and rivers that are our own.

Israel Zangwill, 8 December 1904

***

A commission of three members, whose names will be made public in the course of the week, is to start for East Africa in a fortnight. Their report will be submitted at the next meeting of the Zionist Congress, when the acceptance or refusal of the British Government's offer will be finally decided.

Manchester Guardian, 7 December 1904

Leeds Mercury,
17 December 1904

It is announced that the Commission will consist of Major A. St. Hill Gibbons, Professor Kaiser, and Dr. Wilbusch. All are well qualified for the task committed to them. Major Gibbons is the well-known African explorer, and has written much on the district. It is expected that they will reach 'the promised land' about the second week in January.

Cyrus C. Adams,
New York Times

If their report is as favorable as there is every reason to expect, a pioneer party of Jews is likely to be sent out to Africa later next year.

Chapter 10

Even the torrid heat of the past week or two has not availed to keep the Zionists from holding their usual Conference at Basle.

Sketch, 9 August 1905

The preparations for the seventh congress of the Zionist movement, which begins tomorrow, are rapidly approaching completion. Basel is transformed into a Jewish city for the time being.

Syracuse Journal

When I entered the portals it was at once apparent that nothing had been changed since I last attended a congress. There was the same bustle as of yore, and a veritable Babel of tongues assailed the ear, from English with the Yankee accent to the pure Hebrew of Jerusalem. Many familiar faces met my eye; but one face was missing, and though most of the hundreds of men and women who streamed through the lobbies and rooms were engrossed in the one topic which will dominate the entire Congress, they could not fail to be reminded of the dead leader, never again to be seen in their midst. Picture-postcards of Dr. Herzl, urging Zionists to take his bones with them, are meeting with a ready sale.

Jewish Chronicle

The difficult question of leadership has to be decided at this congress.

Syracuse Journal

Next to the personality of the leader to be chosen, the definition of the movement itself will be watched with interest. The world is waiting to know whether Zionism and Uganda-ism are synonymous.

American Israelite

Maurice Leon,
Cincinnati Enquirer

This morning, amid impressive silence, Max Nordau declared the seventh Zionist congress open. Seven hundred and sixty delegates, representing 23 countries and including 36 Americans, were present. Over 200 journalists were on hand and the floor was filled. Two thousand spectators, who had come from as many lands as the delegates, crowded the galleries. Hundreds who had traveled days could not get in. The hall presented a somber aspect in keeping with the day, for this is the first anniversary of Theodore Herzl's death. Black is seen everywhere. The garments of the men and women, the decorations, even the large Zionist flags on the walls bear black bands.

New York Sun

The great congress hall was draped in black. Over the vacant chair which he had always occupied hung a large portrait of Herzl by Joseph Milziener, the young American painter. A great audience packed the hall to suffocation, as Nordau, amid perfect silence, took a stand near the president's chair and delivered a eulogy, which for style and feeling will be judged to have few equals.

Maurice Leon

With admirable oratory, Nordau eulogized the dead leader to an immense audience, standing with bowed heads, the Jewish mourning attitude.

Julius H. Greenstone,
Jewish Exponent

A request was made that there should be no applause. It was a moving sight, worthy of the pen of a great writer. A Zangwill or a Nordau could do justice to it. It was a scene which few who witnessed will ever have erased from memory.

Maurice Leon

Then the great crowd filed out. All is peace, but the calm is deceiving as before a storm. The congress must provide Herzl's successor, and must vote on England's offer of territory. Zangwill is working like a Trojan to convince the majority into acceptance.

When I asked Mr. Zangwill whether he would urge the acceptance of his resolution on the congress, he said: 'Yes, certainly.' 'And what do you expect?' I asked. 'Defeat,' he replied, laconically.

Leon Zolotkoff, *Chicago Tribune*

In the afternoon began the series of sessions which makes this congress the most memorable in the history of Zionism.

New York Sun

Delegate Leopold G. Greenberg of London presented the report of the expedition sent to East Africa.

Syracuse Journal

The report lays stress on the extremely formidable difficulties in the way of successful colonization rather than on the opportunities the country offers. The land is absolutely uncultivated and the colonists would be compelled to transform immense extents of virgin soil and of thick forests into a habitable country. The territory has no roads and no paths except elephant tracks. It is approached by extremely difficult routes through dense forests infested by wild beasts and dangerous native tribes.

The commission had returned with a report which was anything but encouraging.

Leon Zolotkoff

Unfortunately for the project, the territory is by no means a land flowing with milk and honey.

Leeds Mercury

Committee Sent to Africa Finds That Tract Is Not Adapted to Plan, Owing to Savages and Wild Beasts.

Chicago Tribune

The formal debate began on Saturday evening at 9.20 o'clock.

Julius H. Greenstone, *Jewish Exponent*

A special sitting of the congress was called last evening, four orators supporting and four opposing Great Britain's proposition.

Maurice Leon

Nordau was in the chair, his wife and his little daughter, a beautiful child of nine years, were on the platform.

Gotthard Deutsch, *American Israelite*

Gotthard Deutsch,
American Israelite

Mrs. Zangwill was also in constant attendance at the Congress. It is a peculiar fact that these two leaders of Zionism, by marrying Gentiles, have shown a way out of the 'Judennot' which would soon do away with the need for Zionism. It was said at the Congress that Nordau's daughter had been baptized in the Catholic Church and that Zangwill had confessed his resolution to raise his children, if he had any, as Christians.

The discussion was heated from the start, although none of the speakers succeeded in winning the audience by the force of his eloquence or by the originality of his arguments. German, Yiddish and Russian alternated. The speakers, feeling that this was the opportunity of their lives, held onto the platform and had to be reminded several times that their time was up.

New York Sun

Israel Zangwill, who favored the acceptance of the offer, was everywhere pleading his cause but all in vain. The opponents of the East African scheme listened stolidly to Zangwill's speeches as they were translated into

German sentence by sentence, but declined to budge from their position.

The debate lasted for more than six hours and President Nordau eventually suspended the sitting at dawn.

Maurice Leon

The Congress was resumed on Sunday midday. To secure order, the galleries were kept closed, no visitor was allowed to enter, and the cards of delegates and journalists were rigorously scrutinised. Dr. Max Nordau took the chair, and implored the Congress in the name of the Jewish people to preserve decorum in voting on the question of East Africa.

Manchester Guardian

Just after noon, the Actions Committee suddenly produced a resolution of their own which embodied everything I had been fighting against.

Israel Zangwill

The committee presented the following resolution. 'The congress thanks Great Britain for her offer of African territory, the consideration of which, however, is terminated, and hopes that Great Britain will continue to aid in the solution of the Jewish question.'

Maurice Leon, *Cincinnati Enquirer*

Immediately upon the reading of this resolution Israel Zangwill, the novelist, offered a substitute.

Syracuse Journal

I beg to move a resolution in reply to the offer of the British Government, and I must ask you, out of respect, not for me, but for the British Government, to hear me peacefully, though many of you will not agree with me. You have nearly all of you come here decided how to vote, and as I do not see the use of wasting my breath, my speech will contain only what the gravity of the subject demands. We have duties, not only to Zionists, but to all Israel. We have to save our people, even against their own will.

Israel Zangwill

Therefore, I beg to move: That the Congress resolves gratefully to accept the magnanimous offer of the British

Government; but with the expectation that the Guas Ngishu Plateau shall be supplemented or replaced by other territories.

If we gave up this chance, I know not when we shall have another. It will prove the salvation of tens of thousands, perhaps hundreds of thousands, of wandering Jews. When East Africa is gone, you will be glad that the aching tooth is out, but afterwards you will remember that it was your only tooth. I beg you to ponder these things before you reject the greatest opportunity the Jewish people has had for eighteen centuries.

Syracuse Journal   The congress was in uproar in a few moments and it finally became necessary for Chairman Nordau to adjourn the sitting, owing to the great disorder which prevailed.

Gotthard Deutsch   Finally the question was put.

Shmarya Levin   Speeches were now superfluous. The delegates spoke with their hands – that is, just voted. Almost unanimously, the Congress voted, together with its refusal of the offer, an expression of profound gratitude to the British government.

Chaim Weizmann   At the seventh Congress the Uganda project was liquidated.

New York Times   Zionists, in a Tumult, Reject British Offer.

Scotsman   The Uganda Project Dropped.

Pall Mall Gazette   Scenes of extraordinary emotion have lashed the Zionist Congress for six-and-thirty hours. Certainly the British Government did not anticipate such a reception for its innocent offer of colonisable land, especially as Mr. Zangwill and other influential Jews were very glad of that offer.

Sketch   Even the most ardent Zionist should have admitted that such a *pied-à-terre* would have enabled the refugees to recover self-respect and practise self-government while waiting for the return to Zion. But no; the enthusiastic Zionists will have Zion or nothing, and so they have dismissed the offer of His Majesty's Government, and they are left waiting for Palestine.

From Basle I hear that the differences among the Zionists in Congress there exceed the most gloomy forebodings of the pessimistic. The leaders are hopelessly at variance, and the general condition of the unborn Jewish State is, if the phrase may pass, one of anarchy and chaos. *Yorkshire Post*

The Zangwill party was beaten, and the victorious delegates, those who still turn their eyes toward the Holy Land, exchanged the salutation: 'Next year in Palestine.' *New-York Tribune*

The victors restrained themselves, and it was not until the meeting had been formally closed that they gave vent to their enthusiasm by cheering and singing 'Hatikvah'. But before this peaceful close to a memorable meeting a painful scene occurred. Mr. Zangwill, labouring under intense excitement, entered the tribune and said: I appeal to the bar of history that you have committed treason against the Jewish people. I will only repeat what Herzl said to me at the end of the Sixth Congress: 'The Seventh Congress will be the last.' (Uproar.) *Jewish Chronicle*

Zangwill was granted the floor, but his remarks were so sharp that he had to be interrupted in the middle by the President and was ordered to his seat. *Julius H. Greenstone*

Mr. Zangwill himself, having said that he hoped this Congress would be the last of Zionism, and impeached its President for treason, was dragged from the tribune furiously. *Pall Mall Gazette*

Thirty delegates, voicing their protests and cheered by the supporters in the galleries, marched out of the hall, seceding from the congress. *New York Sun*

Shmarya Levin

A group, consisting of the English and a few Russian delegates, under the leadership of Israel Zangwill, broke away at once from the Congress and the movement.

New York Sun

From that time on peace reigned. Meantime the thirty seceding radicals were laying the foundation of a separate organization and were pressing Zangwill to accept the leadership.

Ithaca Daily News

Zionists Split. Israel Zangwill and His Territorialists Leave the Main Body of Jews at Basle, Switzerland.

Syracuse Journal

The Territorial Zionists have founded a separate organization of their own, and they are now holding meetings in a hall adjacent to that in which the original congress is meeting.

Brooklyn Standard Union

Israel Zangwill, the noted author, has decided to accept the presidency. The offer of presidency was made to Mr. Zangwill yesterday when the new organization was launched, but the novelist at first declined. He has since reconsidered his decision.

Should there be any objection to Mr. Zangwill's leadership, he will gladly retire in favor of somebody of greater influence, business experience and communal popularity.

American Hebrew

The homing instinct that is asserting itself among the Jewish people and which has found an expression in the Zionist movement, has resulted in the formation of the ITO by I. Zangwill, the gifted author of the race. The word ITO stands for Jewish Territorial Organization.

Syracuse Journal

The restriction as to Palestine, set up by the Congress, is formally abolished. The whole world is within the purview of the new organization. The movement is 'Zionism without Zion,' with a vengeance.

Jewish Chronicle

Chapter 11

Israel Zangwill

A race of some twelve million people has no square inch of land that it can call its own. Just as plants cannot thrive unless they have water, so people cannot thrive unless they have land.

Earth-hunger, the natural appetite of every healthy race, has died away under centuries of compulsory abstinence. So great is this Jewish earth-aversion that even those who profess hunger for Palestine turn away from any other soil with holy horror. But what if, while our eyes are fixed trancedly on the closed gates of Zion, every other opportunity slips away for ever?

ITOism does not specify the particular country. It says with Archimedes, *dos pou sto* – give me a place where I may stand. Give me a place and I will make myself again a people.

There must exist somewhere in the world a healthy, empty or thinly-populated territory, large and fertile enough to hold a population of many millions and not strong enough in its civilisation to melt up the Jewish people into its shape. Is there such a land? A land such as Jews would like – a land beautiful in climate and fertile in soil with shining rivers and smooth far-stretching roads, with mansions and gardens waiting for occupation, yet with no enemies to fear – such a land perhaps exists. But its name is *Gan Iden* or Paradise. On this side of the grave we cannot get to it. On this earth, if a climate is perfect, if a soil is fertile, there will already be inhabitants, the flag of some country will be already flying. First come, first served, and we came very late.

But even had we come the day after the creation, we could have got no such land – for no land exists ready-made. Every land, however delightful it seems to-day, was in the past more or less a dangerous wilderness. Every nation has had the task either of conquering the wilderness or of conquering the nation which had already conquered the wilderness, and if you shirk both these tasks, even then you cannot dodge history's debt, for history presents her bill in the shape of persecutions and pogroms. The Jews must leave Russia, slowly or swiftly. They must build a State for themselves. They must face nature, savage nature, but less savage than the Russian masses.

There lies – or rather there sleeps – a land which has every appearance of being the land of our quest. It is unthinkable that the Jewish people shall not follow up on that quest to the end. If we cannot get the Holy Land, we can make another land holy.

***

Search for a New Judæa.

Globe, 2 April 1909

As everyone knows, the Jewish Territorial Organisation has for years past been seeking a suitable spot where an autonomous Jewish state might be established.

Manchester Courier

Zangwill's New Palestine. It is believed Israel Zangwill and his Jewish Territorial Organization has at last found territory suitable for Jewish colonization.

Chicago Tribune

The Jewish Territorial Organisation, or the Ito, as it is more often called, sent a mission of investigation to Cyrenaica. The expedition left London on July 5 last year, and spent nearly a month exploring the country.

Morning Post

The interior of the country was closed to Europeans, but the I.T.O., under the guidance of the eminent British geologist and explorer, Professor Gregory, penetrated

Israel Zangwill

mysterious regions long untrodden by Christian feet. No expedition ever started with higher hopes.

Evening Standard   Cyrenaica is a great projection of land on the northern coast of Africa between Egypt and Tripoli.

Morning Post   Its most striking advantage is its geographical position, for it can be reached at little expense and in a short time by the Jews from Russia and Rumania.

Daily Telegraph   This beautiful and fertile land has been described as the most wonderful of the whole Mediterranean district.

Yorkshire Post   It would appear, so far as is known, to be well-wooded and watered, besides having an excellent climate. Many ruins of a great past are to be seen in Cyrenaica, and the British Museum contains not a few relics of it.

Irish News   There are forests of pine and olives on the slopes facing the Mediterranean, but there are no rivers.

Freeman's Journal   It is cooled by sea-breezes from the North, and protected by mountains from the scorching blasts and sandstorms of the Sahara. But it has long been abandoned by all the world except the wandering Bedouins. Mr. Israel Zangwill is said to be attracted by this promising substitute for the impossible.

Staffordshire Sentinel   In view of the nearness of the country to Europe the lack of information in regard to it is remarkable. To the world in general it is an unknown land, whose very existence is hardly realised.

Theobald Fischer   Unexplored, almost without any communication with the civilized world, almost empty of population in the face of Europe, whose inhabitants are squeezing and pushing as in the high streets of a metropolis, but everywhere covered with the ruins of a great Past, Cyrenaica may at any moment – and in the jostling and pressing of the peoples of Europe for air and light and elbow room, this moment cannot be long delayed – step into the fore-ground of world-politics.

It is possible that Jewry is now definitely approaching a solution of the grave problem confronting it in Russia and other countries.

Daily Telegraph

The report of the expedition is published to-day.

Morning Post,
2 April 1909

Professor Gregory returned to England with the news that the Cyrenaica project literally could not 'hold water'. The soil was spongy, the rainfall of the wet season sank to irrecoverable depths, so that in the dry season a perpetual menace of drought hung over man and field. To establish a large colony in Cyrenaica was impossible; even irriga-tion was out of the question.

Israel Zangwill

An Unpromising Land. Investigation has torn the veil of enchantment from the face of this territory, as to which many romantic and exaggerated statements were made.

Evening Standard

The report was far from encouraging. 'A dead jackal and a living hare' were the only wild animals seen in Cyrenaica, but a few 'small dispirited donkeys' were found, 'fleas and flies were numerous,' and rats and mice were understood to exist in quantities.

*Sunderland
Daily Echo*

Waterless Cyrenaica Abandoned.

Globe

Cyrenaica turns out to be no fit place for an autono-mous Jewish colony. That great essential human comfort, water, is lacking. Cyrenaica occupies a plateau of lime-stone 30,000 feet thick. Why this should continue, after innumerable centuries, to be so porous as to prevent the accumulation of water is difficult to understand. The dust of the centuries should fill the pores. But the expedition came away satisfied that the glory of ancient Cyrene has been greatly exaggerated by the historians. To be sure, no earthly civilization ever thrived without water.

New York Times

London Daily News

Mr. Zangwill does not conceal his disappointment. He refers to the report as 'tragic and unexpected.'

Israel Zangwill

A few ancient vases and lamps, dug out of their repose of two thousand years, stand on my shelf as a melancholy memento of an abandoned hope.

Manchester Guardian,
3 May 1909

The disappointing report has been followed by some speculation as to the next move of the Jewish Territorial Organization. The general rumour, for which there seems to be pretty good foundation, is that Mr. Zangwill's organization is projecting a big scheme in Mesopotamia.

New York Herald

Mesopotamia New Home for the Jews. Mr. Zangwill declared that in Mesopotamia is to be found the solution of troubles which have beset the Jews since they were dispersed from Palestine. The establishment of the colony between the rivers Tigris and Euphrates will deflect much of the stream of immigration which now flows from Russia and Roumania to the United States.

Israel Zangwill

For the refugee from Russia it lies across the Black Sea, and it will be a far more convenient centre of refuge than New York. Although the bulk consists today of vast swamps and deserts, a region the size of Palestine can be irrigated to support a population of millions. Moreover, when the swamps and marshes are cleared away, the climate may be much more bearable.

We are coming into a period of history when gigantic problems occupy the world's attention. What time has the world to trouble itself with the Jewish question? And what right have we to expect that the Jewish people will emerge from all these coming frictions any less battered than before? Who shall say what the whirligig of time has yet in store for us? But imagine an Itoland established and Mesopotamia acting as a refuge against the evil days that may come.

We are on the eve of an important departure in the work and purpose of the Jewish Territorial Organisation. *Liverpool Daily Post*

It has transpired that the heat of Mesopotamia is terrific and the population hostile. Israel Zangwill, November 1909

Australia is Zangwill's new ITOland. *Jewish Advocate, 5 August 1910*

The irrepressible Israel Zangwill has again rushed into the limelight with another I.T.O. colonization scheme. His latest bright idea is to secure territory for the settlement of a million Russian Jews in Western Australia. Of this province the 'United Editors' Encyclopedia' (1907 edition) says: 'Western Australia is for the most part a barren tract, almost destitute of fresh water. The whole interior of the country presents one vast dreary plain, sometimes stifling, scorching, low-lying, deep-red sand ridges; sometimes matted over for hundreds and thousands of miles with scrub.' Worst of all is the 'spinifex' or 'porcupine grass', lacerating the feet of horses and the clothes and flesh of men. *American Israelite*

The scheme is still, of course, only in its initial stages, but we wish it all success. *Jewish Chronicle*

Some correspondence between Mr. Israel Zangwill and Mr. Alexander Marks is published in the latest Australian papers. Mr. Marks wrote to inform Zangwill that 'any form of independence is quite out of the question for a Jewish settlement in Australia.'

The Canadian government has informed Zangwill, who proposed to establish a Jewish colony in Canada, that any project of the kind is entirely out of the question so far as Canada is concerned.

The Jewish Territorial Association have under consideration a proposal for establishing a Jewish colony in Mexico.

An attempt to get land in Australia failed. Offers in Mexico and Paraguay had to be rejected owing to the unsettled state of political affairs in those countries.

The Zionist party, in a strict sense, has held firm to its original aim, the establishment of a Jewish national state in Palestine. By contrast, the party led by Mr. Israel Zangwill has wandered pretty nearly over all the five continents and seven seas without fixing on any one location for more than a couple of months.

Chapter 12

Morris Waldman

Fifty-two William street is the home of the international banking house of Kuhn, Loeb & Co. Frequently this great financial establishment is referred to merely as Fifty-two William street, just as one might say, the Quai D'Orsay, or Downing Street, or the White House, or even, if you will, the Vatican. I doubt not that a letter addressed in this way, mailed in China, would eventually, even immediately, find its way there. The head of this concern for a generation was Jacob H. Schiff.

Though Schiff was short in stature, indeed, quite below the average in height, the dignity of his bearing created the impression of a taller form. This effect may have been produced by his garb. Apparently little affected by the changes in modes of dress, he wore a flat, starched collar and a flat, white cravat that nearly covered the barely discernible white, stiff bosomed shirt beneath, with the old-fashioned, round, starched cuffs showing at the sleeves. A mild mannered man, with an even milder voice, was he, with the decidedly foreign accent of the cultured German, who pronounces the 'th' like an 's.'

A full, grey, nearly white beard, carefully combed on both sides away from a dimpled chin, lent a dignity and aristocracy to his mien that reflected the manners of an earlier and foreign generation. To a casual observer, benevolence seemed to radiate from his countenance. Yet to those who knew him well, beneath that benevolent exterior were discernible force and determination that bespoke a commanding and even an unyielding leadership. The accumulated wisdom of the ages, combined with

the pathos of the two thousand years of *Judenschmerz*, seemed to be engulfed in the profound depths of his calm, steady, grey eyes, which lent a soulfulness to his otherwise coldly and evenly chiselled features.

Saturday Evening Post, 1909

Mr Schiff is a kindly, accessible, gravely-courteous man who wears the same kind of broad white necktie all year round. He is always to be found at a long, low desk at the end of a stately room that has more of the atmosphere of a salon than the air of a place where whole industrial empires have been financed.

Philadelphia Press, 1903

Mr. Schiff is to-day the most powerful force of any of the so-called high-financiers of New York.

Morris Waldman

His appearance at a board meeting invariably caused a quiet stir and a sudden hush in the conversation, in deference not merely to his great wealth in a generation when wealth was much respected, or because of a powerful public influence his colleagues knew he exerted, but rather because of an aristocratic quality in his personality that palpably, yet subtly, distinguished him and, in a manner, separated him from them. If memory serves me correctly, nobody except members of his family or his senior business partners ever called him by his first name; nor do I recall that he ever saluted his other associates and friends in such an intimate manner.

***

The promised land of the Jew, it seems to me, is America. Jacob Schiff

This nation has gradually been built up from a small colony into a mighty world power, through the constant, unrestricted inflow of the surplus population of the Old World. Who would imagine in the early eighties, when the wholesale Jewish emigration from the land of the Czar first began, that in less than three decades in the city of New York alone the number of our co-religionists would rise to a million? Such, however, is the fact, and still they come.

In the small hours of the morning, when responsibilities weigh particularly heavy, when burdens often appear almost unbearable, the question frequently presents itself to my mind, as it no doubt does to others. Unless we find effective ways to deflect the stream of immigration from New York, the congestion already existing here is certain to grow to proportions where it may become a menace to the status of the Jew throughout the country. This we must not risk.

The Jew of the future is, to my mind, the Russian Jew transformed by American methods. A well distributed population of some millions of our co-religionists, imbued with the Americanism of George Washington, Abraham Lincoln, and Theodore Roosevelt will form the best and most efficient centre our people can desire.

The Jew should not for a moment feel that he has only found an 'asylum' in this country; he must not feel that he is in exile and that his abode here is only a temporary or passing one. As I stand before you, there arises before me a vision of coming days – of a generation not yet born, the children's children of the men and women who in this generation have come from all parts of the globe to these blessed shores.

The vision which presents itself to me shows me a people of our faith, who have thrown off the shackles, the peculiarities and prejudices which have handicapped their fathers. A people among the best in the land, proud of their American citizenship, thoroughly imbued with its spirit, with its obligations, with its high privileges, but just as proud of their religion – almost a new type – true Americans of the Jewish faith. Today looked upon as a foreign element, in times to come, as an integral part of a race of Americans yet in the making. This is the vision which passes before my eyes. My prayer, my hope, my conviction, is that in due time it becomes a reality.

With God's help, in a bright future to come, the descendants of the multitude of our co-religionists who now crowd upon our shores, and whom we scarcely know how to properly take care of, will have assimilated with their American fellow-citizens, and have become part of the bone and sinew of our great country.

***

New York Tribune, 17 December 1905
New York City is just beginning to feel the crest of another great wave of Jewish immigration. The Russian massacres have caused more Hebrews to look hither for a refuge than have ever before turned their faces toward this land of freedom and wealth.

New York Press, 30 September 1906
In New York harbor one day last week thirty-one vessels arrived with immigrants from all parts of Europe. This is not a new story, but is the same week after week.

New York Tribune
Few outside the Jewish world appreciate the vast difficulties involved in the Americanization of the Russian Hebrew. Although there are 3,600,000 square miles in the

United States, with an average population of twenty-five persons to the square mile, he usually prefers to wedge himself into the teeming East Side, where a square mile on average contains 400,000 persons.

New York Press

He finds many of his countrymen already here, possibly some of them are friends. It is pleasant to fraternize with them and hear his native language, follow his native customs and eat his native food. He is not quite sure of himself and this new country yet, and he fears to get away from a seaport. If he gets homesick or ill luck overtakes him he wants to be where a steamship is easy of access, so that he can start for home almost any day. His knowledge of America outside of New York is of the vaguest description.

New York Sun

It is true that New York is to-day the greatest Jewish centre the world has ever known.

Morris Waldman

The East Side had become a state of mind. It was the spiritual power house of the immigrant Jewish life of the city.

***

Frederick Boyd Stevenson, 1901

On the East side of New York is the Ghetto – the home of the poor Hebrews. To most of us – even to those of us who live in New York – it is a name without meaning. That vast district is, to many, an unexplored region. Some of us have seen a glimpse of it as we have passed through Hester street or along Ridge street. We have crowded our way through the busy push-cart peddlers and the vendors who throng the streets like an army. We have brushed against the dirty, ragged, hungry children with the curse of poverty marked upon their faces and their bodies dwarfed and crippled by want.

I have spent some time in the New York Ghetto, as I think it presents one of the hardest problems in city life.

And yet, despite the poverty that is apparent there on every hand, there is a fascination in the life on the street that attracts one.

The sidewalks and even the center of the roadway bear the appearance of a great outdoor bazar rather than the thoroughfare of a metropolis. Hester street is the busiest of them all. It is the Broadway of the Ghetto, and is swarming from curb to curb with push-carts laden with fruit, vegetables, meats and foods of all kinds. In front of the dingy stores, blocking up the paths of pedestrians, are stalls and booths covered with eatables, which the fastidious would question as to their composition, and the names of which are unpronounceable to the majority of people. One place in particular I noticed on Essex street. Nothing but bread was sold there. But it was not the bread that one sees on the tables at the hotels and the high-priced restaurants. It was made into the shape of a cheese over two feet in diameter and was black and uninviting. It sold at three cents a pound.

All tenement places on the East side are practically the same. They consist of three small rooms. The room which one enters from the dark hall – all the halls on the East side are dark as midnight in a day of brightest sunshine – is the kitchen. In the rear are two smaller rooms, each just half the width of the front room. They barely admit a bed in the event that the tenant is fortunate enough to own such a piece of furniture. On one side of the kitchen there is generally a window. If the tenement is strictly modern there will be a similar window in one of the bedrooms; otherwise both bedrooms will be windowless. Generally, but not always, water may be obtained from a faucet in the kitchen. There are no bathtubs or closets. Gas light may be obtained by dropping a quarter in a slot in a meter. The only furniture besides the beds consists of a small cracked stove, a rickety table and two or three wooden-bottomed chairs. In these rooms 10 or 12 persons frequently live. Where they all sleep and how they all eat is one of the unraveled riddles of the Ghetto.

When I recall the intensity of the material picture in the dense Yiddish quarter, there abides with me, ineffaceably, the memory of a summer evening spent there.

It was the sense of a great swarming, a swarming that had begun to thicken, infinitely, as soon as we had crossed to the East side. The scene here bristled, at every step, with the signs and sounds, immitigable, unmistakable, of a Jewry that had burst all bounds.

The children swarmed above all – here was multiplication with a vengeance; and the number of very old persons, of either sex, was almost equally remarkable; the very old persons being in equal vague occupation of the doorstep, pavement, curbstone, gutter, roadway, and every one alike using the street for overflow. Overflow, in the whole quarter, is the main fact of life. The scene hummed with the human presence beyond any I had ever faced. There are small strange animals, known to natural history, snakes or worms I believe, who, when cut into pieces, wriggle away contentedly and live in the snippet as completely as in the whole. So the denizens of the New York Ghetto had each, like the fine glass particle, his or her individual share of the whole hard glitter of Israel.

Henry James, 1905

To counteract the hiving tendency of the Russian Jewish immigrant, a society has been established called the Industrial Removal Office.

New York Tribune, 17 December 1905

The country is large enough to absorb all Jewish immigrants – past present and future – if they could be gotten to realize that America is not a strip along the Atlantic, but a mighty continent, hungry for people to develop its resources. The Industrial Removal Office has done much to introduce the rest of the country to the immigrant of the Atlantic ports.

American Israelite

Such men as Jacob H. Schiff, and other prominent Jews, have the movement in charge.

At the corner of Second avenue and Eleventh street there is a small house in which the Industrial Removal Office is located. Daily from forty to fifty men come asking to be sent to other parts of the country.

He is a strange mixture, this applicant. He is basically a product of Old World conditions with all that this implies. The transition from the simple and almost naïve life in Russia to the complexities of New York has been too swift and sudden.

If the applicant is adjudged to be a suitable person, he is sent away to some place in the United States where he will have an opportunity of earning his living. If he has friends or relatives in some particular town, he goes there; otherwise he goes to whatever place is determined upon by the Removal Office.

A big furniture van a few days ago came to a stop in front of a three-story and basement house in Rivington-st. Several men and women and children appeared, some with trunks, some with baskets, and all ready for a long journey. The trunks and other pieces of baggage were loaded in and then each one was given a supply of hard bread, bologna sausage and canned sardines in a large paper bag. With these the company, which numbered perhaps thirty, mounted to the interior of the van. Then the single horse attached to the van strained at the traces, and the party was off, bound for different cities of the West to begin life anew under more favorable conditions than those to be found on the crowded East Side, and the day's work of the Industrial Removal Office had borne its fruit.

During the past year 6922 removals from New York were affected by the office, the largest number during the six years that the work has been going on. The number of removals is, of course, but a fraction of the newly arrived immigrants who remain in New York.

Jewish Exponent
1907

Those who are engaged in the work of the IRO are fully aware that the sum total of removed persons is not a sum of intrinsic greatness.

David Bressler

Once the immigrant settled in New York City, it was very difficult to persuade him to abandon the congenial atmosphere of the lower East Side for some strange, unknown, dull and, to him, alien atmosphere of a small industrial town in the Midwest.

Morris Waldman

To take the plunge into the Hinterland, where Yiddish may be an unknown tongue, Kosher food an unknown thing, and labor opportunities limited, was left only to the most daring.

David Bressler

Schiff made clear that useful as the work of the I.R.O. was, it had made a shallow dent on the growing mass of Jewish population. More drastic measures had to be taken.

Morris Waldman

Chapter 13

Morris Waldman

Though the somewhat romantic story of the Galveston movement is recorded in various publications, reference to it here is appropriate, in view of the fact that I was its pioneer director. The origin of this enterprise were conversations that Jacob H. Schiff had in London with Israel Zangwill in 1906. Schiff told Zangwill he was worried over the mounting congestion of Jewish immigrants in New York City. Zangwill, eager to realize his dreams for large scale colonization, with the vivid imagination of the poet and novelist that ignores all practical considerations, urged his visitor to seek possession of some large territory in the Southwest of the United States which eventually could be developed into the Jewish National Home. After Schiff indicated that such a plan would be not only impractical but decidedly repugnant to basic American ideals, he suggested what later came to be known as the Galveston Movement.

Jacob Schiff to
Israel Zangwill

It appears to me that in this existing emergency, the Jewish Territorial Organization, if for the time being it will occupy itself with something immediately practicable and sidetrack its cherished project of finding a separate land of refuge, can be of very great service to the momentous and pressing cause which we all have so very much at heart.

What I have in mind is that the Jewish Territorial Organization should take up a project to direct the flow of emigration from Russia to the Gulf ports of the United States – notably New Orleans – from where immigrants can readily be distributed over the interior of the country, I am quite certain, in very large numbers.

A proper and thoroughly organized movement of the Russian emigration, such as I have outlined above, has never been attempted. Surely the carrying out of this project will furnish the relief which is imperatively needed, much more promptly than the creation of a new land of refuge, which at best and even if successful, must take many, many years. I am firmly convinced that if my proposal is properly understood and properly handled, there should be no difficulty in getting two million Russian Jews within the next five or ten years into the Southern, Northwestern, and Pacific states of this country.

The difficulty with Schiff is that he is so charming it is difficult to quarrel with him. — Israel Zangwill

Zangwill compromised – grudgingly, perhaps. — Morris Waldman

My opinion is that Schiff forces us to accept. For if another body undertakes it, public attention will be directed to this work and we shall comparatively be crushed. — Israel Zangwill

The Industrial Removal Office at New York, with the experience and connections it has already secured, would be well in position to undertake the carrying out of my project. With this view, it is proposed that the Removal Office create an organization to receive arriving immigrants and at once forward them to their destination. It would be left to the ITO to father the movement in Russia, to gather the proposed emigrants, to arrange steamship routes, etc. — Jacob Schiff to Israel Zangwill

I shall undertake to place at the disposal of the Removal Office the $500,000 which it is my intention to devote to the initiation of the project. Half a million dollars should suffice to place 20,000 to 25,000 people in the American 'Hinterland', and, I believe, with the successful settlement of such a number, others would readily follow of their own accord.

It is my desire that my name be not given undue prominence. It will by no means be a Schiff scheme. This project is now to a great extent in your own and your friends' hands, and I shall look forward with deep interest to see what can be done with it.

***

Morris Waldman   As the plan was being discussed, the question as to which port of entry was to be selected appeared to be the most perplexing. Baltimore was rejected because it was too near New York, and we feared a general drift of the immigrants. Charleston and Savannah were rejected because the meagre industrial development of the South offered no prospects. San Francisco was hardly considered because of the great distance from the points of origin, combined with the limited industrial opportunities of the Pacific Coast. New Orleans received more consideration because it was the terminus of several of the largest railroad lines of the West.

I advised against New Orleans. It was too large and attractive a city. It would offer temptation to the immigrant to remain there instead of braving the dubious uncertainties of some small place in the Hinterland. We would merely repeat a population congestion as undesirable as the one we were trying to relieve on the Atlantic coast.

I remember the thrill I experienced (I was twenty-seven years old) when my judgment was requested. I felt that I was being asked to take part in the making of history. I ventured a suggestion – Galveston. That out-of-the-way little port, which would hardly have been known except for the sad memory of its catastrophic storm and flood of 1900, was finally selected. 'Well,' said Mr Schiff, 'you've made your bed. You have to go and lie in it.' On November 7th, 1906, I was sent to Galveston to prepare for the arrival of the first boatload of its immigrants.

***

There is something spicy and free and reckless and thriving and unconstrained and hospitable about Texas that captures me. If you feel yourself getting conventional and pokey, and stiff and morbid, and the moss is beginning to grow on the north side of your soul, light out for Texas.

Bill Nye, 10 May 1891

The scenery of Texas strikes one as being amazing, strange and paradoxical. It is a mixture, a combination, a conglomeration of all scenery. It is a region of strange contrasts in peoples and places. You may ride in one day from odorous moss grown forests, where everything is of tropic fullness, into a section where the mesquite and chaparral dot the great prairies; or from the sea loving people of Galveston to a people who have never seen a mast or a wave, and whose main idea of water is that it is something difficult to find, and agreeable to taste when one is very thirsty. Nothing can be more changefully lovely, and the whole is a vast panorama of grandeur. Other states may have more lofty mountains towering heavenwards, more wild and majestic streams rushing on to the ocean, more dusky forests and deeper valleys, but for all that give me the glory of a Texas prairie under a vertical sun.

Ottawa Free Trader, 5 May 1883

The approach to Galveston is one of the most charming sights the southern country affords. By sea it is exceedingly so. To look out upon the deep, there to behold a speck in the distance like a 'mirage' – such is Galveston, the island town, the gem of the gulf.

Galveston is the prettiest city I ever was in. It is like stepping into a new world.

M. J. Moore

Paterson Evening
News
The streets are so clean, the breeze, from whatever direction, is so salt and fresh, the bathing so invigorating, that one feels sure of health and buoyancy. The air is full of the sound of laughter and music and is laden with the perfume of flowers.

Jackson Daily
Clarion
This is certainly a most delightful climate, almost perpetual spring. Ladies appear on the streets Christmas day in linen dresses.

Plattsburg
Republican
Many of the streets are fringed with rows of oleanders which grow in wild profusion, and often attain a height of twenty feet. They are in bloom about two-thirds of the year, giving the city the appearance of an immense flower garden.

Texas Siftings
This is why Galveston is called the 'Oleander City,' as these beautiful flowers are seen and smelt on every side. The perfume is so strong at times that strangers are liable to get the headache.

Weymouth Gazette
On every side peeps out the orange and myrtle, the oleander and fig and delicate rose, with all the brilliant-hued blossoms of a tropic land. I have stood at the head of some wide, sandy streets, and looking down their length towards the blue waters of the Gulf, wondered if there could be a more beautiful sight than this.

Eagle River Review,
21 July 1905
It will soon be five years since Galveston was practically destroyed.

Edward Mott
The world knows the awful story of the Galveston storm of September, 1900, when between 8,000 and 10,000 of her population were destroyed by a tidal wave, and over $20,000,000 of her property was swept away, almost in the twinkling of an eye.

Mount Vernon
Daily Argus
Many asserted it must have been a tidal wave; many called it a tornado; the weather bureau of Washington

recorded it a 'freak storm', something inexplicable. When the hurricane reached its height the wind simply picked up the waters of the Gulf of Mexico and hurled them over the island city.

A similar storm blowing across Lake Michigan would have destroyed Chicago, or if it had struck New York would have submerged that city.

Washington Evening Star

Frame residences were swept away like feathers before the howling shrieking winds. Brick and iron buildings fared but little better, for the wind tore the roofs off as though in play. Every bridge connecting the ill fated island with the mainland was carried away by the fury of the warring elements.

Liberty Southern Herald

The storm swept the ground perfectly clear of residences and piled them up in a conglomerated mass on the beach, strewing the piling with the debris, and the bodies of many victims.

Maysville Evening Bulletin

Every able bodied man was compelled to help dispose of the dead in order to avoid a pestilence. At first the bodies were buried in trenches dug in the sands of the island,

Liberty Southern Herald

but this required too much work and time so the bodies were towed out into the gulf and consigned to the deep.

London Daily News   A beautiful city, truly, was destroyed on the night of the 8th.

Bellefontaine Republican   The story of the rebuilding of Galveston constitutes one of the bravest chapters in the annals of American enterprise. The sound of the hammer and the saw has never ceased since the invading waters retreated into the gulf. The piles of wreckage have been cleared away and the scars of the fatality removed. The palms have been replanted and the oleanders are blooming again. The great enterprise which is on every tongue is the sea wall. It is not at all likely that another such storm will visit this part of the coast in a hundred years, but if another does come it will find an insurmountable barrier surrounding Galveston.

Edward Mott   At the cost of over three million and a half dollars, a concrete sea wall made of Texas granite and Portland cement, 17 feet high, has been raised about the Gulf front of the city. It is one of the most stupendous engineering feats.

John Quill   Today, a new Galveston has sprung up out of the ruins of the old.

J. H. Johnston   Even at this early date we are beginning to appreciate the fact that the great storm of September 8, 1900, was but a blessing in disguise, and in the years to come the citizens of Galveston will look back on their great flood as do the people of London and Chicago on their fires, which really mark the first true beginnings of these great municipalities. With population and prosperity increasing by leaps and bounds, with climate unsurpassed, it is certainly no exaggeration to state that this place is today one of the most flourishing, beautiful and healthful garden spots under the blue vault of heaven.

Chapter 14

Israel Zangwill,
30 December 1906

Ladies and Gentlemen, I am not on this platform to speak soft words and to mince the hard facts of the Jewish situation.

The ITO was founded some seventeen months ago, 639 pogroms have made these seventeen months among the blackest in all Jewish history. The emigration from Russia this year is calculated to exceed 200,000. Can Itoland, can any new land, receive such a number? Of course not. Roads have to be made, houses built, bridges constructed, forests destroyed, marshes drained, fields planted. Rome was not built in a day, neither will a Jewish State be.

Itoland is a provision for tomorrow, not for to-day. But unless we begin to found such a land to-day, our posterity too, may be doomed to stand by and wring their hands.

What is to be done then? The problem divides itself into two halves – to provide for the future, and to provide for the present. The ITO is already hard at work on the first half. Shall it leave the second half alone? Shall it go on as if there had been no pogroms since its foundation, no wild flight of emigrants across Europe? Or shall the ITO boldly seize the other half of the problem, too, and present the Jewish people with an institution which no Jew in the world will deny is its most urgent necessity?

I have the pleasure of announcing the establishment of the Department for the Regulation of Emigration. It is already at work. Our friend Dr. Jochelmann spent his Christmas in Berlin pulling together some of its

Continental strings. Our new department aims, among other things, to answer the question of the immediate *Wohin?* In what direction should the wandering Jew of to-day be advised to turn his foot-steps?

There are enough Jews in New York, and more will be born there. These at least cannot be kept out. But you could not for ever go pouring emigrants into New York, or New York would burst. The Jews come from hundreds of towns in Russia, but the great bulk of them go to only one town in America – it is really rather unreasonable. In Russia, they complain they are confined to the Pale and not allowed to spread all over Russia. But at least the Pale is as large as France. When they leave Russia they hasten to pen themselves into a Pale, and that a Pale no bigger than Whitechapel.

We shall proclaim throughout Russia that New York is not the same thing as the United States, that America is not a town but a territory, and that this immense territory is largely empty. Of this enormous territory only the East is developed, the West is only half out of its shell, while the South is still in the egg. It is in the great *Hinterland* of the West that the Jewish emigrants' best opportunities lie.

The Great American West! That is the new *Wohin*, the *Wohin* for the present day.

***

New York Times,
8 June 1907   Russian Jews For Texas.

Daily Express   ITOLAND, U.S.A. Mr. Zangwill Urges Jews to Settle in the West.

Auburn Citizen   Mr. Zangwill Favors the United States as the Home of Zion.

Argus   The latest attempt to stem the tide pouring into congested New York and seething all sorts of social miseries is along the lines that promise success.

Jews leaving Europe for America will be induced to go on to the country lying west of the Mississippi river. It is the belief that during the next few years a considerable part of the Jewish immigration will arrive in Galveston and not in New York.

Auburn Citizen

Texas Colony for Jews. Israel Zangwill, the noted novelist and Zionist leader, is heading a scheme to send families of persecuted Russian Jews to America. A colony for these exiles will be established near Galveston, Tex.

Columbia Republican

Is America likely to find, in ten or twenty years from now, little towns of self-governing Jews throughout the great West as a result of the new scheme?

David Wise

There is not the faintest idea of establishing a colony in Texas.

Israel Zangwill to the *Washington Evening Star*

Mr. Zangwill denied the reported intention to form a Hebrew colony near Galveston, Texas. All they intend on doing, he said, was to form a department, with headquarters at Galveston, to assist emigrants to penetrate the interior of the United States. To further this purpose, Mr. Zangwill said, an anonymous donor, but not Mr. Jacob Schiff, he added, had contributed £100,000 ($500,000).

New York Herald

Though private rumours had previously been circulated to this effect, it is now for the first time made publicly known that Mr. Jacob H. Schiff has contributed the sum of 500,000 dols. towards the movement for diverting immigration through Galveston. That Mr. Schiff gave half a million dollars to the Galveston movement is made public in an interview with Mr. Zangwill, which appears in the *New York Herald* of yesterday. In paying his tribute to the many eminent Jews of this country, Mr Zangwill said: – 'Then there is Mr. Jacob Schiff, known to Gentiles as a great financier, but known to us as a greater preacher and teacher; really a rabbi at heart, and coming

Jewish Chronicle

from a long line of rabbis. He is one of the finest characters in the whole Jewish world. He gave half-a-million to
a philanthropic scheme I am connected with, and would
not even allow his name to be mentioned.'

Perhaps the most striking utterance in the interview,
attributed to Mr. Zangwill, is the following: – 'My ideals
are a pure Jewish religion and a solid Jewish nation.
What I see is the broken fragments of a homeless race
struggling to maintain its religion and race in the face
of almost hopeless obstacles and prejudices. I see Jews
changing their names, denying their parentage and losing
themselves in the new conditions. I see more and more
intermarriages. As a Jew I may lament, as an artist I can
only record the truth.'

Dexter Marshall

In private conversation Zangwill has made many
sharp remarks about this country.

Washington Post,
27 October 1907

W. R. Wheeler sailed for America Wednesday. A
few days before he left England he had an interesting
interview with Israel Zangwill, the novelist. He saw Mr.
Zangwill at the latter's home in Worthing. Speaking of
Mr. Zangwill's views touching the emigration of Jews to
America, Mr. Wheeler said: 'Mr. Zangwill feels that every
Jew who goes to America makes more distant the realiza-
tion of his dream of a reunited Jewish race. In his opinion,
America does more to counteract the efforts of the Jewish
Territorial Organization than any other country. But with
all this said, I must add that Mr. Zangwill feels that as
matters now stand with his race, America is a better home
for the Jew than most countries.'

New York Herald,
8 January 1907

Mr. Alexander Harkavy, of New York, who has been
travelling in Europe in the interests of Hebrew emigration
to America, was today the guest of Mr. Israel Zangwill at
his country house. Discussing the question of means of
diverting the stream of emigration, Mr. Zangwill said to

Mr. Harkavy: – 'America is the euthanasia of the Jew and Judaism. The stronger force always absorbs the weaker. The great pity is that the richly complex culture of the Russian Jew must be swallowed up in Americanism. If I had my way not a single Russian Jew should enter America.'

American Hebrew

Mr. Israel Zangwill appears to be a difficult man to satisfy. After having made an elaborate arrangement by which the Jewish immigration to the United States should be diverted to the South and West, he comes out with the declaration that the ultimate fate of the Jews in the United States fills his Jewish heart with dismay. He fears that their prosperity in this favored land will in the course of generations remove all Jewish feeling from them.

Mr. Zangwill seems to us too pessimistic. There is evidence around him in England and in this country that even amidst all the temptations of modern life, Jews can exhibit that self-control and spirit of abnegation which is involved in leading the Jewish life. That some fall away only helps to strengthen the energies and ideals of the remainder. It was always a component part of the prophetic ideal that only a remnant of Israel will be saved.

Chapter 15

Morris Waldman

It was with a light heart that I took the train for Galveston.

I shall never forget the delight I experienced of rolling through the wide stretches of Oklahoma, Indian Territory and Eastern Texas, the wealth of color of wild flowers completely covering miles and miles of country, interspersed now and then by large herds of cattle, and at times marred by the ugly super-surface structures of oil well drillers. It was quite exciting as we approached the railroad stations to see the cowboys on their ponies in their picturesque clothes and wide sombreros. I recalled their fictional hair-raising adventures in which I had wallowed as a boy.

Galveston greeted me with open arms. The sun shone brightly, the air was soft with nearly languorous softness, the green leaves of the banana tree – a novel sight – were just beginning to split and droop, the oleanders shed their wine-colored leaves on the greensward of the boulevards, the rosebushes nodded hospitably to me as I walked along, and the birds, of deliciously vivid plumage, trilled a joyous welcome. I was happy enough to be nearly grateful that Czars existed so that there would be Jewish problems and Jewish emigration.

Rabbi Henry Cohen was the first man I called on the morning I arrived. We took to each other at once. Yes, he had heard of the new movement. And he was excited about it. It was wonderful, and he and his community would help in every way. It was because of his eager, enthusiastic welcome that the difficulties we in New York had anticipated were dissipated before we started. He had already, at that time, earned the sobriquet of 'the Rabbi of Texas.' He was 'the Rabbi' not only to his own congregation or even to the wider Jewish community, he was 'the Rabbi' to the whole city. Indeed, he was 'the Rabbi' to a good part of Texas and the Southwest.

Galvestonians are proud of their many natural assets – long, white beaches, multi-colored oleanders, tropical climate and the finest surf bathing in the world – but they are proudest of a personality no other city can claim – the inimitable and beloved Dr. Henry Cohen.

Galveston Week

You can pick up innumerable tales about Rabbi Cohen all through the Southwest. Some of them true, some that may be true, and some that ought to be true if they aren't. It is indeed the measure of the greatness of a man that legends begin to accumulate around him when he is still living.

Webb Waldron

In all the state of Texas, from Fort Worth to San Anton', there's not a man who hasn't heard of Rabbi Henry Cohen.

Irve Tunick

It is an experience never to be forgotten to have walked the streets of Galveston with Henry Cohen. He was small and slight in stature, not much over five feet in height, sallow in complexion, low of voice, always dressed in a Prince Albert coat. There was nothing dramatic about him; he was no showman and flaunted none of the usual stigmata of the great man. He knew and greeted almost everyone he passed; almost everyone knew him. To walk with Henry Cohen was to walk with royalty.

Jacob Rader Marcus

At his home he is constantly having to jump up to answer the phone, answer the doorbell, and to give advice. Always laughing, with his characteristic booming chuckle, repeating phrases of his conversation to emphasize their meaning and importance, he appears always in

Bob Nesbitt

the highest of spirits, with a levity as entertaining as it is unexpected, and a fondness for good cigars.

Galveston News Although born and educated in England, as a youth Dr. Cohen came to the United States, serving first at Woodville, Miss., and later coming to Galveston on June 1, 1888.

Wilhelmina Beane Dr. Cohen, a classmate of Zangwill's in London, treasures an autographed prologue to Children of the Ghetto, entitled, 'From the Author to the Audience,' sent him by the author in 1899.

Rabbi Henry Cohen As boys we were brought together. From the year 1890 till the day of his death, Israel Zangwill and I were fast friends – corresponding ever and anon overseas on many subjects. In 1891 and again in 1899 on my visits to England we saw much of each other and on his first lecture tour in the United States we grasped hands and talked of common interests.

Morris Waldman It was the day of bicycles, and as I think of the dynamic little Rabbi now, I have a picture of him flitting to and fro on his 'wheel', doing his countless chores. When people were in trouble, white or black, Jew or Gentile, aristocrat or plebeian, it was 'the Rabbi' who was first consulted. Mollie, his wife, was a sweet and amiable lady in thorough harmony with her husband's spiritual outlook on life, yet a bit more practical and administratively efficient. Otherwise, the Rabbi would have long before been thrown into bankruptcy, for he acted as if his possessions were not his own, but belonged to anyone who claimed them – and there were many such.

As for me, they were sending for my trunk and reluctantly accepted my compromise to dine with them daily. Usually it was both lunch and dinner. Until my family arrived several months later I virtually was their daily unpaying guest.

***

Temple B'nai Israel was crowded on Friday evening with an intensely patriotic throng. A special service was held in honour of the quadrocentennial of the discovery of America. The Israelites of this city seemed to take much interest in the celebration, judged by the attention that was paid to the impressive service of Rabbi Henry Cohen.

Galveston Daily News, 23 October 1892

From 1776 till to-day this has been a country of freedom, the like of which never before existed, and no body of people appreciates this as completely as the Israelites. In this country we are not cramped and crushed physically or mentally. Although we have lost something of our clannishness, it seems that mingling with people of a different creed tends to strengthen us in everything that we have erstwhile held dear, and at the same time removes that exclusive vein from our nature. We may learn from our status in this country that it was never intended by God that we should dwell only in one portion of the globe. And so to-day we rejoice with the rest of the

Rabbi Henry Cohen

American world. We feel that we have even more cause to exult than they.

Galveston
Daily News

When the address was concluded, the children of the Sunday school sang 'America,' the whole audience rising as if by an inspiration, thus ending a ceremonial that will long be remembered by all who had the good fortune to be present. Mr. Leberman presided at the organ with more than his usual skill.

***

Israel Zangwill

The Galveston idea sounds simple; yet the attempt to change it into a reality was fraught with incredible complications. Many an emigrant, when invited to go to Galveston instead of New York, replies wistfully, 'But I want to go to America.'

But our Russian bureau – under the brilliant guidance of Dr. Jochelmann – rose victorious. After months of doubt and scepticism on the part of the emigrants, a batch of believing Jews was collected.

Alexander
Z. Gurwitz

The time came when we felt compelled to leave Russia. We, my wife and I, began to speculate, 'Why should we remain here? What prevents us from leaving this mud-filled town, with the pogrom agitators? Why shall we continue to endure this frightening scene? Why should we not heed the admonition of our brother-in-law Lifshutz, who had written to us frequently from America?' We decided that we would listen to our brother-in-law, and we would leave for America. Said and done. We would sell everything we could not take with us.

The shtetl was agog when our plan was made known. Many people came to our house. A number of them tried to persuade us that we were making a terrible mistake. 'Why should you flee to America?' was the refrain. 'Poor people flee. But why you? Respectable, productive people like you should not be leaving.'

They gave us no peace. They insisted that we should not do this foolish thing. But their talk did not dissuade us. Our minds were made up. We were going! No one who had the capability should remain in bloody Russia! We had closed our mind against the numerous nay-sayers, dear friends as they were. This turned out to be most fortunate for us. Had we remained in Russia, their friendly counsel would have wrought a great disaster for us. Indeed, we should have suffered the same fate that overtook them. It was only several years later that World War I broke out upon the earth. Less than one-half of our town's Jews remained alive.

Half the town accompanied us to the station. As we said our last good-byes and began to enter the car, my heart was seized with anguish. At any moment now, I was about to leave my native land. True, it was a land that persecuted us. And yet, it was our Mother Russia – well, then, our Stepmother Russia. It was the land that had given birth not only to us but also to our parents and grandparents, for many past generations. It was here that I had spent the major portion of my life, an entire half-century. Ah, how beloved to me were the fields and the woods, the lush meadows in which I had spent so many of my carefree childhood moments.

Thus I mused, and my thoughts grew more somber as I stood there looking out of the train window. The last view I had of our hometown was the waving of handkerchiefs, the inaudible (because of the noise of the train) cries of 'Be well!', and then the enveloping of all our friends in the black smoke spewed out by the engine – and they, and the entire town, disappeared.

Colony of Hebrews Sailing for Texas.

Washington Times,
8 June 1907

The steamer Cassel left Bremen to-day for Galveston with the first detachment of Russian Jews with which

New York Times

Zangwill's Jewish Territorial Organization is colonizing the Southwestern United States.

Alexander
Z. Gurwitz

In the afternoon, we boarded our ship. It was standing peacefully moored at the water's edge. The passengers of all three classes crossed over the little bridge, the plank that connected the land to the ship. First the first- and second-class passengers were permitted to board, and their baggage was taken aboard for them. Then the third-class passengers' turn came. There was a rushing and a shoving, and the din was deafening. Everyone wanted to get on board first, everyone at the same time, for each one wanted to grab the space at the higher level of the boat. It grew dangerous, and often it appeared that some passengers would be pushed into the water. We were among the last. When things quieted down a good deal, we boarded.

At five o'clock precisely, a loud whistle was sounded, signaling that we were about to start out. Then a grinding note of machinery was heard, and a rumbling began – and the water was all around the ship. Its nose sliced the water as we moved out into the ocean. Those on shore,

who had come to say farewell to passengers, shouted and waved hats and handkerchiefs at the departing friends, who responded from the boat's side with the same signals.

All of this happy leavetaking was only from the decks of the first and second classes. The third-class passengers were as orphans. No one had escorted them, and there was no one to whom they should say farewell. The third class was essentially wanderers, people from distant points, fleeing their misery. Their good friends were far away. They had shared farewells before, in their numerous hometowns. Here there was no one who cared about them. They stood a while at the rail, silently, and then hurried back to secure their precious places on deck so that no one should take those hard-won prizes from them.

We descended to our cabin. We ate, and then we went up to the deck to catch some fresh air and to see the first sunset at sea. We watched as the sun descended close to the water, its rays playing over the high columns of spray created by the ship's cleaving of the ocean. The sun finally permitted itself to sink into the water. Suddenly it was dark. The skies were clear, not the faintest trace of a cloud visible. Stars began to make their appearance. But our fatigue from that long and draining day asserted itself and overcame us. We went down to our cabin, slept soundly and well through the night, and arose in the morning refreshed.

We decided to go out on the deck and see how our fellow immigrants were faring. There was the jovial noise of camaraderie. Metal tea and coffee pots were out everywhere, and almost everyone was dunking hard rolls. The hot coffee and tea were contained in large community urns, and so there was a general pushing and shoving – but pleasantly spirited – to get close to the source.

The deck became calm after a while, with each family group breaking the fast. After this refreshment, the mingling resumed. The children played as though they were

on dry land. Their parents sat in circles, getting to know each other – Jews from numerous lands, speaking many tongues. Each one recounted what had happened to him as he stole his way across the border with his family. Others told of their fright and of the horrors they suffered in the pogroms.

Gradually, these personal sorrowful reminiscences cast a sadness over the gatherings on the deck, but not for long. Their faces took on smiles and joy, as the sound of the young people's singing filled the deck. They were singing songs of freedom. They were free! The hands of the Russian Bear could no longer seize them.

The morning was lovely, without a cloud in the blue sky. The great Atlantic Ocean was calm, and the sun's rays glistened on the serene waters. The ship, therefore, sailed in complete tranquility. All of the passengers, from all three classes, were out on deck, savoring this delightful scene. This scenario was replayed each day of our voyage. There were no storms the entire way. Once in a while a bit of wind would come along, and the more delicate stomachs would react in natural fashion. But on the whole, the agenda consisted of eating, drinking, chatting, singing, enjoying the pleasant hours.

On the twenty-second day of our setting foot on the ship, the captain informed us that at noon we would arrive in Galveston. With mounting and happy excitement, we began preparations for our landing. We packed our belongings, washed ourselves, had our hair trimmed. For some this hair trimming was a rejuvenation! There was an older man, with whom I had discussed the Torah on deck daily – he was a learned, pious Jew – who suddenly came out on that last day completely shorn of his grey, long, luxuriant beard! He looked like a young man! Only a thin moustache was on his face. He was virtually unrecognizable.

We teased him a bit. He was unperturbed. He said, 'Why do I need to have the Americans laugh at my beard until I take it off? Better to have you laugh at me for a little while here, and an end to it!'

We stood at the rail eagerly watching the ship's progress as we neared the American shore. At one point we heard the ship's whistle proclaiming our imminent arrival in port. Immediately the commotion began. Everyone grabbed their packs and rushed to the rail to be closer than anyone else to the exit, to be the first to set foot ashore.

After spending a month crossing the broad expanse of the Atlantic, stopping for a brief view of Baltimore and then plowing the waters of the gulf of Mexico, future citizens of the United States obtained their first view of the land of the Stars and Stripes – their future home. When the boat was safely warped alongside the dock a rousing cheer went up from the strangely clad yet happy faced throng which lined the steamer's rail on the land side. *Houston Daily Post*

The ship stopped at the dock, whistling all the while. The sailors put down the plank, and all the passengers rushed to the opening in the rail. Alexander Z. Gurwitz

Houston Daily Post In less time than it takes to tell, the gangplank was lowered, the ship's papers were delivered and the work of disembarking the passengers begun.

C. H. Abbott Dressed in the picturesque garb of the land from which they came, they marched down the gangplank, faced the authorities, opened their baggage for inspection, and were assembled.

B'nai B'rith Messenger Nearly all were Russian Jews and their homes ranged from the southern boundaries of the empire to the dreary frozen wastes of Siberia.

Houston Daily Post To a stranger the landing of a load of immigrants is a strange sight. The scene around the wharf is well worth seeing. The strange headdresses, the strange appearing boots and shoes and the burdens which the newcomers are carrying are at times amusing. These wend their way down the gangplank – men and women and children laden with bags, bundles and baskets containing their belongings which they carry with them to the new country.

Alexander Z. Gurwitz We had to exit singly and pass through a space where two doctors examined each immigrant. They looked carefully into our mouths, our eyes, searching for some flaw. If they did discover some physical deficiency, that person was instructed to stand at the side, awaiting the awesome judgment. 'Who will enter, and who shall be denied entry?' Only an immigrant can appreciate fully what this fearful moment of doubt means. Whoever was found in complete good health was permitted to disembark, free to become an American. But whoever was found to be flawed was detained and not allowed to enter the Promised Land. No arguments or pleading made any difference. There were no exceptions.

My family, thank God, went through the inspection without difficulty. But when it came to me, the immigration officials cast a jaundiced eye. They regarded my silver-grey hair and began to mutter among themselves. But, praised be the Lord, they let me through! My relief was indescribable.

The immigrants, after they had passed the United States medical inspector and immigration authorities, were taken to the bureau building, and the active work of the day began.

B'nai B'rith Messenger

Every preparation for the reception of the small band of pioneers was made. There was a rush for postal cards. Around a long table they clustered, marking in a most peculiar script the messages to friends in Russia. It was a babble of tongues, but while they were speaking German, Yiddish and Polish they laughed all alike. 'America' in a dozen different accents sounds always like 'America.'

C. H. Abbott

The sound of splashing came from the bathrooms. It had been three weeks since any of the party had enjoyed a fresh water event of this nature. It wrought a transformation. High Russian boots that had been worn outside went inside of wide Russian trousers. Blouses and shirts that had once waved full length in the breeze were stowed away in the manner of an American.

Each one had a bath, a good substantial dinner, an hour or two to smoke their cigarettes and drink their tea à la Russe and write letters home to their dear ones. They were a very tractable lot of people and were profuse in their expressions of delight and gratitude for the comfortable reception we gave them.

Morris Waldman

The intelligence of the large majority of the aliens is marked. One has but to observe the general vivacity at the first meal at table after twenty-five days from Bremen to appreciate this. Quick to understand, their minds run in the grooves of intelligent thought. At the first opportunity they ask for newspapers – Yiddish, German or Russian; and then follows another question – as to the possibility

Rabbi Henry Cohen

of procuring a Yiddish–English or a Russian–English dictionary! A request came to me from the detention hospital where a few of the immigrants were awaiting further examination – would I kindly send them a game of chess? This country need have no fear of this class of alien. The brawn and sinew – and for that matter the brain – of the United States will be strengthened by those Jews that pass through its Galveston portals.

B'nai B'rith Messenger

Rabbi Cohen was indefatigable in his efforts from the time of the arrival of the ship early in the morning until the last of those leaving yesterday had departed.

Rabbi Henry Cohen

The distribution of mail long looked for by the aliens, the refreshing bath and the wholesome and generous meal; the purchasing of railroad tickets; and then, supper; the apportionment of food sufficient to last each immigrant for the whole up-country journey and a little longer; then the departure of those who are to leave on the night trains; the checking of baggage to destinations, and the leave-taking from one another after a month's constant companionship; the comfortable placing of the travelers in the railroad coaches, then telegrams so that they should

be met at the station; the retiring of the remainder to bed (what a change from the steerage bunks!) to leave on the morrow or thereafter, according to circumstance – all this and more must be seen to and be realized.

I was busy with receiving and sheltering and talking with our charges. Rabbi Cohen also was busy with me; indeed to make sure no one would miss his train he even helped lug their baggage into the baggage trucks. Nothing was ever menial to this man, who, idolized by the community, could have played his part with the formal dignity that usually characterizes men of his calling and stature.

Morris Waldman

The spirit of a single line in an ancient Hebrew prayer has been wafted over the world. For centuries up to a few years ago it was repeated nightly by millions of the scattered nation. Now with less repetition it has come to be more perfunctory. 'May next year see me in Jerusalem,' is the literal translation. The 'next year' of the prayer does not represent 12 months or 365 days, but an epoch. Zion

C. H. Abbott

may be the ultimate destination, but the United States is a stopping point en route. A few days ago, more than half a hundred Jews climbed the gangplank of the steamer Cassel to the soil of Galveston Island. The episode represented one of the greatest philanthropic events of the century.

Chicago Tribune

The first load was comparatively a small one. The Cassel probably did not carry to Galveston as many Jews as entered New York on the same day. But everything must have a beginning, and this first load must be taken merely as proof to intending emigrants from the old country that there are other ports in the new world than New York. If these first refugees find in Texas a realized land of promise there will be enough to follow.

Detroit Free Press

With the arrival here this week of the detachment of Jewish pilgrims whom Israel Zangwill is sending out to Texas, Galveston begins her real history as a great immigration port.

Alexander Z. Gurwitz

As soon as we landed and looked around, we spied our nephew Solomon Lifshutz. He had come from San Antonio to meet us in Galveston. We were delighted to see him, knowing that he would take care of all the necessary arrangements. The moment we set foot outside of the immigration center, we breathed deeply of free air.

We went out to explore the city, to see Americans, to enter a restaurant and see what Americans ate. Then we made our way to the train depot, to see at once the difference between an American and a Russian train terminal. The coarse and brutal police were not there, the filthy rooms and benches were missing, the ragged peasants with their dirty clothes and foul mouths were absent. No curses, no shouting could be heard. There were no divisions in the station; all were alike, and the cars of the railroad were glistening clean. The conductors, unlike those to whom we were accustomed, were the soul of politeness. Only one thing disturbed us and diminished our joy. We were totally dumb. We understood not one word of what these Americans were saying, although their glances were friendly and sympathetic. The conductors took up our tickets with such graciousness that we were enchanted with the whole situation.

We arrived in San Antonio, and we took a streetcar to our nephew's father's house. Through the streetcar's windows we looked out upon the streets and the stores of the city. We saw also the homes and the opulent shop window displays. Seeing these, I thought, 'It is true that America is the golden land.' But, riding on a little while, through some of the side streets, and as we came closer to my brother-in-law's house, the attraction of America lost some of its allure.

What I saw disturbed me so much that I said to my nephew, 'Is this your golden America? Muddy streets, unpaved, with miserable little shacks lined along both sides, with small and poverty-stricken shops, just as in Russia's *shtetlech*! Was it worth all the trials and difficulties and money to come all the way here, to this? Dirt roads with poor people we had there in Russia, so why did we have to make the long trek here?'

I was angry at Columbus and at my brother-in-law, who had counseled our coming here. Even though my nephew explained that this was not typical of America – that this was a newly developing city in its infancy, recently settled, only lately taken from the Mexicans, but that other cities were wonderfully developed, as San Antonio soon would be – the first heartwarming blush of America, I confess, was dissipated and I was disappointed.

The city had a half-wild appearance. It did not look like an orderly, settled community with planted trees growing in rows along the streets. It was more like some wild wood where, for some inexplicable reason, houses had been set up here and there. The streets were overgrown with thorny bushes. Horses, cows, and goats wandered freely there. Dirty puddles were everywhere in the streets, all of which – except the few where the great business establishments were located – were unpaved, and therefore muddy after every rain. Indeed, there were many places where one could not extricate the foot from the lime mud. When a carriage drove past, its wheels could not be seen for the mud. There were miserable little Mexican shacks, constructed of boards, covered with rusted tin. The wild cries of the burros that stood at the front of these shacks pierced the ears. The air was filled with vicious flying little beasts, mosquitoes, which fattened themselves on the filth. Summertime they permitted no sleep, and they carried many diseases.

We were given the hospitality of my brother-in-law, Z. Lifshutz. His children had brought him over several years earlier. At home, in the small shtetl in Lithuania where he lived, he was a respectable, pious Jew. He brought to America all of his small-town ways, casting none of them into the ocean on the trip over. In fact, he gathered up all the old-world obsolete nonsense that the other passengers left on the ship, made a package of them, and brought them with him, intact, to America.

My brother-in-law received us with warm friendliness and made us most welcome. His wife, my wife's sister, was a good, religious Jewess, of excellent character. No matter that they were hospitable and kind to us, we saw that we could not stay there long. And so we selected a house for ourselves.

I confess that it is difficult for one who has lived steadily in one place, as I have, to note the daily changes that come over a city. The city changed so gradually that I was scarcely aware of it. But were a man who had not seen this city for these years suddenly to return here, he would cry out with astonishment, 'Is this the city? Is this really San Antonio?'

The city has changed so very much, in so many ways, that it is hardly recognizable from the vantage point of those years. The little wooden homes, the unpaved muddy streets, the wilderness, the crazy-quilt pattern of the trees – these are no more. Gone also is the peace, the tranquility, that prevailed then. No more horses, donkeys, wagons dragging their way through the mud-filled streets. Now thousands of automobiles speed on the slick, paved roads. And on either side of our streets, orderly rows of trees, carefully planted, shield the passerby from the burning Texas sun. Of those old, decrepit little houses clustered in what is the downtown of today, nothing is left. In their place there now stand large, modern, beautiful buildings, some thirty stories high.

The city is regarded as one of the most healthful in the country, because no factories are here to becloud the skies with bad smoke. The rays of the sun shine through unobstructed in the pure blue heaven. The air is clean and dry. In midwinter, when the bitter frosts and freezing storms rage elsewhere, we have green fields, and flowers bloom.

Our first group of immigrants arrived on July 1, 1907, and subsequent groups at three weeks' interval.

Rabbi Henry Cohen, 1908

There is always something to see that is new. This morning among the arrivals was an old Russian couple. Dressed in clothes that better belonged in a land of snow and ice, and laden with heavy luggage, they were the center of attraction. He with his heavy whiskers and bushy hair, and she with her strange dress, looked like a pair of strange beings which could not be classed. They were beaming with good nature, however, and submitted to the examination and passed it all without trouble. While one of the inspectors was going through their baggage he found a sack filled with something that rustled like leaves. Opening it he found curled pieces of dried bread, brought from their native land in far away Russia.

Houston Daily Post, 18 September 1909

To show that it was not contraband the big fellow grabbed up a handful and throwing it into his mouth began to chew on it demonstrating that it was nothing but food.

H. J. Haskell,
Kansas City Star

All sorts of occupations are represented among the immigrants. There are tailors, shoemakers, bricklayers, tinners, blacksmiths, butchers, bookkeepers, locksmiths, woodworkers. A capmaker, who in Russia had made only a few dollars a month when he could get work, was started in Kansas City at $10 a week, which soon was raised to $12. That was opulence, and he lived with the joy of a millionaire until he made a discovery. Then he went to Mr. Billikopf with a grievance. 'What's the matter?' inquired the superintendent. 'Aren't you getting on all right?' 'Yes,' was the reply, 'only I have heard that Cohen, who isn't any better a capmaker than I, is getting $18. When shall I be getting $18?' That discontent was the evidence of the Russian capmaker's Americanization. And that is one of the fruits of the Galveston movement.

Israel Zangwill,
December 1907

There is scarcely one of our emigrants who does not bless the day he landed at Galveston. We have now created in Russia no fewer than 150 centres of information and selection, and Galveston is now a household word and a word of hope throughout the Pale. Never in Jewish history has there been a longer chain of brotherhood. Beginning in the lands of persecution, and passing through Germany, it stretches across the Atlantic and reaches by way of Galveston to all the Western States of America. Let us hear no more therefore of Palestine as a field for our emigration. Unless you mean Palestine, U.S.A. For Texas possesses a place called Palestine, quite near to Galveston, with two Jewish families and one synagogue between them, and to this Palestine we shall cheerfully conduct the emigration.

Chapter 16

One of the most picturesque figures in Jewry is Mr. Israel Zangwill. Dreamer and man of affairs; idealist and pragmatist; novelist and playwright; essayist and journalist; humorist and serious thinker; orator and sphinx; Zionist and anti-Zionist.

Jewish Chronicle, 12 June 1908

Our most distinguished man of letters, for the past few years he appears to have abandoned the triumphs of authorship to devote his brilliant powers to the development of a gigantic scheme for the benefit of his oppressed brethren. Mr. Zangwill is busy in controlling the vast machine which he has set going.

It was at the London office, in Portugal Street, that I found Mr. Zangwill on a recent occasion, when, having succeeded in making my way past three secretaries, I gained access to an inner sanctum, and besought an interview for the *Jewish Chronicle*.

'One must not forget, unless you have already forgotten it, that there was a time when you wrote books.'

'It is quite true that I have written scarcely anything the last few years. But as the work of the Ito is now going on so satisfactorily, I am hoping this summer to be able to finish a play I have just begun on a theme my emigration work has shown me is urgent. If I can finish it, it will be produced in New York before the end of the year.'

I shut my eyes one night, and there before me saw in one vivid flash the whole play, just as it should be on stage. I saw people fighting, striving, working out their salvation, groping in the dark – and there I had my play!

Israel Zangwill to the *New York Times*

That's the way all my plays come to me: on the flash of an instant, then the whole thing is clear and is three-quarters done. That is how the 'Melting Pot' came to be written.

***

Israel Zangwill, August 1908

Dear President Roosevelt, I don't know if the fifth of October will find you in Washington, but if so, I should like to offer you or any members of your family a box for the first performance of my new play 'The Melting Pot' which dramatises your own idea of America as a crucible in which the races are fusing into the future American.

Theodore Roosevelt, 1896

The mighty tide of immigration to our shores has brought in its train much of good and much of evil, and whether the good or the evil shall predominate depends mainly on whether these newcomers do or do not throw themselves heartily into our national life, cease to be European, and become Americans like the rest of us. But where immigrants or the sons of immigrants cling to the habits of thought of the Old World which they have left, they harm both themselves and us. If they remain alien elements, unassimilated, and with interests separate from ours, they are mere obstructions to the current of our national life, and, moreover, can get no good from it themselves.

In fact, though we ourselves also suffer from their perversity, it is they who really suffer most. The man who does not become Americanized nevertheless fails to remain a European, and becomes nothing at all. The immigrant cannot possibly remain what he was, or continue to be a member of the Old-World society. If he tries to retain his old language, in a few generations it becomes a barbarous jargon; if he tries to retain his old customs and ways of life, in a few generations he becomes an uncouth boor. He has cut himself off from the Old-World, and cannot retain his connection with it; and if he wishes ever to amount to anything he must throw himself heart and soul, and without reservation, into the new life to which he has come.

He must revere only our flag; not only must it come first, but no other flag should even come second.

***

On board the steamer Teutonic, which is scheduled to arrive in New York today, is Israel Zangwill, the well-known author, who comes to America to assist in the staging and producing of his play, The Melting Pot, the premiere of which is to occur at the Columbia Theatre, Washington, D. C., Monday October 5. The Melting Pot is said to be one of the most remarkable plays that has yet been given to the public.

Billboard, 1908

As a general rule nowadays, the announcement of a new play excites but little and languid expectation. But this is not the case when the author's name is Zangwill.

Chicago Sunday Tribune

Several friends and interviewers awaited the arrival of the boat at the dock, but it was delayed unseasonably by the dense fog which hung over the lower bay and harbor.

American Hebrew

Mr. Zangwill was immediately besieged by the interviewers of the New York newspapers. He is pretty much the same Zangwill in appearance and in characteristic speech, though indications were not lacking that the last few years of his life must have been the most strenuous of his existence. For the raven locks of the author of 'The Children of the Ghetto' are more than tinged with gray, and there are a few lines in his face that were not there at the time of his last visit.

Jewish Exponent

There is still the same strong, plain face of the familiar newspaper illustration, one of those faces that instinctively cartoons itself upon one's memory forever. In the profile, homelier than Abraham Lincoln's – and that is claiming much for the homeliness thereof – there has

Noel Y. Harte

grown a suggestion, a faint tinge of the grim and mordant sadness of Dante.

Reuben Brainin,
American Hebrew

His face has grown more spiritual, and his look more concentrated.

Brooklyn Daily Star

Zangwill Melts Us Up Into Play. Not in years have Washington first-nighters been so interested in a new drama, and it is likely that the premiere of 'The Melting Pot' will be witnessed by the most distinguished audience ever gathered in a theatre in this city.

Washington Post,
4 October

Tomorrow evening, at 8:15, the curtain will rise on Israel Zangwill's new play. Walker Whiteside will be seen in the leading role.

Walker Whiteside

A great audience crowded the house, including President Roosevelt and Mrs. Roosevelt, and all the notables at that time within the capital.

Allen D. Albert,
Washington Times

The President sat facing one of the leaders of American Jews, the Hon. Simon Wolf.

Simon Wolf

President Roosevelt occupied a box next to Mr. and Mrs. Zangwill. I never could tell which caused the greatest applause, the play or the President. He kept up an animated conversation with Mrs. Zangwill.

Even Washington might be pardoned for dividing its attention between a new play and such auditors; but not only did the great number of those present forget these dignitaries, but the dignitaries seemed to forget themselves.

Allen D. Albert

Mr Zangwill shows us a typical Jewish family in New York. The old grandmother is a wizened crone, who speaks only Yiddish, pores over her Hebrew books, and puts all the force of her hardened nature into the minute observance of every jot and tittle of the ceremonial law. Her home is still a Ghetto of the Russian Pale, though fate and family ties have transported her to New York. Her son, Mendel Quixano, is a second-rate musician, polished into an outward conformity with Gentile manners. His nephew, David, belongs to the younger generation. He came to the land of promise while still a lad. He thinks of the Old World behind him as nothing but a nightmare of massacres and oppressions.

Nation

The hero of the play is David Quixano. He comes to America, the land of his hopes, he decorates his rooms with its flag, sings its anthem in the streets, and writes a symphony in its honor.

Current Literature

David is rather an uncouth fellow. His hair is tousled, his necktie all awry, his clothes ill fitting, and one suspects that his finger nails are rough.

New York Tribune

Walker Whiteside preserved with remarkable consistency the touch of foreign accent natural to an immigrant.

American Hebrew

David Quixano has come to this country after seeing his family massacred at Kishineff. The face of the officer who ordered the murder is constantly in his mind. He

New York Times

WALKER WHITESIDE IN THE MELTING POT

falls in love with a Russian girl – the daughter, of course, of the officer.

New York Press

David loses no time in falling in love with Vera Revendal. The play revolves around these two, David representing the Jew, Vera the Gentile.

Alan Dale

The real crux of The Melting Pot occurs at the close of the third act. It is then that the thing becomes a play.

New York Evening Post

At the sight of Baron Revendal, David is seized with his chronic hallucination of Kishinev and he casts Vera from him.

Chicago Daily Tribune

In the climax of the play, wherein the young Jew and Russian baron meet, Zangwill has brought out with thrilling force all the woe, bitterness, and pity which an entire civilized world felt concerning the Kisheneff episode.

New York Evening Telegram

Walker Whiteside was received with the utmost enthusiasm. His effective presence, beautiful voice, appealing eyes and method of admirable reserve, caught and held

151

the audience throughout. His description of the massacre, half revery, half epic, which might have been made blatant by a less skilful actor, was in his hands a genuine bit of poetry.

Mr. Whiteside is still a young man, although he has been on the stage for more than fifteen years, having played *Hamlet* in Chicago when he was only seventeen. He is a native of that Western State so prolific of talent – Indiana.

Matthew White, Jr.

Out of nowhere, a genius came last night to stir and stun an audience by the swift and terrific power of his acting: in an instant he proved his greatness. Sometimes his acting was like the lightning flash, sometimes like sweeping flame, again like the glow of smoldering ember.

O. H. Hall,
Chicago Journal

He has a resonant voice in texture, beautiful with the tonal shadings of an imaginative mind, and vigorous with the conviction of the message of the play.

Christian Science Monitor

CHRISTAL HERNE AS "THE MELTING POT" AT THE COLUMBIA

Baltimore Sun	The heroine is enacted with equal success, though for different reasons, by Miss Crystal Hearne. Miss Hearne possesses the rather rare art of listening dramatically, since she is called upon to listen far oftener than to speak.
San Francisco Chronicle	The fourth act is Saturday night – the Fourth of July – and David's symphony is being performed for the first time. He has crept away to nurse his grief alone, and to him comes Vera. Their greeting at first is of a most formal character, but as they talk they begin to realize that race and creed are as nothing when they are but fragments tossed into 'the crucible' as part of the material that the Almighty is using in his construction of the American people.
Hartford Courant	His symphony can be heard from the roof garden in which this last act occurs. The sun is setting. Lights appear on Ellis Island and the Statue of Liberty.
Christian Science Monitor	He realizes that he is no longer Jew, but American, and that the page of the past is to be turned and fastened down.
New York Times	David Quixano delivers himself thus: 'America is God's crucible – the great melting pot – where all the races of Europe are fusing and reforming. Here you stand, good folk, think I, when I see them at Ellis Island: here you stand in your fifty groups, with your fifty languages and your histories and your fifty blood feuds and rivalries. But you won't be long like that, brothers, for these are the fires of God you have come to – these are the fires of God! A fig for your feuds and vendettas! Germans and Frenchmen, Irishmen and Englishmen, Jews and Russians – into the crucible with you all! God is making the American.'
Jewish Chronicle	David and Vera are finally reconciled; the dead hands of the victims of the massacre which they have felt creeping between them are removed by their devotion to the

ideal of the new American humanity. America has freed them and made them one, and the last curtain drops to the singing of their praises of the new land.

We hung in the balance throughout the first two acts. There was that quiet, however, that told us the play was being watched and heard with respect if not with complete satisfaction. But when the curtain fell the entire audience rose and cheered.

Walker Whiteside

The audience was most enthusiastic and repeated curtain calls had to be taken. Mr. Zangwill did not appear before the audience until after the last act, when Walker Whiteside pulled him to the foot-lights.

V. Gilmore Iden, *The Show World*

The enthusiasm amounted to an ovation for Mr. Whiteside and for Mr. Zangwill. President Roosevelt manifested his appreciation with frank spontaneity.

Washington Evening Star

Certain strong lines caused Mr Roosevelt to lean forward in his box and say in a perfectly audible tone: 'That's all right!' It was the President who led the applause.

New York Times

President Roosevelt was a most enthusiastic spectator. At the end of the play he leaned over toward me and clapped his hands, exclaiming, 'It's a great play, Zangwill.'

Zangwill to the *Jewish Exponent*

Again and again the Chief Executive led in the bursts of appreciation, while leaning from his box to talk to a young woman in the next.

Baltimore Sun

Nearly every person in the big audience wondered who was the attractive young woman to whom the President talked so long. President and Mrs. Roosevelt occupied their accustomed box while Mrs. Zangwill was in the adjoining. During two intermissions, President Roosevelt chatted with the wife of the playwright across the intervening railing, and seemed to enjoy every minute of the conversation. Mrs. Zangwill is extremely attractive-looking and smiles continually as she talks.

Washington Times

Edith Zangwill

The first night was a great success, but it is too soon to tell whether the play is going to be a popular hit. There were cries for 'Zangwill' after every act. The President was most enthusiastic. He had hailed me over earlier in the evening to sit next to him and positively raved. However the President's opinion does not make any particular difference. Only it is encouraging, from a box office standpoint, because I always feel that Roosevelt is a glorified 'man in the street', a sort of commonplace person raised to the nth power, and what would appeal to him would also be likely to appeal to the masses. Among other things Roosevelt said to me, 'I'm not a Bernard Shaw or Ibsen man, Mrs Zangwill. No, *this* is the stuff.' I thought everyone recognized Ibsen as a great genius. Poor Israel. I had to repeat it to him to keep him humble.

American Hebrew

On the following day, the English author and his wife took luncheon with the President.

Brooklyn Daily Eagle

Mr. Zangwill said that he will have his play printed in book form and dedicate it to President Roosevelt.

Theodore Roosevelt to Israel Zangwill

I do not know when I have seen a play that stirred me as much. That play I shall always count among the very strong and real influences upon my thought and my life.

Augustus Thomas

I have seen a great many plays, and I have never seen men and women more sincerely stirred than the audience that was present when I saw 'The Melting Pot.'

Washington Post

Has it remained for Israel Zangwill, an Englishman, to accomplish what American authors have so far failed in? Is 'The Melting Pot' 'The Great American Drama'?

Independent

The Melting Pot, written by an English Hebrew, is altogether American, more American than Americans, for even on the Fourth of July we hardly dare be so unqualifiedly optimistic over the future of the country, so wildly enthusiastic about the success of our great experiment of amalgamation, as Mr. Zangwill is.

'The Melting Pot' has led to discussion throughout the nation. *Current Literature*

Some persons think it a 'great' play, and say so; some others think it not even a good play, and because they say so are denounced as odious creatures little short of being traitors to their country. *New York Tribune*

New Zangwill Play Cheap and Tawdry. Even a President may be mistaken. 'The Melting Pot' is sentimental trash masquerading as human document. That is the sum and substance of it. *New York Times*

Candidly, 'The Melting Pot' is a heavy, dreary, presumptuous and preachy affair. The Jewish hero is an impudent young cad. He is so delighted with his own voice that he goes prosing on, and on, and on, until you long to throw your opera-glasses at him. Such a pleasant girl as Vera should get up and leave him to do his talking to the empty chair. *Cosmopolitan*

What is this glorification of the amalgamated immigrants, this exaggerated contrast of the freshness of the New World and the staleness of the Old, this rhapsodizing over music and crucibles and Statues of Liberty, but romantic claptrap? *The Times*

Call it sentimental, satirical, melodramatic, clap-trap, what you will, the fact remains that the third act grips you, thrills you, and that is a sufficiently rare achievement in the modern drama to insure success. *American Hebrew*

The emphasis upon Americanisation is, of course, surprising to those who have followed Mr. Zangwill's activities. *Jewish Chronicle*

American Hebrew Is it not strange that Mr. Zangwill's utterances and writings glisten with brilliant paradoxes? He is himself a more brilliant paradox than any of his own creation. Erstwhile a Zionist, now a leader of the ITO, he gives us in his newest play assimilation as the answer to the Jewish question.

Washington Post Nations, creeds, and colors, diverse and conglomerate streams of blood, reach our shores; they step in and are lost forever, fused into one indistinguishable mass called the American people.

Bernard G. Richards, American Hebrew We shall be melted whether we like it or not. All our ancient traits and characteristics, our 'hankering for the past' and even our religious beliefs shall vanish in the great process of the crucible. There is no use arguing about it. What spiritual identity will the Jew have when he emerges out of the 'melting pot'? I infer from Quixano's rhapsodies that the Jew will no longer be a Jew. I protest against his pronouncement of our doom.

Washington Post It is hard to see the body of Mr. Zangwill's people accepting this as their material salvation, and equally difficult to credit the author with advancing it; yet surely nothing less can be adduced from his play.

Jewish Chronicle It is suggested that Mr. Zangwill has meant to utter a strong warning to the Jewish people, to those of America as well as to those of other lands: get a country of your own and create your own life or else – 'into the crucible with you all.' The pity is that this warning is not contained in the play itself.

The Times Naturally enough, its one really valuable element passes almost unobserved. I refer to its delicately sympathetic and quietly toned picture of old-fashioned orthodox Judaism, forlorn but faithful amid strange and hostile surroundings, the simple, solemn ritual of the

Sabbath, the pathetic clinging to what to outsiders seem 'lost causes and forgotten beliefs,' to be seen in the aged Frau Quixano and her son Mendel.

Here, of course, Mr. Zangwill is at home; he knows the beauty of Jewish character and tradition, handles it reverently, and makes of it an exquisite thing. So exquisite a thing that, on one observer at any rate, his play produced just the opposite to its intended effect. What are 'melting pots' generally used for? Is it not to melt down choice old silver, masterpieces of craftsmanship, the heirlooms of the ages, into a mere mass of metal? Well, it seems to me not a good thing, but a grievous pity, that these fine old products of the ages, these richly-toned masterpieces of tradition, the authentic orthodox Jews represented by the elder Quixanos, should be cast into the melting pot to come out – what? Americans, if you will have it so, but at any rate crude, shiny, brand-new Americans. Here is Mendel Quixano, the son of a learned Rabbi, wearing his shabby black frockcoat with something of Oriental dignity, speaking with a solemn simplicity that has in it an echo of Isaiah. You cast Mendel into the 'melting pot' and out he comes chewing gum and drinking cocktails, holding on by one hand to a subway strap and reading papers in the other. Is the Jewish immigrant, is America, is anybody to be congratulated upon such a transformation as this? Mr. Zangwill of all men, one feels sure, does not really think so.

Chapter 17

Henry Berman

By the late spring of 1910, immigration at Galveston reached encouraging proportions. The Movement had at last arrived at maturity – only to receive a formidable blow. The department of Commerce and Labor (as it was then known) held up a boatload of men at Galveston, and by the deportation of a number of the immigrants called a halt to the entire work, and stood ready to destroy at a stroke a patriotic endeavour which had required months of upbuilding.

Alfred Hampton

Upon assuming charge of this district recently, I was surprised to learn that it had been the custom each month to admit at this port many destitute Jewish aliens, that is, Jewish aliens without money, and without friends or relatives in this country.

New York World, 22 August 1910

Jacob H. Schiff's Immigrants Held Up. Official Inquiry Shows Lax Conditions at Galveston, Where He Shipped His Proteges.

Benjamin S. Cable

These aliens were excluded on the ground that all of them have been induced or solicited to migrate to this country. There is no reason why the law should not, within a short time, be administered at Galveston as at other ports, and this will be done.

Morris Waldman

It was at a meeting in one of the board rooms of Kuhn, Loeb & Co. that I first perceived Schiff's dominant personality. Israel Zangwill was his guest. A number of serious obstacles had arisen, chief among which was the disturbing suspicion that some of the immigrants had had part or the whole of their transportation paid by the Jewish Territorial Organization. The committee had assured our government authorities that these immigrants' transportation was not being paid.

I had seen Zangwill years before, when he had left the impression on my mind of a young, restless, ill-mannered, ungainly product of the East End ghetto of London. I was pleased to find him now nearly handsome in comparison, attractive, impressive in a well-built loose-fitting grey suit that harmonized with his bushy iron-grey hair and his somewhat ruddy complexion and more mellowed, though still sharp, hawk-like features.

Schiff began his references to this subject in his usual mild, deliberate manner and well-modulated voice. But as he went on, his voice assumed a sterner timbre and his face became set and solemn as he emphasized the imperative necessity to leave not the shadow of a doubt as to the good faith of the committee with the United States authorities. His lips closed so tightly behind his patriarchal beard that I, sitting quite close to him, was startled. His mild benevolence had for the moment given way to an almost cruel resentment at Zangwill, who, he suspected, had in his eagerness to promote Galveston immigration, failed to observe that meticulous respect for the committee's assurances to our government which to Mr. Schiff was a high and sacred duty.

And what a relief to us all when, after Zangwill earnestly assured us that the suspicions that had been aroused were utterly without foundation, Schiff quickly relaxed and again assumed the aspect of the kindly, gentle philanthropist whom we knew so well.

Great and far-reaching movements like the one we have on hand can seldom be worked out without difficulties of some sort. It appears we were mistaken in our

Jacob Schiff to Israel Zangwill

assumption that we could count on the goodwill of the administration. But we shall not give up without a fight.

Jacob Schiff to Benjamin S. Cable, 22 August 1910

Sir: The recent action taken by you in connection with Russo-Jewish immigrants arriving at Galveston induces me to address you as follows. Our work can in no wise be described as inducing or illegally assisting immigration. Those behind the so-called Galveston movement had every right to expect the good will of the authorities, and, until recently, this appears not to have been withheld. Of late, however, and for no satisfactory reason, the Department of Commerce and Labor has changed its attitude, and is now throwing needless difficulties in the way of the admission of those who arrive at Galveston, a course which, if persisted in, is certain to break down the Galveston movement.

Henry Berman

It required almost six months before the Department of Commerce and Labor finished debating the matter. Withdrawal from its position was inevitable; but the cost to the Galveston Bureau's work was heavy, nevertheless. The Movement had been partially discredited in Russia. Galveston became synonymous with uncertainty. While conditions were unchanged at New York, Philadelphia, Baltimore, and Boston, immigrants who arrived at the Texas port were in danger of being thrown back to Russia. Confidence gave way to doubt, disbelief, and distrust. And these could not easily be dispelled.

Israel Zangwill to the New York Times, 4 June 1911

'The Jewish Territorial Organization is doing excellent work now. It has passed some of the dangerous ailments of infancy. It has withstood the onslaughts made against it. The United States immigration authorities have given us a clean bill after their investigations. When we have about 20,000 immigrants in the southern part of the United States, the stream of Jewish immigration will turn in that direction.

Chapter 18

Kieff, an important town in the south of Russia, has become a center of great activity for Jewish emigration. Properly organized parties of emigrants are being dispatched thence periodically to Galveston, by way of Bremen. For $40 the organizers guarantee to transport a Jewish emigrant from Kieff and land him in the Port of Galveston.

Brooklyn Daily Eagle, 22 October 1909

The Emigration Regulation Department is divided into four sections, English, Russian, German and American. And I should like to say here, without underrating the work of the other sections, that the Russian work is by far the most arduous, and without undervaluing the work of other men, that the success of the Galveston movement is primarily due to Dr. Jochelmann. If, in the teeth of malicious misrepresentation, in the teeth of the difficulties of organisation under Russian law, and capricious rejection of large bodies of immigrants by Washington, if in the teeth of all this, large parties are now booking for Galveston by every steamer, the credit must be ascribed to the genius and self-sacrifice of Dr. Jochelmann.

Israel Zangwill, 27 June 1912

Dr. Jochelmann, Vice-President of the Ito and Russian Director of the Emigration Regulation Department, sailed from Bremen on Tuesday, by the 'Kaiser Wilhelm II' for America, where he goes to study questions of emigration and colonisation.

Jewish Chronicle, 11 October 1912

According to a cable just received, Dr. Jochelmann is now leaving New York for the West and expects to be in Galveston on November 7th.

Jewish Chronicle, 25 October 1912

Houston Post,
7 November 1912

Dr. D. Jockelmann of Kiev, Russia, arrived in Galveston today. He immediately went into a conference with Rabbi Henry Cohen and several others interested in immigration here.

Brenham Daily
Banner

When the steamship Koeln lands her cargo of human freight at the port of Galveston, Dr. Jochelmann will be shown each detail of the manner in which the immigrant aliens are received upon their arrival in the New World.

Israel Zangwill

Dr. Jochelmann, our Russian organiser, after his recent journey through the area of immigration, reported that emigrants of ours, whom he had known in Russia as crushed, worn-out, hopeless and prospectless pariahs, he found again in America, holding up their heads, decently dressed, living in bright, clean flats, their children at school, themselves often attending evening classes, and invariably aspiring to American citizenship. And the lesson of this success is that the same organisation which has proved itself capable of cutting out a new channel of emigration for our wandering masses is no less capable of guiding them to an ITOland.

***

It is precisely because I soon discovered that Itoland could not be an immediate refuge, if only because of the years necessary to find it, that the Ito, while making the quest of such a land its central line of activity, established also a branch line to America in the shape of the Galveston work.

Israel Zangwill, *American Hebrew*, 18 April 1913

Now, this branch line carries within itself a secondary solution in the event of the primary proving impossible. For America has ample room for all the six millions of the Pale: any one of her fifty States could absorb them. And next to being in a country of their own, there could be no better fate for them than to be all together in a land of civil and religious freedom.

This very Galveston work made it clear to me why Itoland will not attract any large number of Jews while America remains open. But, it will be asked, if the branch line is more important practically than the central line, why not close up the central line? If Itoland will not attract the Jewish masses, why go on to build it?

All the Jews on the branch line are going nowhere. The Jewish people has been preserved almost exclusively by its religion, as a tortoise is protected by its shell. With the decay of the shell, the organism it guarded must go. I do not say the Jews will disappear in a day, or at the wave of a conjurer's wand. A people dies as slowly as it is born. But just as a tortoise turned three hundred may be said to have seen its best days, though a century of torpid existence be still before it, so we may say of ourselves that we are at the beginning of the end.

America is the land of refuge, but it is also the 'melting pot.' No people in history has ever been able to live unmelted in the bosom of a bigger people, except when safeguarded by a separate religion. And the religion of American Jewry is not strong and separate enough to save the American Jews from absorption. Even the East Side of New York speaks Yiddish with a twang.

There is literally no land on earth which has not been brought to our attention during our long quest. One gentleman recommended to me an island that seemed indeed large and empty, only it was in the Antarctic.

The salvation of the Jews cannot be achieved without a territory for the Jews. One of the great sayings of the Talmud teaches, 'It is not thy duty to complete the work, neither hast thou the right to neglect it.' The work must be begun, and begun to-day. Were a territory acquired for Jewish colonization, the Jewish problem would not indeed be 'solved,' but every year and every century would see it getting nearer and nearer to solution instead of further away. Disappearance would be a comedy, continuance a tragedy, reappearance an epic poem.

Chapter 19

For some years the Ito, under the leadership of Mr. Israel Zangwill, has been seeking a 'land of refuge' that will enable the Jew of oppressed countries to live his life after his own fashion. Almost every corner of the civilised world has been scoured in the hope of securing a land for the less fortunate members of the 'tribe of the wandering foot.' The very latest project will deal with Angola as a land of Jewish settlement.

Sheffield Evening Telegraph, 22 June 1912

Angola is a country on the west coast of Africa. The country is mountainous and well-watered. Most of the soil is very fertile, producing palms, citrons, oranges, lemons, bananas, tamarinds, mangroves, and sugar cane in great abundance. Lead, sulphur, petroleum, and iron are plentiful, and gold, silver, and copper are said to exist in the interior. Gum, wax and ivory are now the most important articles of trade. Angola was discovered by the Portuguese in 1484, and they have maintained their possession ever since.

New York Times

Portugal, it is well-known, is in hard straits just at present and would be willing to yield some of her colonial possessions. But hitherto, the experience of the Ito has shown that when a territory is offered it, it generally turns out to be unsuitable. Let us hope that this may not prove the case with the Angola project.

American Hebrew

Die Welt of last Friday prints an account of an interview with Senhor Magalhaes Lima, the first President of the Portuguese Republic. Questioned as to the motive

Jewish Chronicle, 6 December 1912

which prompted the Portuguese Government to offer a portion of Angola to the Jewish people, Senhor Lima replied: 'The question is put under a misapprehension. The Portuguese Government has never offered a foot of Portuguese territory to anyone. It has, however, repeatedly declared that it will hospitably receive European settlers in its non-European possessions. We do not make it a point to have Jews or only Jews as settlers. Whether Jews, gypsies, negroes, or other peoples settle there is all the same to us. But we demand that the colonists shall live as Portuguese.'

Hamilton Daily Times, 18 July 1913

The official report on the proposed colonization of Angola is now out. As anticipated, the report does not recommend an attempt to colonize the country. There were various difficulties whose importance was impossible to deny, not least of which was the likelihood of trouble with the natives. In short, it appears clear that the Angola scheme will join the Cyrenaica scheme in the realms of the 'might have beens.'

Israel Zangwill

Where lies the Ito's defect? Precisely in that sphere where no human power can avail – the sphere of geography. The dryness of Cyrenaica, the tropical heat of Mesopotamia, are examples of the destructive realities of geography. I believe less and less that the required territory will be found. We have knocked on all the most promising doors and everywhere we received the answer: 'too late, too late, ye cannot enter now.'

Chapter 20

Galveston Immigration Bureau to be closed.

American Hebrew,
29 May 1914

The announcement has recently been made that the scheme of the Ito for diverting Jewish immigration is about to be dropped. The statement marks the end of an interesting experiment.

Jewish Chronicle

As for the chief facts of the bureau and its discontinuance, they are briefly told. One of the strong objections to the Galveston bureau was that the ships touched first at Philadelphia, then proceeding to Galveston. And to people cooped in the steerage the voyage of nearly six thousand sea miles was insufferably long.

Jewish Voice

A steerage voyage is none too pleasant when only a week in duration. To face three or four weeks of it calls for an amount of grit and determination which only a limited number of emigrants can be expected to have.

American Hebrew

If Baltimore could not serve as a distributing point because of its nearness to New York, a city like Charleston, South Carolina, was in the path of the German boats, and could have avoided twelve hundred miles of ocean voyage.

Reform Advocate

This, coupled with other reasons, was deemed finally sufficient to abandon the bureau.

Jewish Voice

The bureau succumbed to obstacles which could not be overcome. But it is in no sense a failure; 10,000 people

David Bressler

will have arrived at Galveston by the closing date. The way is pointed; the route is open. The human contribution cannot be overestimated.

Henry Berman

From Corpus Christi, in Texas, to Duluth in Minnesota, from Atlanta, Georgia, to San Francisco, one may come upon the Galveston immigrant. From the individual who presented himself on boat-day, to the same individual upon whom one might later chance in a western or southern city, there was a difference so wide that the beholder was divided between wonder and satisfaction. It was as if the immigrant was saying with all his being: 'I have come into my own!'

Reform Advocate

Towns which had never known Jewish residents acquired groups of them to which there are constant additions. Industries were confronted with Jewish workmen who proved tenacious, sober, and earnest. Schools which had never contained Jewish children, found them carrying off prizes for scholarship. The Jewish immigrant has at last pushed his way across the Mississippi River – where he should have come at least a decade before. In Houston, Fort Worth, Dallas, and San Antonio in Texas; in New Orleans and Shreveport in Louisiana, in Little Rock, Pine Bluff, and Fort Smith in Arkansas, in Wichita and Topeka in Kansas; and in a host of towns, the Jewish immigrant coming through Galveston has made himself part of the community life, far removed though it might be from his previous environment in the Russian pale. With the entrance of the Galveston pioneer, this Western country lost its remoteness and strangeness for his kin and friends.

American Hebrew

The name Galveston is now so well known in Russia that a certain percentage of immigration will inevitably seek this port of its own volition.

The 'Galveston movement' is certain to continue and
ultimately work out silently, but effectively, the problem
for which it has been started. I believe we have a right to
feel that we have, in a measure, succeeded.

The Jewish Immigrants' Information Bureau of Galveston discontinued its activities Thursday, October 1,
1914. For seven years this bureau has been operating,
financed by Jacob H. Schiff of New York. And, though
the gifts of the great financier and philanthropist to this
organization have been many, there has been devoted
to the welfare of the bureau the time and thought and
work of a Galvestonian whose name is a household word
among the immigrants the bureau has handled in the
seven years of its existence. Though lacking the millions
of dollars to give, this Galvestonian – Rabbi Henry Cohen
– has given a personal service that it would indeed be
difficult to measure by monetary standards.

Since the bureau was organized, in the spring of 1907,
hardly an immigrant ship has touched the Galveston
wharf when Rabbi Cohen has not been as familiar a figure
as the United States immigration officials themselves.
The extent of his activities in assisting the newly-landed
immigrant during that seven-year period covers a range
hardly conceivable. Few men could be better adapted to
the task. Speaking fluently practically every European
language, he has been able to place himself in instant
touch with the needs of the immigrant.

From Galveston to Seattle are strewn the men
and families whose names are on the bureau records.
Throughout its entire history, from inception until the
day its doors close for the last time, moves the dynamic
little figure of Rabbi Henry Cohen, casually spattering
languages as a machine gun spatters lead, acting instan-
taneously as father, uncle, confessor and adviser to men

of all sorts and conditions, proving at the cost of infinite work and worry his belief in the ancient commandment 'Thou shalt love thy neighbor as thyself.'

Jacob Billikopf . It was my privilege to be associated with the movement from its inception. I was on the Galveston docks that thrilling July 4th, 1907, thrilling to us on the docks, thrilling to those on the steamer who realized the significance of the day, when the 'S. S. Cassel' arrived with the first group of Jewish immigrants. My cooperation with the movement, in one form or another, endured from that memorable 4th of July until the outbreak of the world-war and the virtual cessation of trans-atlantic passenger traffic compelled its termination. This work brought me into intimate contact with Mr. Schiff.

As is so well known to everyone who is in the least familiar with Mr. Schiff's outlook on life, he gave something more than the large sums of money for which he was noted. With his contributions went his personal interest. He was eager to know what was being accomplished. That was true of the many institutions to whose support he so lavishly contributed. But it was true to an even greater degree with regard to the 'Galveston' movement. He was unable to content himself with mere documentary evidence, no matter how voluminous. He was bound to see for himself.

One day in 1915 I received a telegram from Mr. Schiff who with Mrs Schiff was visiting the San Francisco Exposition, apprising me that they desired to visit Kansas City and several neighboring towns in order to meet the immigrants, preferably in their own homes, and to hear from their own lips the story of their progress.

Mr. Schiff and his party arrived in Kansas City on April 12, 1915. Spending a minimum of time at the hotel, he at once started on a long, and to anyone else, tiresome

171

round. But as we went from house to house, in the poorer sections of the city, he seemed to gain energy, vitality. The sight of these men and women winning out in the struggle to adjust themselves spiritually and economically to their new environment, the contentment, the determination he saw in so many faces, gave him tremendous satisfaction.

But his greatest joy came when, after hours of this gruelling but gratifying labor, he visited a night school where a large group of immigrants had gathered, after a hard day's work, to grapple with the intricacies of the English language, its accent and construction.

It had been planned that Mr. Schiff should deliver an address at a meeting of the Missouri Bankers Association, which had been moved forward a day in order to take advantage of his presence in Kansas City. The expectation was, of course, that this famous banker, talking at a meeting of bankers, would dwell on some important phase of the subject of banking, or speak on some economic or financial subject. Now those who knew Mr. Schiff have a very vivid recollection of his punctuality. But at this meeting of the assembled bankers of the state of Missouri, of his western colleagues, he was late. He was late because he had been unable to tear himself away from that classroom full of immigrants. He made that explanation of his tardiness, when finally, after nearly an hour's delay, he arrived at the bankers' meeting. And then, touching only casually on the subject he was expected to discuss, he told, in detail, the wonderful story of the Galveston movement. It was plain that he had been stirred. So too was his audience. For he took as the text a composition written by an immigrant who had been in this country only six months. The subject of the essay was 'Abraham Lincoln,' and from it Schiff read, and proceeded to develop his own conception of Americanization. To him, Americanization was a matter of soul, not of outer conformity – of clothing, of speech, of manners. Love for America, for its institutions, for its ideals – that was Americanization.

***

Edith Zangwill

I have often thought of those early days of the I.T.O. The first idea came from Dr. Jochelman. At the Zionist Congress of 1905, which rejected the offer of a great plateau in East Africa, there were scenes of extraordinary emotion. Israel Zangwill pleaded passionately for the acceptance of the offer. The voting went against him. All through that long nerve-wracking session, my husband had been supported by a man hitherto unknown to me, a black-haired, square-browed Russian, vehement but calm, capable of anger, but with a gentle smile. His name was David Jochelman.

After the Great Refusal, the brief remainder of the night was spent by small groups of people in excited talk. David Jochelman was pleading with Israel Zangwill to head a new movement. Of course it would have been

impossible for Dr. Jochelman, who was then an unknown youngish Russian Jew, to found the I.T.O. himself. My husband demurred. He had never been physically strong. Only two years before he had been seriously ill. But there was no one else, they told him, and, indeed, this seemed to be true. At last, gravely, almost sadly, he consented. To this cause, he said, he should devote his life. A deep relief lit the face of David Jochelman, a joy that was almost rapture.

This amazing Russian apparently throve on sleepless nights of never-ceasing argument. Was his youth sustaining him, I wondered? In those days I was young myself and I believed Dr. Jochelman to be my junior. It was amazing that only four birthdays separated his age from that of my husband. I now realize that David Jochelman's vigour must have been of the soul rather than of the body.

Dr. Jochelmann is lying seriously ill with heart failure in my village at East Preston. He came over here in connection with the winding up of the Galveston work, and is in a state of nervous breakdown from anxiety. It adds to the tragedy that his wife and children are separated from him in Russia. But Mrs. Zangwill is now nursing him, and I hope by the time the war is over he will have recovered. Israel Zangwill to Jacob Schiff, 1914

Dear Jochelmann, Serious as is the state of affairs, still more serious for me is the state of your health. Let the Galveston emigration perish. But Jochelmann must be saved. You have plenty of working and thinking yet to do for the larger world. If possible, I think your wife and children should now come over here. The girls could go to school or have a governess at home. They are destined to become English. Israel Zangwill

Jews, I know, have little faith, but try for once to cultivate the belief (of which I am sure) that you will be reunited with your wife and family, will make a good living, and lead a more peaceful and happier life than any time in the past. Your future belongs to England.

Now please be sensible, consider your health, consider your wife and children, and consider also a little

Your affectionate friend, Israel Zangwill.

Part Two

New York

Chapter 21

Variety,
18 November 1925

Young Playwright Who Talks Much; Knows Little.

*Brooklyn
Standard Union*

The Provincetown Playhouse, near the dividing line between Greenwich Village and Little Italy, has begun this season with 'Adam Solitaire.'

Oakland Tribune

'Adam Solitaire' is authored by Em Jo Basshe, which, you must admit, is something of a name.

Messenger

The author is a young man who makes no bones of calling himself Em Jo Basshe.

Theophilius Lewis

The author's name is Em Jo Basshe. It is the kind of play you would naturally expect a man with a name like that to write.

Em Jo Basshe

The identity of Em Jo, which is a nom de plume, is a particular mystery.

Variety

There is still a good deal of bewilderment in the minds of those who saw 'Adam Solitaire' at the Provincetown Theatre Friday.

Walter M. Oestreicher, *Brooklyn Daily Times*

When the final curtain drops, one cannot avoid a feeling that whatever Mr. Basshe's meaning may have been, he took the long way round to express it.

New York Times

To detail the story as it unfolded in fifteen scenes would be quite useless in this limited space.

Commonweal

Adam is accused of a crime that he did not commit. A new steel bridge gives way under him and he is merely injured. He tries to kill himself and fails. Just as he is about to be re-united to his wife, he dies.

Drama Calendar

He suffered almost as much as his audience.

Burns Mantle

The settings form the pièce de résistance of Adam Solitaire. These, at least, are clear and comprehensible, and one or two of startling beauty. That silhouette of the great suspension-bridge against a night-sky with the figure of Adam outlined between its webs will not soon be forgotten. And the street scenes – of houses askew, crazy, about to topple – are an index to the tempest that shakes the mind of the halfcrazed protagonist.

Drama Calendar

There is one scene in which Adam, confused and defeated, stands upon a bridge and cries to heaven to show him his destiny. At that moment the bridge collapses. This symbolism seems to apply to this play and its author, one Em Jo Basshe. The play seems to collapse on several occasions when the author is exhorting loudest.

Freeport Daily Review

Here is a play in which the author seems to be trying cryptically to say something about life, destiny, the problem of evil and of human suffering. Is Mr. Basshe trying

Drama Calendar

to express something actually comprehensible? Or is he clutching at the really inexpressible?

Dixie Hines

The impression one gets is that the author himself was not quite certain of his path, and made many turnings, bringing himself up against stone walls or forests of bewilderment.

Richard Dana Skinner,
Independent

Personally, I found this play a profoundly stirring work.

Brooklyn Standard
Union

'Adam Solitaire' will delight thinkers and life-problem solvers and delvers into the whys and wherefores of human existence.

Brooklyn Daily Times

The author is a man of big thoughts and, perhaps, of big talent, too.

New York Herald
Tribune

The play is either a subtle masterpiece, too advanced for the average mind, or it is a chaos of distorted playwriting. There is every reason to suspect that the second alternative is correct.

Drama Calendar

Now how far are these scenes actual, how far symbolic? Did the bridge really give way or was that a symbol? We give it up. For we have at length been visited by a horrid suspicion that the writer deliberately chooses to beat about the bush, to baffle, merely in order to produce the awesome effect of profundity, to leave us guessing at the utterly utter that lies beyond the beyond.

***

Mordecai Gorelik

A happy experience of those days was the beginning of my friendship with the young dramatist Em Jo Basshe, who liked to relate that he was the son of a London banker and a Russian peasant woman. He had an appealing, simple quality, and he did look like a Russian peasant, although his original name was Emanuel Jochelman.

When I realized that one could not carry around so many names without tripping I took Em from my first name and Jo from my second, and Em Jo came to life. Foolishly I did not join the two, and a lot of critics had a holiday with them. But I did later, and Emjo became my name, legally and otherwise.

Emjo Basshe to
H. L. Mencken

I predict formally that in another fifty years Emjo will be as popular in this great Republic as Kenneth or Elmer.

H. L. Mencken

Little of the work that has emerged from the expressionist theater in America has proved as exciting, as charged with an untamed emotionalism, as full of rich potentialities as the plays of Em Jo Basshe. Basshe was born in Russia in 1899, the son of Dr. David Jochelman, a noted social service worker, a philanthropist, leader of the ITO, and a very intimate friend of the late Israel Zangwill. At the age of thirteen, Em Jo was brought to America.

Aben Kandel, 1927

Em Jo Basshe told me yesterday a few things about himself. 'I arrived in this country from Russia with my father,' Basshe related. Now barely 27 years old, Basshe has worked alone in America since he was a boy of 12. For

Sender Garlin,
*New York Daily
Worker*

his father remained in this country but a short time before returning to continue his work of Jewish colonisation as an escape from the pogroms of czarist Russia.

Jewish Chronicle   One of the very first impressions which I formed of this interesting figure was of a restless, roving nature, a sincerity of conviction, and an utter disregard of conventionality. There is no doubt that this young dramatist, with his passionate love for the theatre and his vital, restless presentment of the moving stream of life, will give great things to contemporary American art.

Aben Kandel   That Em Jo Basshe will go far as a pioneer in the American theater is no wild prophecy.

Variety   Twenty years from now, Emjo Basshe will be internationally known.

Chapter 22

In 1925 Em's tragedy, *Adam Solitaire*, was seen by Otto Kahn, a millionaire theatre patron.

Mordecai Gorelik

Emjo was kept from falling to the dreary level of the characters in his own dramas by the kindly intervention of Mr. Otto Kahn.

Alexander King

Theirs was a curious relationship. Basshe got to him, I was told, because Kahn knew his father, who was an important but a mysteriously (and deliberately) unpublicized personage in the European Zionist movement.

Bernard Smith

Em Jo has received an allowance of $1000.00 for the year from Otto Kahn. This will mean a lot to Em. He is going around looking very cheerful. I'm surprised he got the money. I've had an idea there was that kind of money floating around, but I never thought anybody but artists and pale poets saw any of it.

Mordecai Gorelik, 1926

After the opening of 'Adam' everything was pretty black. I was down and out – spiritually and mentally. For years I had prepared myself in most of the branches of the theatre, had written close to thirty long and short plays and this was the result. Therefore when word came about your reactions to the play . . . up until that time you had been a mythical figure . . . A complete change came over me.

Emjo Basshe to Otto Kahn

I have a medieval appreciation of dreamers.

Otto Kahn to Emjo Basshe

***

Jewish Criterion, 1922

Otto Herman Kahn is the aristocrat of Wall Street.

Theodore Roosevelt, 1918

Mr. Kahn has his face set toward the light.

Thomas Edison to his secretary

Will you please ask personally of Kahn for his photograph autographed. Say Mr. Edison thinks you are one of the very few men known to him who can think straight.

Beverley Nichols

Otto Kahn was my ideal American millionaire. He used his millions with taste, kindliness and understanding. Needless to say, he had the inevitable mansion in Fifth Avenue, and the equally inevitable château on Long Island; naturally, he owned diamonds and yachts and railways. There was a cosy feeling, when travelling with him, that one could request the engine driver to stop so that one could admire the view. (Once we actually did this, to the fury of a number of earnest business men who, for reasons best known to themselves, were desirous of arriving punctually in – of all places – Philadelphia.)

I have met during my life a quantity of millionaires, but I have only met one millionaire who is true to the ideal standards of fiction. Otto Kahn gave a perfect display of the fictional millionaire. (I do not mean that he was acting – I only imply that he is one of those refreshing people whose lives, by the force of their own personality, seem as though they were dictated by a master story-teller.) I cannot recall any man the rhythm of whose life is so consistently set to music.

I have never seen a more beautiful house than here on Fifth avenue, the Roman palazzo of Otto H. Kahn.

Emil Ludwig,
Boston Advertiser

Artichokes, artichokes! Artichokes are what stick in my memory most. This is at a luncheon meeting, where for the first time I experience what a colossal inconvenience it is to have a footman behind the high back of your chair. Hands appear from beyond the range of vision and simply paralyze your digestion. Moreover, these endless,

Sergei Eisenstein

countless sets of forks and little forks, spoons and little spoons, knives, little knives, and littler knives! And on top of everything there are artichokes!

I sit down. Behind me is a footman. Beside me, the white mustache of Otto H.; on the other side, his daughter's welcoming smile. The shimmering silver services, the exotic flowers (orchids? camellias?), the diners' dinner jackets, run together into blurred concentric circles. The buttons on the footman's green livery glint insipidly. And there it is, against the blinding white of the tablecloth, before me.

Why does the artichoke on Otto H.'s white tablecloth keep coming to mind? The difficulty lay in how to swallow this strange fruit of the earth, whose petals forming the cupola are each crowned with a small sharp spike maliciously pointing upward. More precisely, how this is accomplished at millionaires' tables. For one remembers from childhood that tsars eat only chocolate, and every other dish must be sweetened with sugar. How, then, do millionaires eat artichokes? Only the soft, tender base? Or do they, like other mortals, have to suck the fleshy bottoms of the separately torn-off leaves?

Edgar Hay,
Miami Herald

Otto H. Kahn is known in every civilized city of the world that has a bank. Yet Mr. Kahn is the most unbankerlike banker ever we have met in our vague and scanty contacts with the financial world.

New Yorker

He looked more like the head of something ornate and polished – a restauranter, a successful modiste, a jeweller – than a man up to his neck in financial welter.

Alexander King

On first impact, Mr. Kahn's coloring seemed deliberately theatrical. His hair, which he parted in the middle, was pure white, as was his beautifully groomed and waxed mustache. But his eyebrows were two astonishing patches of black charcoal. He was small, like a bullfinch, and his clear hypnotic stare, his tiny well-shod feet, and his quick emphatic movements gave him a sprightly, bird-like quality.

'Ottokahn' so those who regard him with greatest awe pronounce his name, with one three syllabled effort, is of gravely smiling mien. His gaze is a fixed regard, dark and bright from beneath cavernous overhanging of brows. *Theatre*

There is about him an air of the aristocrat of European culture. Seeing him anywhere and not recognizing him for Otto H. Kahn, one would nevertheless set him down as a man of distinguished bearing and power. *New York Telegraph*

By no means a big man, Mr. Kahn gives the impression of greatness. *Daily Mail*

German by birth, German by culture, he found himself in America while he was still a youngster, and in a few years he took his place as one of the big financiers who control the destinies of so many men and so many things in America. *T. P. O'Connor*

He is known to the world of finance as the head of the international banking house of Kuhn, Loeb and Company. It was he who lifted the banner of that famed house when old Jacob Schiff died a few years ago. Like Mr. Schiff he was born in Germany and married into the firm. *Clinton Gilbert*

Wall Street! What a host of ideas rush in with these two words. How much of American life has centred there for over a generation. And yet how little the average American knows about the district. Financiers are usually men of few words. In their private offices hovers a spirit of dignified seclusion, and a massive impression of silence hangs in the hushed atmosphere of their heavily furnished reception rooms. Finance, one thinks, desires *Louis Levine, New York World* to be shrouded in mystery and to maintain the enchantment that only distance is supposed to lend. Well, this is becoming a dead tradition, and Mr. Otto H. Kahn made me realize it. Nothing seems more foreign to him than the spirit of mysterious seclusion or of chilled dignity. The man's personality is shot through with amiability, vivacity, responsiveness.

T. P. O'Connor   Few Americans have left a profounder impression upon me. You could not talk to this man for five minutes without being impressed by his masterly intelligence.

New York World   He will drop a Latin quotation here, a French epigram there. He will discuss with lively eye the points of a Holbein, the political situation in France or the dramatic reforms of Ibsen. His brains seem to be divided into compartments, any of which he can open at any time and from it produce a document of interest. His versatility is almost weird.

Newsweek   He would far rather discuss the paintings of Matisse or the music of César Franck than talk about stocks and bonds and foreign loans.

Alfred M. Frankfurter   There can never escape my memory the picture of his desk as I saw it on repeated occasions: covered with books, stacks of books of which a few titles were visible – new plays, new works on economics, the orchestral scores of a symphony or an opera, art books on the primitives and on modern painting, even an occasional novel, and also, highly scientific works on finance and government. Where, was the irresistible thought, did this man find time to attend to his business?

T. P. O'Connor   Do not picture to yourself an insolent and masterful Wall Street figure in the person of Otto Kahn. He is artistic to his fingertips.

189

Mr. Kahn's mind was always restless, imaginative and sentient to whatever ideas were in the air. To use up every day all his energy; to come in contact with many minds and people in different walks of life, perpetually interested him.

Olin Downes

There is another side to Mr. Kahn that is known to many deserving, struggling actors and singers. He is most open-handed in assisting them financially and any number are indebted to his generosity.

Charles H. Joseph, *Detroit Jewish Chronicle*

Coming away from his large flat-top desk at the end of a long room in the banking house at the corner of William and Wall Streets, he takes a subway uptown to his Fifth Avenue home. And it is a good chance that awaiting him at home, awed by the magnificence of his surroundings, will be a young and most esoteric artist looking for a loan.

Newsweek

He was a patron of the arts in a sense that has been little understood since the days of the Renaissance.

Beverley Nichols

There are millionaires who, recalling the Gospel reference to the difficulties of the rich man in entering heaven, have sought to make amends. They have contributed to universities, hospitals, libraries, museums, established foundations for scores of purposes. I believe Otto H. Kahn wishes to make amends. He has himself used the word 'atone' in an explanation of his services to art. And atonement by means of patronage of the arts is perhaps a little more distinctive than burdening a university with an endowment or founding another hospital.

Harry Salpeter

Otto Kahn has done more for cultural America than perhaps any other man living.

Edgar Hay

For years, he has been recognized as the 'angel' of the Metropolitan Opera Company, meeting deficits like a true

Charles H. Joseph

sportsman. At the end of each season the directors assemble. The treasurer of the company, Mr. Ziegler, reads the annual deficit, usually about $38,000. There is a silence. The directors present smoke abstractedly. Year after year the silence is broken in the same way. 'Charge that to my personal account, Mr. Ziegler,' says Otto H. Kahn.

*Huntington
Long Islander*

Mr. Kahn may frequently be seen sitting in the low priced seats in the Metropolitan Opera House with the audience there, fraternizing with those real lovers of art who are willing to wait in line for hours to gain admission and who go to hear, not to be seen. His activities are not confined to New York. In addition to being chairman of the Metropolitan Opera Company, he is also honorary director of the Royal Opera, Convent Gardens, London, and is equally well known in other operatic circles. He is in reality the foremost figure of the world in grand opera.

Herbert Knight
Cruikshank

He is an actor – a star with varied repertoire, playing every rôle with ease and finesse, and always looking the part – whatever the part he plays. The perfect Wall Street type, he is likewise the cultured boulevardier, the artistic dilettante, the social lion, the benign benefactor. Let him walk on in any show depicting one of these, and every audience will smile its recognition.

***

Otto Kahn

If the doctrine of self-determination had prevailed when I was 17 years old I would have been an artist instead of a banker. At that age I had written two immortal tragedies of five acts each – in blank verse. But my plays were consecrated to the flames, and I was consecrated to the heart of a business school.

I came to this country thirty years ago. The not very bulky equipment which accompanied me included a great love of art. My feeling for it, reverence toward it, interest in it, and a little knowledge of it, constituted a precious possession. I was asked the other day whether the initials of my name, 'O. H,' stand for 'Opera House.' Now, I can hardly give my parents credit for having foreseen sixty years ago that at some time in my existence I was going to be the President of the Metropolitan Opera Company of New York. But I do give them credit, and I do give them thanks, for having taught me from my earliest youth to cultivate and love and revere art, for having enjoined upon me never to let it go out of my life, wherever I might be and whatever my career. I owe them a great gift. To have appreciation of and understanding for art is to have one of the most genuine and remunerative forms of wealth which it is given to mortal man to possess.

In the course of one of the all too few hours which I have had for contemplation, it occurred to me the other day how significant is the original meaning of the word recreation. Our theatrical managers speak of offering us entertainments, they speak of attractions – a hideous term – but recreations, re-create, how true a definition in one word of what our pleasures, our leisure hours ought to do for us. To re-create the wasting tissues of our souls, the worn fibres of our brains, to re-create the zest and courage for life, to stimulate, to move, to cheer – that is the purpose of recreation, and art, particularly art of the stage, has the power to accomplish that purpose.

We all, rich and poor alike, need to give our souls an airing once in a while. What both men and women, tired or idle, do want is to be genuinely moved and stirred, either to laughter or to tears, in short, to be lifted out of the rut and routine of their daily life and thoughts.

In this vast country, with its unprecedented mixture of races, all thrown into the melting-pot of American traditions, climate, surroundings and life, underneath what the surface shows of newness, of strident jangle, of 'jazziness,' there lies all the raw material of a great artistic development. Every kind of talent is latent here. All that we have to do to bring it to fruition is to call to it, to look for it, and to see that it gets fostering care, and guidance and opportunity.

A great stirring and moving is going on in the land, a searching and groping for the attainment of a richer, fuller, intenser life. America in the last century had the formidable task of conquering a continent, physically, industrially, economically. That consummation has been accomplished. America stands today the most prosperous nation in the world. We can afford – and ought – to occupy ourselves increasingly with art, science, culture and other things of the spirit. And there is every evidence, in my opinion, that this evolution is, in fact, taking place. Nowhere else in the world nowadays does the stage fill so large a place as New York, nowhere else does it show the same vitality and vigor, nowhere else is there such a profusion and variety of offerings. The sap is running strong in the tree of American dramatic art.

The ranks of American playwrights are filling up signally. And, what is particularly and auspiciously significant, the general tendency and character of these plays have not been imitative of European models, but they have aimed to be racy of the soil, expressive of American life, pervaded by the tang and the atmosphere of America.

I am indulging in the hope that there may be, in the not too distant future, at least one theater in New York devoted exclusively to youth – a stage where Young America shall have its innings. My imagination pictures a playhouse, where understanding, guidance, encouragement and opportunity shall attend young talent; where the delicate bloom of its hopes, dreams and aspirations shall be nurtured. There is no people anywhere more malleable than this new race of ours, a race which is the composite and resultant of strains so multifarious, and still in full process of evolution and development.

The book of American art is young. Few of its pages have been written as yet. That book is destined to tell, I feel sure, of high and fine achievement, worthy of a great and high-souled people.

Chapter 23

Mike Gold In 1926 I received from the most regal art patron of New York an invitation to call. I borrowed a good suit, shaved, had my shoes shined and, shaking like an Autumn leaf in a tornado, called on Mr. Kahn.

After five minutes of conversation with him I lost my fears. He has the strangest, most inexplicable instinct for all that is new, experimental and revolutionary. He said in his thick German accent that the theatre had become a mausoleum, nothing but a mausoleum, he repeated.

'We must have a new, young theatre, of young people,' he said. I agreed with him. He said, 'Why don't you organize such a theatre? I'll help you.' So I said, 'All right, thanks, I will,' and staggered out into the street. I think it was about midnight that I called up three other playwrights, John Howard Lawson, Emjo Basshe, and Francis Faragoh. Each of them had produced what might be called a Modern play recently.

Otto Kahn Dear Mr. Gold, If convenient all round, I should be glad if you and your prospective associates would lunch with me at the Bankers Club (29th Floor, The Equitable Building, 120 Broadway) on Tuesday of next week, the 18th of January, at half past twelve o'clock. Faithfully yours, Otto Kahn.

***

Carleton Beals Mike Gold is a Hungarian Jew using a pseudonym, a product of New York ghettos and of Greenwich Village.

Mike was dark-eyed, handsome, with wide, lush lips, uncombed hair, and a habit of chewing tobacco and keeping himself a little dirty.

Max Eastman

He affected dirty shirts, smoked stinking, twisted, Italian three-cent cigars, and spat frequently and vigorously on the floor – whether that floor was covered by an expensive carpet in a rich aesthete's studio or was the bare wooden floor of the small office where Gold's desk was littered with disorderly papers. These 'proletarian' props were as much a costume as the bohemian's side-burns and opera cape. They enhanced Gold's loveable qualities; his assumed naïveté, dark animated face and deep laughter, and his ironic mode of speech won people easily.

Joseph Freeman

He was liked by everyone for his gipsy nonchalance toward time, tide and food. Through his nature ran the song of poetry, like a Hungarian melody, but a song that often cracked on harshness. Mostly terrifically hard up, he never worried about his next meal.

Carleton Beals

He had shaggy black hair, sleepy black eyes, and a dazzling white-tooth smile – he could write like a wizard.

Charles Shipman

I learned from him that he was a product of East Side Jews without money.

Lewis Mumford

As a lad of nineteen, I would visit my friend Irwin Granich, later Michael Gold, who lived far down on the East Side on Chrystie street. Only one room received outside light, and whole colonies of cockroaches and bedbugs had had time to entrench themselves in the woodwork.

Dorothy Day

I was eighteen years old and used to spend a great deal of my time with Mike exploring the streets of the East Side, or sitting at the edge of piers over the East River and talking about life and the miseries of the working classes. Every now and then he would break into a song, whether in Hebrew or Yiddish I do not know. Once in a while he would take me up to his home where his Orthodox mother wore the traditional wig of the Jewish women who cut off their hair at marriage. She used to look at me with great sorrow. All three of her sons, it seemed, were running around with Gentile girls. After we had eaten at her house, she conscientiously broke the dishes that we had eaten from. It would not be kosher to use them again. I was not interested at all in religion at the time and so understood very little about the Orthodox Jews and the grief they felt at the falling away of their children. I did feel, however, the intensity of their religious belief.

Mike Gold

I was born in a tenement. That tall, sombre mass, holding its freight of obscure human destinies, is the batten in which my being has been cast. All that I know of Life I learned in the tenement. The tenement is in my blood. When I think it is the tenement thinking.

I can never forget the East Side street where I lived as a boy. It was a tenement canyon hung with fire-escapes, bed-clothing, and faces. Always these faces at the tenement windows. People pushed and wrangled in the street.

There were armies of howling pushcart peddlers. Ragged kids played under truck-horses. An endless pageant of East Side life. Horse cars jingled by. A tinker hammered at brass. Junkbells clanged. Whirlwinds of dust and newspapers. A prophet passed, an old-clothes Jew with a white beard. The sound of my street lifted like a blast of a great carnival or catastrophe. The noise was always in my ears. Even in sleep I could hear it; I can hear it now.

There was always somebody arriving from Europe in search of new luck; endless caravans of bustling cousins and their families, bunches of uncles and aunts and distant and near relatives, *landsleute*, village neighbors of Hungary and Roumania, friends of our friends. When I woke of a morning, I was never greatly surprised to find and smell and see a new family of immigrants beside me, sleeping in foreign baggy underwear, pale and exhausted, all of them stinking of Ellis Island disinfectant, a smell that sickened me like castor oil. Around the room were strewn and piled all their wealth, all their monumental bundles of featherbeds, pots, pans, fine peasant linen, embroidered towels, queer blanket clothing.

Every tenement home was a Plymouth Rock like ours; the hospitality was taken for granted until the new family rented its own flat. The immigrants would sit around our supper table, and ask endless questions about America. They would tell the bad news of the old country (the news was always bad). They would worry the first morning as to how to find work. They would be instructed that you must not blow out the gas (most of them had never seen it before). They would walk up and down our dismal East Side street, peering at policemen and saloons in amazement at America.

The Civil War was still close to my generation. The principal of my public school was a grand old white-bearded Colonel Smith who liked to tell us anecdotes of the war at morning assemblies. Many Civil War veterans were still alive, and the father of one of my friends was Corporal Michael Gold, an upright, fiery old man who survived until the age of 95. I took his name for a pen-name when I needed one, and he never seemed to mind or to reproach me.

I was born and raised in New York, but hate the town. So does everyone else who has to live in it. Human beings cannot permanently live in this kind of artificial prison. As I write, I can hear the riveters clattering next door on a new skyscraper. The bedlam has been going on for weeks. It is the harsh, cruel song of New York. It poisons the sleep of thousands of people, pulls down their health. The workers who must jam the subways twice a day certainly have no desire for a more futuristic New York. No one in hell longs for hotter flames. Yet New York remains the most interesting city in America. Why must hell always be more interesting than heaven?

***

John Howard
Lawson

In 1926, Mike Gold asked me to a luncheon with Otto Kahn to discuss the founding of a theatre. Gold invited two other playwrights, Em Jo Basshe and Francis Edwards Faragoh.

We stood nervously in the lobby of the club at the top of a skyscraper high above Wall Street. We were above all the surrounding buildings; we could see the Hudson River and the harbor. While we waited for Otto Kahn, I examined my three companions. I knew Mike Gold slightly. It was my first meeting with Francis Edwards Faragoh and Em Jo Basshe.

I was puzzled by Mike: in appearance, he was like a typical Greenwich Village artist. He was dressed more carelessly than the others. From what I knew of his temperament and background, he was talented, vaguely aesthetic, with a rough-hewn, earthy quality which was attractive but not altogether authentic.

I knew something of Basshe, and my first impression of him strengthened my hope that we could work together. His beautiful and baffled play, *Adam Solitaire*, had appeared at the Provincetown in 1925. Basshe was like his play, moody, difficult, boiling with energy for which words were inadequate. A few of us regarded Basshe's play as the most promising work by an American playwright since the emergence of O'Neill. Kahn inclined to this opinion.

Faragoh was startlingly different – a small, dapper man, carefully dressed. He was born in Hungary and came to the United States with his family when he was fourteen.

The luncheon was uneasy, and slightly absurd. Em Jo wore old clothes because he had no others. Mike had a sock in his pocket, and kept taking it out nervously under the impression that it was a handkerchief. Kahn did his best to make us feel at home. We talked spasmodically, at cross purposes, unaware of each other's opinions, united solely by our fervor. Fortunately, Kahn was rather pleased by our incoherence. It was clear that we had not met before and had made no effort to develop a unified approach. The awaited moment came, when Kahn sat back and announced that he would give us $30,000, with no strings attached.

I proposed an additional member of our committee, John Dos Passos. He was traveling somewhere, but I had no hesitation in pledging his participation. Dos, writing from Europe, agreed to be one of the five New Playwrights.

***

I like to remember Dos Passos as I saw him from time to time in the middle 1920s. People gathered round him at parties in the Village and strained to hear the understated but uproarious stories he told; but soon he would

Malcolm Cowley

drop out of the group, as if its homage made him uneasy, and stand in the background to watch and listen.

He had straight black hair, a wide forehead growing a little higher each year, and a wide mouth curving upward at the corners into apologetic grins. He suffered from extreme shortsightedness. He had to peer at people and carried his head forward like that of a shy, inquisitive bird. Sometimes he offered opinions in a tentative fashion: 'Gosh, I d-don't know about that,' he would say, or, 'D-don't you think that perhaps–?' Sometimes, with a timid but mischievous smile, he stuttered out a devastating remark.

In Greenwich Village, he was taken to be an elusive and even a mysterious figure. Very few of his companions knew where he was living in any given week. He never seemed to have a nest, but only to be perched on a branch, as if he were a migrating bird. At parties he left his soft brown Harvard hat near the door 'so as to be ready to bolt,' he said, 'at a moment's notice.'

Sinclair Lewis

I met Dos Passos once. I have a recollection of lanky vitality and owlish spectacles.

Archibald MacLeish

I met Dos Passos because I kept running into him. He would walk along, without seeing where he was going, and you had to get out of the way or introduce yourself.

Carleton Beals

Dos rarely recognized friends on the street, being too short-sighted. In social gatherings he is not always sure until he peers and listens to a voice whether he knows someone or not. He speaks in staccato jerky sentences and with eager enthusiasm, interspersed with 'Oh, yes . . . yes . . .' When about to speak, he has a peculiar way of lifting up his cigarette and examining it closely with a little frown and gulping several times before saying anything. Often he says sharply truthful things to people, then hastens to soften any personal sting his words seem to

carry. People invariably are on to him with instantaneous affection. At first his pleased chortling comments give him an aspect of rare innocence and gullible naïveté.

Dos is so shy that he seems cold as an empty cellar with the door locked when you meet him. Those flames of passion and sky-licking imageries that illumine his novels are damped down so that they don't even smoke in social intercourse. — Max Eastman

Though still in his twenties, just four years older than the century, he had published half a dozen books including *Three Soldiers* and *Manhattan Transfer*. — Malcolm Cowley

Often I wondered how Dos, with his poor eyesight, could see so much, for his prose reeks with the richest sensitivity of sight, colors, shapes, laid on lavishly. — Carleton Beals

In *Manhattan Transfer*, Mr Dos Passos does, really does, what all of us have frequently proved could not be done; he presents the panorama, the sense, the smell, the sound, the soul, of New York. — Sinclair Lewis

D. H. Lawrence

It is the best modern book about New York that I have read. It is an endless series of glimpses of people in the vast scuffle of Manhattan Island.

Mary Ross

I can still feel beating in my memory its bright, sharp rhythms, the jangled, unorderly music of the Manhattan of dusty or rain-swept streets, taxis, trucks, steam riveting, jazz and symphonies.

Mike Gold

This novel flies and hurries so, like an express train, it has such a stiff schedule to maintain, it swoops and maneuvers like a stunt aeroplane. I have always admired this gorgeous writer John Dos Passos. His senses are so fresh; he smells like a wolf, sees like a child, hears, tastes and feels with the fingers. I was born in New York, it is in my bones, but he has made me see and feel and smell New York all over again in this book. John Dos Passos seems to know capitalists, and crooked stock brokers, and factory hands, pimps, lonely young thieves, waitresses, morbid newspapermen, army captains, manicure girls, actresses, detectives, briefless young lawyers, milk-wagon drivers, bootleggers, sailors, cabaret singers, – he knows them, the way they make a living, their slang, the rooms they live in, the food they eat, their lusts, their hates, their defeats and hopes. He knows them.

Dos Passos knows the good and the bad, and tells both. Through him one can enjoy a great experience – one can roam the wild streets of New York, and climb up and down the fire-escapes, and see and know all that happens in this mad, huge, fascinating theatre of seven millions, this city rushing like an express train to some enormous fate.

***

John Dos Passos

I had come back from the war and the Near East not quite sure whether I wanted most to paint or write but with no idea of making a career of either one. I had a faint hankering after the theatre. I was fresh from the great days of modernism in Paris when I got a cable from a friend in New York telling me that a Medici-minded financier was putting up some money to start an experimental theatre. Would I become one of the directors? Sure. I took passage back to New York.

Four directors were already operating. Their prospects seemed rosy. Jack Lawson had already made a name for himself with *Processional*. Francis Faragoh, a small tart man with a charming pair of exiled Hungarians for parents, had won critical acclaim for his *Pinwheel*. Em Jo Basshe had some reputation as a coming dramatist. It was Mike Gold, with his Yiddish charm, and his air of the East Side Gorki, who had talked Otto Kahn into putting up the money.

Chapter 24

St Louis Daily
Globe-Democrat

Five rebellious young dramatists have banded together with the declared intention of giving expressionistic drama a chance. And the suspicion is rife that Otto Kahn has agreed to give their venture such backing as it may need to get a start.

New York Sun

The organization is to be known as the New Playwrights Theater.

The Bookman

They are Em Jo Basshe who once wrote a concoction called 'Adam Solitaire', John Dos Passos who wandered from the novelist's path, Francis Edwards Faragoh whose 'Pinwheel' is now spinning at the Neighborhood Playhouse, Michael Gold whose past achievements escape us, and John Howard Lawson, chiefly noted for his 'Processional'. That should be sufficient warning to anybody curious to know what type of thing the New Playwrights Theatre will do.

Mike Gold,
New York Sun

Most of our art theaters in New York have become timid and bourgeois. They are afraid to experiment. They are afraid of guts and passion and revolutionary harshness in the theater. They like to produce dainty little costume trifles, and decadent European problem plays.

John Howard
Lawson

We have the theatre existing in a feeble trance totally removed from the rush and roar of things as they are, a sanctuary with doors barred against the world.

Mike Gold

The New Playwrights' Theater is to get away from all this. It will try to break down the walls that separate the street from the theater. It will try to get close to the earth of America. This theater may fail, but it will make the first heroic attempt to prove that the old theater has come to an end.

It will insist that the playwright forget the impotent middle class, the perfumed social register. We want working class audiences to direct our efforts. Then they can claim us as their own, as we sincerely hope our theatre can claim them. Emjo Basshe

The theatre is not a temple, not a lecture-room, not the rich man's parlor. This, which they tell you is theatre, is old. Too old. Old theatre for old people. You don't belong to it, and it does not belong to you. The new theatre is coming. Help us build it. We don't know what it will look like, what it will sound like, we have not yet found the voice for it. But we know that this theatre is going to be young. Francis Edwards Faragoh

Theories, iron, dynasties, song, man, ships eventually come to an end. But they must not be forgotten. Therefore histories and records fill our libraries and museums. Archaeologists are digging up everything in sight, searching for mementoes of the past. Scientists are roaming over valleys and mountains recording the songs, manners and superstitions of dying peoples. The past was great, rich, fertile; its heritage incalculable. It must be preserved. The true artist never derides or rejects this heritage and pays homage to its creators on every occasion. But he does feel that the present is as important as the past – even more so. Emjo Basshe, *New York Times*

The contemporary spirit of the theatre does not hide himself in a corner, hoping against hope for the return of the glories, color and pageant of the past. He stands shoulder to shoulder with the mentors of this age: the Einsteins, Goethals, Curies, Michelsons, Edisons. He accepts their nuts, bolts, cranes; he listens to the tune played by their acetylene torches, cutting through steel, rock, bone; he trembles as the earth trembles when their shoring engines shriek and pound away. Does the earth welcome it? Probably no more than man. The show will go on. We are in the presence of the present. We visualize a theatre where the spirit, the movement, the music of this age is carried on, accentuated, amplified, crystallized. A theatre which shocks, terrifies, matches wits with the audience; whose emotion runs parallel with those of the flapper, the tabloids, the radio, the screeching advertisements. All in all, a theatre which is as drunken, as barbaric, as clangorous as our age.

Irwin Swerdlow Emjo was the stormy petrel of the New Playwrights.

***

Ernest Hemingway to John Dos Passos Well kid how does it feel to be back?

John Dos Passos to Ernest Hemingway I'm in deeper and deeper in the drahma every moment. I'm now one of five directors of a little Otto Kahn-undernourished playhouse on W. 52nd street. I do a lot of carrying about and painting of scenery and switching on and off of lights which is very entertaining – but I don't feel it's my life's work. Anyway it keeps me from writing or worrying and I'm merry as a cricket.

Ernest Hemingway to John Dos Passos from Key West As soon as the drama has you on your ass or as you get the drama visa versa come down here.

John Dos Passos The work that appealed to me most when I was a director of the New Playwrights was planning and painting scenery. To tell the truth, at that time I was more interested in scene designing than in the drama per se.

Edward Eliscu The group leased a former ballroom with a stage, located on West 52nd Street. Dos Passos did not appear at the depressing auditorium for weeks. He took one look at the stippled yellow-green walls, turned around and left without a word. Hours later he returned, driving a rented horse and wagon with a load of huge, garish paintings of New York scenes painted by his friend, Louis Lozowick. Without consultation or help, Dos Passos nailed the canvases up on the walls where they emphasized the incongruity between the grimy old interior and the shining new venture.

Chapter 25

John Dos Passos | The enterprise started with a bang.

Mike Gold | Maybe I'm prejudiced, but I think the most interesting theater in New York is going to open its doors Wednesday, March 2.

John Howard Lawson | The first production of the New Playwrights in 1927 was my play, Loudspeaker. I was numb as the curtain went up – from fatigue, from a fear that too much depended on the opening, and too much was wrong.

Harbor Allen | 'Loud Speaker' is a satirical epic on American fakery. Every American fake is here. Fake religion, fake romance, fake politics, fake news, fake women, fake booze.

Variety | The plot: a man running for Governor of New York gets drunk and over the radio tells the American public to go to hell. The citizens think he is an honest man, so he's elected.

Weekly People | It is a play in the radio spirit – much noise and static, turned on and turned off, perpetual excitement. The stage fits the play. It begins nowhere and has no boundaries. It is all stairs and chutes and trap-doors and twists and turns.

Alexander Woolcott, New York World | 'Loud Speaker' was staged with scenery so scrupulously eccentric that nothing so humdrum as a wall or a ceiling was tolerated for a moment.

Mordecai Gorelik | I designed a constructivist monstrosity, full of steps, platforms, ladders, and Coney Island chutes. The New

209

Playwrights were all pleased. Along with the actors and the ushers they took rides down the chutes. Those were the happy days of a new American theatre.

The seats pitch forward violently. Unless the theatre-goer clings to the arms of his chair he is likely to be catapulted on to the stage at any moment. The playgoer's lot is not a happy one.

New York Times

True, in 'Loud Speaker' they enter and make their exits on chutes and runways, and they gallop up and down spidery green stairs indifferent to heart strain, but this, we presume, is simply the playwright's method of saying that we have subways, elevators, and live too fast. So we do. And what of it?

Bookman

It is beyond the powers of this scribe to present a word picture of Loud Speaker in such a manner as to make it clear to the reader because it isn't quite clear to him. However, there is no theatre in the United States quite like this, now known as the New Playwrights Theatre.

Dixie Hines

It was fairly natural that the audience didn't like it. Hatred of novelty is one of the main characteristics of the human organism. But if you want a new theatre, there's nothing to do but to have one and to let the audience recover its equilibrium as it can. You can't make an omelet without breaking eggs.

John Dos Passos

***

For the second season, in an attempt to put on productions more economically, the theatre was moved down to the little Cherry Lane Playhouse on Commerce Street.

John Dos Passos

New Playwrights Theatre Find New Home in Greenwich Village.

New York Daily Worker, 26 August 1927

John Dos Passos

The tunnel-shaped auditorium, gloomy at best, containing two hundred and forty uncomfortable seats, and some of them busted, is about as far as anything could be from the circus-shaped hall we would like to have. On one side of the auditorium is a yard stacked with the debris of last season's sets which are to be rebuilt into this season's sets, upstairs is a workbench where the props are made, some cans of paint, a gluepot and a series of cramped dressing rooms where the long-suffering actors have to sit motionless and silent waiting for their cues, as every step on the floor sounds from the auditorium like an elephant doing a cakewalk.

Alan Reed

The New Playwrights was the kind of theatre where everybody pitched in and did everything. My duties as stage manager found me spending entire nights in the theatre, building and painting sets, cleaning, and preparing the book for the next play to go into rehearsal. It was an exhilarating experience.

John Anderson,
New York
Evening Post

Five New Playwrights Take Their Hammers in Hand and Do a Little Carpentry. The New Playwrights are conducting an experiment not only in the production of modern American plays but also in human relationships within the rather modest confines of their little theatre at 40 Commerce Street. The five playwrights have been elbow deep in work. Curiously enough, these men, all primarily writers, have come to an unspoken agreement to forget writing for the major part of this season at least, in order to be able to do the thousand and one things that crop up around a theatre.

Who would expect that the author of 'Manhattan Transfer', a widely known literary figure and a man whose works have been widely translated – who would expect to find him in a workroom of the theatre, supervising the building of the stage settings? Yet Dos Passos, who has driven many a nail in the construction of these settings, finds himself thoroughly fascinated by this new and quite unliterary work. 'It is like a vacation from writing,' he said, 'and it gives me a chance to do something that has been at the back of my head for many years.'

Francis Edwards Faragoh is now the business director of this theatre. The naïve might have fancied him a poet, utterly unaware of the prosaic routine all around him. But that picture vanishes at once when Mr. Faragoh negotiates any deal involving the expenditure of the New Playwrights' money. John Howard Lawson is probably the last man one would expect to find worrying about concrete floors, the kind of chairs with which to reseat a new house, and other mundane details. Em Jo Basshe comes a little closer to his own field in the work detailed to him. He is remembered for his 'Adam Solitaire,' which the Provincetown produced. Mr. Basshe concerned himself with many of the staging problems. Michael Gold concentrates upon arousing conscious interest in the program of the New Playwrights.

Here, then, is the spectacle of five writers, strongly individualistic in their own work but all trying together to build a permanent theatre for American plays that are at once experimental, vibrant and abreast of the times. One might well expect clashes of temperament – in fact, it is a tradition of artists that no two can work under one roof, let alone five.

One incident illustrates this complete submergence of artistic 'hauteur.' The night before the first dress rehearsal it was suddenly discovered that some floors had to be swept out and painted. It was after midnight, following a long conference. Were there lusty cries for porters or others to whom menial labor generally falls? Indeed, not! All five playwrights promptly got into overalls, gathered brooms and paint brushes, and at 5 o'clock the next morning the work was finished.

John Dos Passos to
Ernest Hemingway,
1927

Hem – I am busy doing sets for this so called theatre. Are you coming to New York or through it? I'm tied down until the theatre goes belly up or uptown – we're now on Cherry Lane & Commerce St. (God save us. He won't.)

Ernest Hemingway
to John Dos Passos

For God's sake come down.

Chapter 26

Variety is the spice of playwrighting for Em Jo Basshe. Two seasons ago this young playwright, who, though he is but 27, has been writing drama for ten years, had a fantasy of metropolitan life called 'Adam Solitaire' produced at the Provincetown Playhouse in New York. Now Basshe's setting will be entirely different. He has written 'The Centuries,' a drama of Ghetto life which traces the metamorphoses of Jewish immigrants in their mad flight from the pogroms in Europe.

Brooklyn Daily Eagle, 13 November 1927

Em Jo Basshe's play made its bow last night at the New Playwrights Theatre, only a stone's throw from the portrait the author has painstakingly painted.

Brooklyn Daily Times

It was rather interesting to watch Otto Kahn, banker, philanthropist and patron of the arts, entering the theatre on opening night.

T. J. O'Flaherty

I saw him in cloak and high hat, gold-knobbed stick and all, being escorted in lonely magnificence to a whole block of empty seats. Not even his best friends would go with him. He paid for the play, but he paid it the higher compliment of his presence.

John Anderson

Smiles and whispers of 'That is Otto Kahn' are amiably ignored by him.

Theatre

A cynical first-night audience that included Otto Kahn, the white-moustached angel, laughed occasionally and applauded vigorously at the end.

Daily Worker

Brooklyn
Daily Times The plight of the immigrant bursts upon you with the rise of the curtain. Driven to this country by a series of pogroms, huddled like cattle on trains and boats, their conception of the Land of the Free is first formed in the immigrant house on the East Side where an enclosed wagon dumped them.

Weekly People The play portrays their gradual change as the years pass and they are absorbed into the life of Hester Street. The whole life of the East Side eddies and swirls around them. Pushcart peddlers, old clothes men, factory workers, cops, harlots, housewives, beggars, the rabbi – nobody is left out.

Kelcey Allen The dramatist has caught the tang of East Side life. This play of feverish bustle and kinetic movement shows the emigrants as hawkers of vegetables, horse-radish and Sabbath candles; it shows them as rag pickers and pawnbrokers; it shows them bustling to and from the factories.

Stage One's interest is taken haphazardly from group to group, from the love of the young immigrant girl up to the pathetic spectacle of the old-world Rabbi and his holy men slowly reduced to beggary on the streets, still clinging to the rigid unchanging Mosaic laws of the centuries – laws which are neither suited to nor respected by the Israel of the New World.

Sacramento Bee Characters come and go, and scenes change in rapid kaleidoscopic fashion. It is as though everything were going on at once, and the focus of the audience only changes.

Weekly People The set is built on three levels; something will be happening on the street in the lower right hand corner, the center of interest will suddenly shift to the synagogue in the upper left, from that to the factory in the still more upper center and from there down to the lower left. Complicated? Oh, not at all: just stay wide awake and you'll follow the action with perfect ease. Only don't look for realism in time and space.

John Dos Passos shares honors with the author in the marvelous ingeniousness he displayed in designing the setting.

Daily Worker

The steep, imaginative set is peopled by patriarchs who seemed to have climbed straight out of etchings.

Gilbert Gabriel, *New York Sun*

The actors even have the intonation down pat. The costumes, which surely were gathered together at a rummage sale, are just too perfect: everything contributes to a vivid picture, presented to both eye and ear, of the noise, the bustle, the squalor, characteristic of the East Side.

Weekly People

The author knows his East Side. There is no doubt about that.

Detroit Jewish Chronicle

The stir, the confusion, the brutal beauty and grotesque humor of Jewish life was caught in this vivid play. Presented on a tiny stage, it achieved an epic quality.

New Masses

Weekly People As for the name, 'The Centuries,' we didn't see where that came in at all till the last act. The rabbi has tried in vain to stop his people in their inevitable development, and has had about as much success as he would if he tried to turn back the ocean tides. So he reflects on how the centuries have driven the Jews from Egypt to Palestine, from Palestine to Spain, from Spain to Kishinev, from Kishinev to Delancey Street and from Delancey Street to – the Bronx. Whereupon he too departs Bronxward.

Kelcey Allen The hope is held out that as the emigrant attains material prosperity and moves away from the ghetto, his dissatisfaction with his American haven is decreased and he becomes assimilated in the great melting pot.

Stage One finds in 'The Centuries' an element of personal sympathy and grief that Mr. Basshe's other plays did not quite achieve.

Gilbert Gabriel,
New York Sun It has a massy knit impossible to discover in his first effort, 'Adam Solitaire'. Out of his own life and memory and brewing convictions much of it seems to have clawed.

Sacramento Bee It is possible to observe a certain bitterness the author, perhaps not unjustly, harbors against the present order of things. He would intimate that the immigrants jumped from the frying-pan of pogroms and wholesale annihilation in the old countries into the fire of what he looks upon as a spirit-crushing, vice-breeding land.

Stage 'The Centuries' is not only a far more poignant work than 'Adam Solitaire,' but also, I believe, the most significant thing the New Playwrights group have yet done.

John Howard
Lawson For me, *The Centuries* was the soul of our theatre. It stirred my soul to a more intense and painful consciousness of my Jewish background, my half-lost and yet

inescapable Jewish identity. As I watched and listened to the rhythms of Jewish speech, I felt that I was discovering a heritage that was mine and yet wholly alien to me. I was sure that Em Jo had made a contribution to a new kind of theatre.

Chapter 27

New York Times, January 1928

Down in Commerce Street, where the playwrights have pretty much their own way about things, the New Playwrights' Theatre presented on Saturday night the latest work of the generally interesting John Howard Lawson. Here, certainly, is something experimental – even Mr. Lawson does not seem to be quite sure where he is going. It is a tale of oil in Thibet and war-makers in Wall Street, the threat of Moscow, revolution on the streets of New York. Perhaps an elderly conservative may be pardoned for preferring the old-fashioned methods of about 1926.

Alexander Woollcott, New York World

'The International' seemed to me almost excruciatingly uninteresting.

New York Evening Post

We would have given a good deal to be able to like any part of it, no matter how brief. We tried our best, and sat sympathetically in the gathering darkness of its twenty-one scenes, but there wasn't a spark. Not one. Once in a while we wondered if we were perhaps listening to a language we were not fitted to understand, but then this self-mistrust gradually melted away. We are willing to try harder to understand and make allowances for the New Playwrights Theatre than most others. They are intelligent, they have original conceptions, and they are digging hard in the sub-soil from which, one of these days, a new kind of theatre may grow up.

Robert Benchley

The International may very well be good something, but it isn't good theater.

The International, I feel, was the most interesting experiment we made. Many people disagree with me I know.
People still shudder at the mention of the play's name.

John Dos Passos

No one, except my associates, had a good word to say
for it. I could not ignore the hard fact that my play had no
appeal to 'the masses.' I recall an evening when the auditorium was sold to a union of window-cleaners. I moved
to strategic points around the theatre to study the faces of
these workers. They wanted earnestly to enjoy themselves,
but they would have been happier at a movie. These faces
were more troubling to me than the diminishing returns
at the box office.

John Howard
Lawson

Otto Kahn was less disturbed by our attacks on the
bourgeoisie than by our failure to attract audiences. He
understood and approved our aims, he delighted in the
bohemian joys of our parties, but Kahn was a realist, and
it was taken for granted that our second season would be
our last. It was clear to everyone except Em Jo.

One evening in the spring, I cooked a spaghetti
dinner for Kahn and Em Jo. The dinner was intended to
give Em Jo a chance to outline his plans for a third season.
The rest of us were discouraged, but Em Jo felt that his
life depended on the New Playwrights – and in a way
he was right. He expressed his faith eloquently to Kahn,
who applauded as if he were witnessing a show. Kahn was
not insincere: he was moved by the passion of the artist,
moved by his own lack of it, and he was more touched by
Em Jo than by me or my other colleagues. But he avoided
any promise of future funds.

***

The 'New Playwrights,' the group of young authors
who have attempted to make sophisticated New York
swallow 'new' ideas in words, plots and staging, are again
at it – i.e., they are still holding together.

Weekly People

John Dos Passos

Next season, and there's going to be a next season, in spite of the heartfelt prayers of our many wellwishers, we are opening with a production of Singing Jailbirds by Upton Sinclair.

Thomas Dickinson

'Singing Jailbirds' dramatizes the mental sufferings of a prisoner bound in an underground cell. Most of the action of the play takes place in the mind of the prisoner, which gradually breaks under the strain.

Donald Mulhern,
Brooklyn Standard
Union

The prisoner's delirious dreams are queerly and arrestingly revealed.

Brooklyn Daily Eagle

Whether or not you enjoy 'Singing Jailbirds' lies in your own state of mind. If you are strong for the proletariat, no doubt you will leave the theater firmly convinced that you have seen one of the world's great dramatic masterpieces. If you belong to the much despised bourgeoisie, you will leave under the impression that you have seen a 'mighty rotten show.' And that is what you have seen.

Brooklyn Daily Star,
20 February 1929

The New Playwrights Organization is offering a play by John Dos Passos tonight. The title is 'Airways, Inc.'

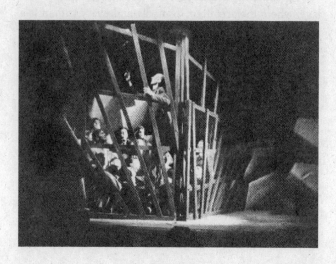

It was the name of John Dos Passos which drew me downtown to see 'Airways, Inc.' I had read a remarkable novel by him called 'Three Soldiers,' in which I saw signs of a sensitive intelligence. The novel had fine quality in it, and, after nine years, remained so well remembered that I went with eagerness to see its author's attempt on the stage. But alas for the vanity of human affairs. I found that the sensitive Mr. Dos Passos had been supplanted by one who is incoherent and muddy-minded. Two acts of this piece were more than enough for me. I fled from the theatre before the opening of the third act unable to bear any more of the dismal yammering which Mr. Dos Passos calls a play. St. John Ervine

The critics guillotined me, and the great public to whom we offer our works made no sign of life. John Dos Passos

By the end of the summer of 1928, everyone knew that the New Playwrights Theater wouldn't live much longer. Bernard Smith

***

Considering the intellectual advantages of the Village, where the arts flourish madly and every ruffian is a strolling poet, boredom there becomes a sort of triumph all its own. For example, how can the New Playwrights possibly succeed in boring their audiences? How can such an organization succumb to dullness? J. Brooks Atkinson, *New York Times*

Smashing dramatic form into fragments and then trying to create drama by pitchforking the fragments onto the stage is not a proceeding which is getting the theater or society much nearer the millennium. In fact, after seeing two or three such plays, one forgets the millennium entirely and sobs for ear muffs and aspirin. Walter Prichard Eaton, *New York Herald Tribune*

There is getting to be something heroic in the way John Howard Lawson and Em Jo Basshe (and the rest of the rebel dramatists) go on. 'The International' by the former and 'The Centuries' by the latter are the latest attempts to create a new form of stage play in which the melting pot can boil, or men can pull civilization down about their ears to the strains of a jazz band and the capering of a chorus. I have tried to keep an open mind, but now I have frankly given up the attempt. They are too much for me, and I admit it. They seem to me not only to lack order but to lack the ability, or certainly the patience, to understand and strive for order, and if they represent the drama of the future, for me the fireside and slippers. However, I don't believe they do.

Stark Young,
New Republic

The playwrights have shown themselves time and again much too indifferent in the mere little matter of the audience enjoying itself. Too often at the New Playwrights' Theater you get the sense of being slapped in the face.

John Dos Passos

The critics went into a sort of hysterical chorus; nothing pleased them, not the plays nor the productions nor the acting nor the seats.

Mike Gold

We were submitted to a crossfire of venomous, personal abuse. Never a word of mature blame, praise or advice. Our crude sincerity they could not endure. We learned to forgive them, even to welcome the feeling that we had won the hatred of the weary and the conservative.

Herbert Corey,
Brooklyn Daily Times

This paragraph is being written because of the names. Listen – 'Messrs. Lawson, Farragoh, Dos Passos and Em Jo Basshe' – are those names not luscious? Have not these pioneers of the New Playwrights Theatre romantic rhythms? Wouldn't you think that Mr. Kahn would be delighted to lose money with them? But he isn't. There seems to be no pleasing Mr. Kahn. He has withdrawn from the New Playwrights and the rest of the story writes itself.

Chapter 28

The New Playwrights Give Up the Struggle. The New Playwrights Theatre, that obstreperous infant terrible of the New York dramatic world, is dead. At the bedside stood Otto H. Kahn, godfather and backer of lost causes in the arts. Rigor mortis set in shortly after.

Charles Vale Harrison, *New York Evening Post*, 27 April 1929

New Playwrights Abandon Productions. Em Jo Basshe the Last of the Founders to Quit.

New York Times

Jo Basshe Quits; Village Theatre Ends Existence.

New York Daily News

Just whom Basshe handed his 'I quit' notice to is a mystery. Em Jo must have had a hard time finding him.

Sam Love

Of the theatre's five founders, John Howard Lawson and Francis Faragoh are writing for the motion pictures, while Mr. Dos Passos and Michael Gold are preparing books for Fall publication.

New York Times

Basshe and Faragoh were the most gifted playwrights I have ever known. All three of us found it difficult, after 1928, to find a place in the theatre. Faragoh followed me to Hollywood, but he never abandoned writing plays. Basshe continued to write brilliant, erratic, inspired theatre pieces – he could not discover or create a theatre that would meet the challenge of his imagination.

John Howard Lawson

It is a pity . . . a great pity. There is need for a theatre like this . . . I am very sorry that you got a rough deal here . . . You certainly deserved a better hand . . . but the good guys always get it in the neck all the time. Believe it or not but it's true. Bitter? Yes I really am.

Emjo Basshe to Otto Kahn

I am not a great guy but at least I learn as I go on . . . the theatre and music and acting and everything connected with it . . . my constant study . . . and I believe in it . . . believe in the theatre . . . play closes in ten days . . . theatre dies . . . a noble experiment gone wrong . . . it did some good . . . some learned much . . . others a little . . . and the rest went to the movies.

***

John Dos Passos

The theatre didn't suit me really. I was by nature and training a morning worker, while in the theatre everything gets done after midnight. I lived in Brooklyn, and we always finished so late that I had to walk back home across the Brooklyn Bridge. I never got home before three a.m. and being someone who's never been able to sleep later than seven in the morning, I just couldn't keep up the schedule. The New Playwrights got my head to spinning so I decided to pull out of New York for a while. I craved fresh air and I had to have some sleep.

I've forgotten whether I told Ernest about Key West or whether he discovered it on his own, but the second time I landed there, I found Ernest and Pauline established with their two small boys in a frame house on a sandy back street.

You arrived by ferry from the mainland. It took half a day and was a most delightful trip, with long cues of pelicans scrambling up off the water and man-o'-war birds in the sky and gulls on the buoys, and mullet jumping in the milky shallows.

I arrived worn to a frazzle. Hem always did have a gang of people with him. He wasn't alone when he came down to see the steamer dock that sunny afternoon. He just gave me time to leave my bag at the Overseas Hotel and to change out of my clothes and then we all had to go tarpon fishing because the tide was right.

Hem was the greatest fellow in the world to go around with when everything went right. What made his company so delightful was that outside of his literary gifts he had real talents. There was a passionate accuracy about his knowledge of hunting and fishing. I was never much of a fisherman. I freely admitted that. The part of it I enjoyed was being out in a boat and the sights and the smells and the sounds. Hem had brought along a couple of bottles of champagne which perched on the ice that kept the mullet fresh in the bait bucket. The rule was that you couldn't have a drink until somebody caught a fish.

Sometimes we kept fishing right on into the moonlight. I remember the ark of the dark silver against the moon's sheen on the water when the fish jumped. We would drink and fish and talk and talk late into the moonstruck night. It was a delight to be able to chatter amiably on all sorts of topics. Everybody said the first thing that came into his head. After the ideological bickerings of the New York theatre Key West seemed like the Garden of Eden.

Am down here licking my wounds, fishing, eating wild herons and turtle steak, drinking Spanish wine and Cuban rum and generally remaking the inner man, somewhat shattered by the encounter.

John Dos Passos to Edmund Wilson

Chapter 29

Asheville Citizen-Times, 27 August 1929

Miss Doris Troutman Married in New York. Announcement has been made by Mrs. L. A. O'Neal of the marriage of her daughter, Miss Doris Elisa Troutman to Mr. Emjo Hode Basshe at Wurtsboro, N.Y. on April 1st.

Miss Troutman graduated from Asheville High School in 1927 and during her high school days took leading roles in many of the high school dramatic presentations. Following her graduation here she went to New York.

She married the Russian dramatist after doing dramatic work at the New Playwright theatre. Presentations in which she has had parts have been 'Singing Jailbirds' and 'Airways Incorporated,' both of which were directed

by Mr. Basshe. Mr. Basshe is a playwright, director and author of 'Earth,' 'Adam's Solitaire' and 'The Centuries,' also a large group of one-act plays. Mr. and Mrs. Basshe are now at home at 'Rock Tavern,' Orange County, New York. They will return to New York City about September 1st.

I got married yesterday, to Miss Doris E. Troutman of Asheville, N.C. I figured that if I am an intelligent human being I'll never be totally and really happy so what's the difference. In January a child will come into the world to create a little disturbance. I wonder if the world can stand another like me after all the trouble I've given it?

Emjo Basshe to Otto Kahn

***

My parents were married in 1929, and I was born in February 1930, at a quarter to midnight, at East 15th Street Lying-In Hospital, New York. I was born first, and then my mother heard the doctor say, 'Knock her out, here comes another one.' My twin brother was born at 12.15, and he was born dead. My mother said I had two birthdays – one for him. The ninth and the tenth of February.

In those days there was a waiting room for men. She told me that when my father held me, he said, 'I finally feel responsible for someone else,' which pissed her off tremendously.

If my brother had lived, I would have been named Jane, after my mother's favorite aunt. Almost all Southern children are named after someone, like Jewish children. I'm not a Jane, I don't think.

My mother obviously let my father name me what he wanted. I'm named Emjo Hode Basshe II. I didn't know what the hell all those names were for. It was something to saddle a little kid with, believe me. Even though I loved my father, I didn't really want that name.

I knew his real name was Emmanuel, but I thought of him as Emjo. My father wasn't handsome. He had a nice

Jo

228

face, because he was a lovely man, he was a lot of fun, from a child's point of view, but he was no beauty. He looked like what he was, an Ashkenazi Jew from Eastern Europe. He had a nice headful of dark-brown curly hair: in the morning he used to slick it back with water, because it was unruly, but he would also run his fingers through it, and it got curly again. He wore tailored suits, and he always wore a hat.

My mother was a real beauty. She had a classic face, and perfect features. She presented herself like an actress. She projected her voice, she was always elegantly dressed, always aware of herself. Her back was dead straight. She was always hitting me on the shoulders to make me stand up straight.

She just bowled people over. At a parent–teacher evening my mother walked into the room, and my English teacher, Mr Katzenbach, just about dropped his cup and saucer, and in my mind I remember him leaping over a table to get to her. She was something. She had Southern manners, which are gorgeous manners. She could charm a pussycat out of a tree.

My mother never bought a dress in the Depression. She had a wealthy friend, Gertrude Chase, who passed on a lot of dresses, virtually unworn. I remember one of them, she had it for years. It was black, and it had rows and rows of little braids hanging down, and they shimmered when she walked. My mother looked gorgeous in it. She wore it with black patent sandals, inch-and-a-half heel.

One of her great disappointments was me – that I was not a Southern Belle. I couldn't have been, I'm a New Yorker to the core. Southern women have a charm that Northerners don't have. You don't just ask somebody to do something, you say, 'Will you be so kind to …' 'Oh, darling Mother.' That was what she wanted, and I couldn't do it. It would be phoney on me. My temperament was so practical, and so disliking any kind of nonsense – just the opposite of my mother. It was one of her sorrows that I could never be elegant. I had scraped knees all the time, and I've never had gracious manners. I knew I was, in temperament, just like my father and totally different from her. She did say to somebody, about me, 'She's just like her father, and it drives me crazy.' We were so very different. It must have been hard on her, because I was not the daughter she would have wanted.

She went to New York in 1928. She wanted to get out of North Carolina because it was small town, it was narrow, it was racist, although you didn't use the word in those days. She was contemptuous of religion, and in North Carolina, God is everywhere. She got out of high school and her father said he'd send her to university if she'd become a lawyer, and she said, no, she wanted to become an actress, so she went to New York.

Her accent was heavy when she first came, so she got rid of it. On certain occasions she would get it back. If she

had a cocktail party and was trying to be a gracious host-
ess, she would be more Southern. It always went over well.

She took the usual jobs that actors and actresses do.
She was a sales girl, she modeled clothes on Seventh
Avenue, she modeled for artists. Robert Henri was a fairly
well-known painter and she modeled for him. She's nude
from the waist up, and she looks straight out. He painted
dark eyes, but her eyes weren't dark. She mentioned
Robert Henri, only in passing, but she never mentioned
the painting.

She never mentioned acting, never mentioned being
in the theater, never mentioned a role she had played. She
gave it up when she married. My mother gave up quite
easily. She loved the theater, she had the talent and the
looks, but she lacked stick-to-itiveness, as they used to
call it in the South.

***

All my mother's and father's friends were in the Village. Most of them were writers, artists. We had friends who were puppeteers. It was the best childhood a kid could have, because nobody was normal – there were no businessmen. My mother eventually knew a businessman, and she was so proud of herself. I think his name was Bill, or Bob, or something dismal like that.

Everybody I knew came from somewhere else. The Otas were friends of my parents: Aunt Gin was from Virginia, and her husband, Takashi, was Japanese. Remo Bufano was Italian. My mother had a good friend named Clara Coffey – Clara was from Wisconsin, John Coffey was Irish. Mike Gold and George Granich were Jewish. My mother was from North Carolina, my father was from Russia. People came to New York, and mostly their background faded away.

People used to say to me, 'Wow, you're a real New Yorker.' But they were typical New Yorkers, in that they came from somewhere else. I wasn't typical.

I knew the city quite well, but mostly my life was in the Village. There was enough there to keep me occupied. There were plenty of horses, pulling old clothes wagons and milk wagons. We had an ice man: he drove a wagon covered with straw that protected his great square chunks of ice. On Saturdays Bleecker street would be full of pushcarts. There were always people yelling in Spanish, German, Yiddish, Russian, Italian. My friends and I would throw in Yiddish words now and then. Little turns of phrase. 'Oy vey.' 'Vey ist mir.' 'Bei Mir Bistu Shein' was a very popular song – 'by me, you are lovely'. Yiddish was in the air.

We played with chalk, we played hopscotch, we played ball, we played jumping rope. On the streets we sang, 'East Side, West Side, all around the town. Boys and girls together, me and Mamie O'Rourke, we tripped the light fantastic on the sidewalks of New York.'

I remember a lot of music in the house. When my mother could afford it, she'd rent a piano, and play Mozart and Bach and Haydn, Beethoven, and Schubert, and she sang the old English ballads she had learned as a child. They had gone over to the South with the people in the seventeenth and eighteenth centuries. 'Gypsy Davy', 'Lord Randall', 'Barb'ry Allen'. My mother taught me enormous numbers of songs and poems. Whenever we saw a ladybug, we would say, 'Ladybird, ladybird, fly away home, your house is on fire, your children are burning.'

My father had a beautiful baritone voice. I don't remember the two of them ever singing together – he only sang Russian songs. I remember my father singing 'Dark Eyes'. 'Ochi chernye, ochi strastnye, kak lyublyu ya vas.' He used to sing the 'Bozhe, Tsarya khrani': God save our noble Tsar. I learned the song of the Volga Boatmen from my father. I remember his walking around the house singing it in that beautiful voice, and I just sang along. 'Ey, ukhnyem.' I can almost hear him singing it.

My father had a Victrola gramophone, a large heavy thing with a horn that stood about four feet off the ground, and you wound it up at the side. The gramophone was in a cabinet, then underneath there were lots of shelves for records. He loved Russian composers: Tchaikovsky, Rimsky-Korsakov, Chaliapin. He would dance the Kazotski – the Russian bear dance – in the dining room or in the living room. It's very hard. You squat down and kick out your legs very fast while you're still squatting. You see Russian soldiers doing it in opera, it's really for young men to show off how strong they are.

Yiddish is very rich, particularly in curses: 'May a trolley cart roll on your stomach.' 'May you have lice and short arms.' 'May the worms dance the Kazotski on your head.'

We hope that before the season is over you will find the time to have dinner with us and see the little girl 'conduct' the music emanating from the phonograph. She often gets a perfect beat and if she is out of time she stops and catches up with it. Kindest regards and the best wishes in the world to you from the three of us. Emjo.

Emjo Basshe to Otto Kahn, February 1931

* * *

Jo

My mother couldn't cook anything before she got married. She was a Southern girl, and Southern girls didn't cook. My father taught her to make cabbage rolls – stuffed cabbage in a tomato sauce, with sour cream. We had karcha with fried mushrooms and onions in cold weather, and borscht in the summer, every day, or clabbered milk. We ate it as a cold soup. My father would slice cucumbers and throw them on, with a little bit of salt. It was lovely.

There was one dessert which my mother invented, and I've never known anybody else to do it. You take half a canned peach. There's a hole where the pit was, and you fill it up with macaroons, mashed with some peach juice. You put whipped egg whites on top, and it goes in the oven to get brown. The peach is warm, and the meringue is toasted on top. That was Depression Peaches. My mother always objected when I called it that – she didn't like the name.

We went to the Jewish delicatessen every Saturday. That's where we got lox, and smoked fish, and pickled herring in a glass jar, and gefilte fish, and bread and corned beef, and anything else we wanted to pick up. There were great big barrels of half-sour pickles, still bright as fresh-picked cucumbers. The pickles were always good. I ate them with a ham sandwich, which was not very kosher. My mother was a Southerner, and Southerners eat pork.

They had huge round loaves of black bread. We usually bought a quarter of a loaf. My mother loved white bread, because she'd grown up with it, but I got black bread, which was the only thing I would eat anyway.

In New York, you put mustard and mayonnaise on one side, and mayonnaise on the other. You never put on butter, because you know you never mix 'fleisch' with 'milsch'. Not because we were Jewish, but because that's New York. I was brought up knowing that you had mayonnaise on sandwiches, and my mother was not. When she had a roast beef sandwich, she wanted butter. I was just horrified.

My mother didn't have a New York accent, and she wouldn't let me have one. She corrected my pronunciation if I ever slipped. 'Toidy toid street and toid avenue', 'So I says to her' – those were things I would never say, but I heard other people say them. She was very persnickety about pronunciation, vocabulary, and not sinking into New York City language. 'My grammar is Latin grammar': that's what I was taught.

I knew a lot of Southern expressions because she would use them. The South is a very colorful place for speech, more colorful than the North. 'Leave it lay where Jesus flang it.' 'If a frog had wings, he wouldn't have been bumping the earth all this time.' You say that to somebody who says 'if'. 'If I'd only done something.' If someone says 'I wish' something or other, you say, 'Wish in one hand and spit in the other, and see which one gets filled the quickest.'

Chapter 30

Asheville
Citizen-Times,
17 February 1933

Wife of New York Producer Visits Here. Mrs. Emjo Basshe and daughter, Emjo Hode, arrived in Asheville on Wednesday for a few weeks' stay. Mrs. Basshe is the wife of Emjo Basshe, dramatist and theater director of New York City.

Jo

My mother took me down to North Carolina sometime in 1933. I met my great-grandmother, Agnes Matilda – a very old lady dressed all in white, with skirts to the floor, sitting in a rocking chair on the porch. She was eighty-three, and I was three. She put her hand on my head and said, 'Poor little Yankee.'

It was left over from the Civil War, or the War of Northern Aggression, as the South called it. To be born in the North was a tragedy. There was a shadow over my little life.

I got the idea her family never realized my father was Jewish. I think they thought he was some different kind of Protestant that they hadn't heard of before. They weren't interested in the outside world: they never desired to travel abroad, or even to the next state, or even to the next county. Their only contact with Europe had been in World War One, when my Aunt Sarah's husband had been a soldier in France. They found Europe very strange and offputting, and didn't want to know anything more about it. They didn't think of him as Russian – he was a New Yorker, New York was strange.

In the North my mother was Doris, but in the South she was Doris Elisa. My great-grandmother was Agnes

Matilda, and my grandmother was Frieda Bel. Doris was an odd name at the time. My grandfather named her after the Doric columns in Greece. That's typical of the South, to drag in Greek and Roman. They imagined themselves an aristocracy, and aristocracy was English, and the English studied Classics, so the South did.

My mother's family had been in North Carolina since the eighteenth century. The ancestors went to one place and they stayed. My grandfather had sixteen brothers and sisters, and they were, as they always said, farmers, teachers, and preachers. They went to church on Sunday, they farmed the land, they married and had as many children as God sends you. On her mother's side they were fancier. They were FFV, which is 'First Families of Virginia'. They had money and slaves and property. By the time I knew them, the Civil War was over and they were all penniless, but they held their heads high. In the South there's a great deal of holding your head high in spite of everything. My mother remembered the last of the Civil War veterans – she sat on their laps when she was a little girl.

My grandfather was regarded as a thundering atheist, because he didn't go to church. He was a deist: he believed God created the world and then said, 'Well, folks, you work it out on your own,' and this created a great deal of consternation among his relatives. His brothers and sisters fought with him all his life. When he was dying, they wanted to bring him preachers, and he wouldn't let them. He refused a minister on his deathbed, which took a lot of guts there and then.

My mother had an older brother, and an older sister. The eldest was Sarah, and then there was brother Fred. She would always say brother Fred. They all had the same eyes – Troutman eyes. I have a picture of the three of them: these three sets of gray eyes looking at you. It was very disconcerting.

Her younger brother was Gene. He was a half-brother, but you never counted that in the South. We called him Tiny Bitty Uncle, because he was closer in age to all of us nieces and nephews. He was from Grandaddy's second marriage. He was so handsome – he looked like an English aristocrat from the eighteenth century. He would leap onto a horse with no saddle, scoop up his daughter, Jane, who was about four or five, and gallop off. She screamed, and everybody said, 'Put her down, put her down,' but he didn't. It was a really impressive sight.

My mother was not nostalgic. She loved New York, she never wanted to go back to North Carolina. She didn't like the race relations, she didn't like the politics, she didn't like the lack of freedom. But she always called it 'down home.' She would say, 'I heard from down home.' Where you were raised really has its hands on you. You are what you're brought up, no matter where you go.

She taught me the Carolina toast: 'Here's to the land of the Long Leaf Pine, the Summer Land where the sun doth shine, where the weak grow strong and the strong grow great, here's to 'Down Home,' the old North state.'

Chapter 31

My father could be friends with anybody. There was a woman named Fanny King who sort of adopted him. When I was born, she said, 'This child will call me Grandma,' which I never did.

She was like a little old Victorian lady. She always wore gray or lavender dresses that seemed to me in the 1890s style. They were embroidered, they were tucked. She wore stockings and proper shoes, and a hat if she went outside.

She was a fairly wealthy woman, and she gave my father a house. I have no idea why. We would drive up in the summer. It was way-the-hell-and-gone in the country, about sixty miles from New York, which in the thirties was a long distance, because cars were not too reliable.

The house was built into the side of a hill in 1776, and never improved. There was no heating, there was no electricity, there was no running water. We had a well, and my mother cooked on the fireplace. It was a very plain little house, made of wood. In those days you had trees that were enormous – our floorboards were two feet wide. We had a folding bathtub made of gray rubber. We opened it up on the stone patio just outside the downstairs room, and poured in water from the well, and let the sun heat the water. However warm it got, that was the bath you took.

In Rock Tavern my mother taught my father to drive, or tried to, because she never managed. I sat in the back, they were in the front, and I can see him in my mind's eye, waving his arms about. She was trying to grab hold of the steering wheel, because he didn't take his foot off the pedal. A bee had got in the car, and so he took his hands off the wheel to catch it – he didn't want it to sting me. My father was totally incapable of driving. He couldn't drive worth a damn, and he never learned. Mechanical things like cars were beyond him.

We were there long enough to have a garden in the summer, and have it produce things we could eat: lima beans, cucumbers, tomatoes, lettuce, spinach. I remember working in the garden with my father when I was four or five. He was teaching me how to know when a lima bean was ready to be picked. When there were two or three beans in a pod, they'd be big enough to be worth picking. He was telling me that I had to get them when they were fat. That was his word – fat. And I said, 'Is this a fat one, Emjo?' Why I remember that, I don't know. I have some memories that have always been in my mind.

Emjo Basshe, 1932

Look how fat and rich the land is. The land, the earth, the ground to your left, to your right. The trees to the East, the clover, the grain, the fruit, the copper to the South, the iron to the North, the birds, the animals, the wheat to the West. Listen to the wind through the rye. Listen to the wind through the oak leaves. Forget for the moment the machines, the wheels, the smoke stacks, the clink of the Dollar, the hissing of the locomotives. Just remember the earth itself.

Chapter 32

I never knew my parents didn't get along, until they broke up. If they quarreled, it was never in front of me. They were unsuited to each other. I imagine he was difficult, and I know she was. All Southern women want to be worshiped, and they want to be catered to, and they want to be treated like frail ladies. But they're strong as iron. My mother liked to be worshiped, and my father was not in the mood for worshiping anybody.

I have very little memory of my parents together. Out at Rock Tavern my father and I would be in the garden and my mother would be in the house. I think mainly they didn't speak – it seems very silent in my memory, between the two of them. There are no pictures of them. I have pictures of many other things in my childhood, but not of them together.

I went off to summer camp when I was six, and when I came back, my parents had separated. They never divorced. I think there wasn't enough money for divorce, or maybe there wasn't any point. Neither of them ever said a word to me about it, so I made up an explanation: for some reason my father needed to live uptown, and we needed to live in the Village. It had to do with the theater. I didn't really know what it was, but it satisfied me, so that was enough.

He lived at 105th Street, which was very far up for us in those days. I remember lying in that little bedroom on 105th Street, and him telling me about Schnoots from New Jersey.

He was a wonderful storyteller. He was more flamboyant in his gestures than my mother, because he was Jewish. He waved his arms around. I don't know who Schnoots from New Jersey was, and I don't remember any of the stories. New Yorkers look down on everything, but New Jersey in particular – it's sort of a little brother. I don't know how that fit in, or if it did. I just remember him sitting by my bed telling me about Schnoots from New Jersey before I went to sleep.

I saw plenty of my father – I never got the feeling I was separated from him. The Lower East Side was full of Jews and Jewish restaurants. We would go to a nightclub called the Russian Bear, where there were all sorts of Russians, singing and eating. You normally never take a child to a nightclub, but the Russian Bear was different. It was small, it wasn't garish like most nightclubs. They had people on the stage playing balalaikas, playing the violin and the tambourine, dancing.

He would take me off on trips to see various friends of his in upstate New York. I remember riding in the back of a car in the open air. Instead of a trunk it had a two-person seat which you pulled out with a handle. I remember riding in the rumble seat with one of my father's friends, and he taught me a song in French – something about planting cabbages. 'Savez-vous planter les choux?' He had to entertain an eight-year-old, and he was a grown man, he probably didn't have children, and didn't hang around them very much. My father took me everywhere, and it was up to other people to make the best of it.

Chapter 33

Jo   I remember people talking about whether there was going to be a war. In summer, when I went to camp, we sang World War One songs. 'Mademoiselle from Armentières, hadn't been kissed in forty years, hinky dinky parlez-vous.' It was English, and the Americans picked it up. 'What's the use of worrying, it never was worthwhile, so pack up your troubles in your old kit bag and smile, smile, smile.' They were mostly English, except for 'Over There', which is American. 'Over there, over there, send the word, send the word to beware. We're coming over, we're coming over, and we won't come back till it's over, over there.' Those were the ones everybody knew.

The Great War was constantly with us in the thirties. People we knew had lost boyfriends or husbands or sons during that war. I remember one woman, Catherine Reigard, saying she was a one-man woman, and that man was gone.

My father was drafted into World War One, in the very last days. He was called up, he had a physical exam, and he was sent to a camp for basic training. The Armistice was two months after he was drafted, so he never went anywhere, but he kept his raincoat – that's what my mother told me. I can't imagine my father would have made a good soldier, but who knows.

Even I knew things were not right in Europe. It was in the air. I can still feel the atmosphere, of knowing things were going to happen. There was a Walt Disney cartoon: 'When Der Fuehrer says *We ist der master race*, we heil,

heil, right in Der Fuehrer's face.' In New York all the kids knew it. That brings back the war to me.

The distance between countries was greater than it is now, mentally. In 1938, when Neville Chamberlain was dickering with Hitler, he said of Czechoslovakia, 'A faraway country of which we know so little.' Czechoslovakia was too far away from London to amount to anything in those days – and the United States is three thousand miles from Europe. Three thousand miles of ocean means a lot psychologically.

We didn't have television, we had one little radio. We listened to the news every day at six o'clock, for fifteen minutes. That's all you got. I listened to the children's shows – they came on after school, fifteen minutes at a time. 'Mr Keen, Tracer of Lost Persons', and 'Jack Armstrong, the All-American Boy'. And we always listened to Roosevelt's fireside chats. I grew up with him. All my life he was leader: when I was born he was Governor of New York state, and he was President until April 1945. He was always so reassuring.

Everybody read at least one newspaper a day. If we ever went to the movies, there were ten minutes of newsreels. It was called 'News of the World', and a lot of it was preparation for war. I found it fascinating – these great big pictures of Roosevelt, Hitler, Mussolini.

I knew what was going on in Europe, but then again, I wasn't a kid who felt ominous things. It's never inevitable at the time. When you're in it, you don't know what's coming. You don't realize it's a build-up. Looking back on it, I can see the war clouds gathering.

I remember when Hitler marched into Czechoslovakia. My mother was crying. I had a straw hat with an embroidered blue ribbon around the crown, and the ribbon had been woven in Czechoslovakia. She said that Czechoslovakia had been conquered by Hitler, and she took the ribbon off and put it away as a keepsake.

We weren't sure it was going to happen, until September first, 1939, when Hitler marched into Poland. I have no idea what I was doing, but I remember it. I can see him marching into Poland in my head.

Chapter 34

I was always being put on a train and sent somewhere,
and I just accepted it. I had a suitcase, and I was put in
charge of the conductor, and was sent on my way. I'm not
sure I ever questioned anything. In the summer of 1939,
when I was nine years old, I was plunked on a train to go
200 miles down to Pennsylvania.

Fanny King had a school for 'feeble-minded girls',
out in the country. It was called the Brett school, named
after Catherine Brett, a friend of Fanny. They were both
spinsters, and they ran the school. It was a huge house
with yards around it, and it had a schoolroom with school
desks. All the girls slept on the second floor. Families
didn't want to acknowledge they had 'feeble-minded'
children, and they would put them there – it was a board-
ing school that they never left. They hired girls from
Columbia Teachers' College in the winter, and they hired
another batch for the summer.

When I was younger I had gone there with my father
for several weeks at a time. There were two little cabins on
the property, where guests stayed. I went off on my own,
and he went off on his own. He was probably writing in
one of the cabins, and I was off playing with one of the
girls, or wandering around, or reading.

I went there a lot, but the only summer I spent there
was 1939. I wasn't one of the pupils – I ran my own life.
I read, I showed up for meals, I could go anywhere I
wanted. I wandered around the whole neighborhood, and
walked into town. Once I passed a cemetery, and there
was a man with a shovel, taking a rest from digging a

grave. He was sitting on a tombstone, reading *Life* magazine, and I thought that was very funny.

They had a library which seemed to me huge – it was probably just a living room, but there were books on all four sides – and I was let loose in there. I was allowed to read anything I wanted, unless it had small print. That was my mother's only criterion. My eyes weren't good, and you don't want to put glasses on a little girl, it would spoil her looks. I read Shakespeare: one play and one of the long poems. I just did as I pleased. As I later found out, my father was sick the whole summer.

New Masses,
October 1939
Emjo Basshe, the playwright, is critically ill at Bellevue Hospital, New York. He will appreciate letters from friends. They should be addressed to Ward B-2.

Jo
My mother came down to Pennsylvania in October. I remember standing with her in a small hallway off the dining room, with no windows, and she said, 'Your father's been sick.' The instant she said it I knew. I don't remember anything more than that.

New Masses
A week ago we published a notice that the talented playwright Emjo Basshe was critically ill at Bellevue Hospital and would like to hear from his friends. Now there is even sadder news for these friends: Emjo Basshe is dead.

Hollywood Reporter,
31 October 1939
Emjo Basshe, noted playwright and director, died at Bellevue hospital early yesterday morning.

New York Times
Emjo Basshe Dead; Playwright was 40. Emjo Basshe died last night in Bellevue Hospital where he had been a patient since Oct. 11. Born in Vilna, then in Russia, forty years ago, he had lived in this country since 1912.

Jo
I can see myself standing in that hall, and knowing what had happened. I don't remember what went before or afterwards. That just remains a frozen picture in my mind.

Later on I knew he died of bacterial endocarditis. He was in the hospital for three weeks, and my mother was there with him. She said he didn't want me to come – he didn't want me to see him sick. My mother told a lot of lies, but there wouldn't be any reason for her to lie about that. Do you want somebody with you when you die? Maybe you do. Maybe you want to say goodbye. I really don't know.

In those days children did not go to funerals. Nobody ever discussed it with me, I never asked anyone. A few days before my mother came down, I remember seeing Fanny and Catherine going off. Fanny was dressed in gray, and Catherine in black, and I didn't know where they were going. At the time I had a strange feeling about it. Later on I realized they'd gone to my father's funeral. He was buried in Fanny King's Episcopalian churchyard in New York, where her family is buried, and where Fanny was buried, eventually.

After my father died, my mother sold everything and we went to North Carolina. She didn't really know what to do, so she went back home. I think in her eyes she had no choice, but she never mentioned it, and I never asked her. We got on a Greyhound bus, because my mother couldn't afford a train. It was an eight-hour trip.

I have never gotten over my father's death. It's almost as if it happened yesterday, even though it's been eighty years. I used to dream about him all the time. I don't remember the dreams, I just remember it was always nice to see him again. For years, I dreamt of him off and on, and then it stopped.

I miss him more now than I did when I was nine. I miss all those years that I didn't have him. All those years. Oh well. There it is. I don't know how things would have been different if it had been my mother and not my father. Who knows. I've never allowed myself to speculate, because it's pointless. Wish in one hand, spit in the other.

He's almost always somewhere in my mind. Never any specifics, like what he would be doing now, or what he would say. He's just there, in the corner of my mind – a little tiny figure.

People never really go. Even President Roosevelt. He was there my whole life until I was fifteen – on the radio, in the newspaper, in the movies – and so he's in my mind. But he's in my mind on the screen. My father's in my mind in the garden, or in the apartment.

I think about the past just as it drifts across my mind, as I think about the present. I'm not nostalgic. Except for my father. Occasionally I go back and see my father and me, picking lima beans in the garden.

Mordecai Gorelik,
Drama Review,
March 1973

To the Editor, May I call attention to an error in the article by James V. Hatch? On p. 11, the last paragraph reads 'Earth (1927) by Jo Em Basshe.' The name of the dramatist is Em Jo Basshe.

Em, who was a friend of mine, began by calling himself Em Jo; later, as a member of the New Playwrights Theatre, he added Basshe. His name, originally, as I recall it, was Emanuel Jochelman.

Part Three

London

Chapter 35

Sergeant William
Lennard

Special branch, Metropolitan Police, Scotland House,
26th day of January 1921. With reference to the applica-
tion for a Certificate of Naturalisation by David Salomon
Jochelman, an Ukrainian Jew. Memorialist appears to be
a respectable man and states that he intends, if his appli-
cation is granted, to reside permanently in the United
Kingdom, and seeks to obtain the rights and capacities of
a natural-born British subject.

Memorialist speaks, reads, and writes the English language well. He states that he was born at Postavy, Vilna,
1st April 1869, but cannot produce any documentary
proof in support of his statement, and that his ancestors
have been Lithuanians for generations past.

The Memorialist has been married twice. The first
marriage, he says, took place at Vilna, Russia, when
according to him he married Rebecca Tchech, a Russian
subject about 27 years ago. He has no documentary proof
of this marriage. The second marriage was on the 19th of
April 1906. He is shown on marriage certificate as David
Gochelman, Bachelor, age 33, married to Tamara Bach,
Spinster, age 27.

There are two children of the second marriage residing with him, and their names are as follows: Sophie
Jochelman, born at Kieff, 8th July 1908; and Fanny Jochelman, born on the 29th December 1906.

Memorialist states that his first wife is still residing
at Sichalishki, Government of Vilna. His explanation
for leaving her is on account of alleged misconduct.
He assures he put the matter before the Jewish Rabbi

in Russia, and that it was then agreed that they should separate. He only lived with her for a few years.

Applicant describes himself as a Doctor of Philosophy. According to events he was in Switzerland from 1900 to 1906. At this juncture it may be mentioned that the Ito Jewish Territorial Organisation was formed at the Basle Congress in 1905. Applicant became a member of the Committee. In 1907 applicant and his family proceeded to Kieff, Poland, and from that year, he, having been appointed Managing Director of the Immigration department of the above, came to England at least once a year, for the purpose of reporting upon the activities in Russia.

At Kieff on 2nd of March 1914, applicant obtained a passport enabling him to proceed, owing to an illness, to Bodensay Sanitorium for five weeks, and following this period he came to England, residing with Referee Zangwill, at East Preston, Sussex.

Applicant declares his politics to be very narrow, and hinted that his sole ambition is to help all Jewish sufferers.

This has been a very difficult inquiry to pursue, owing to the lack of documentary proofs, and the unsatisfactory manner of applicant, who tells a different story at each interview. On this being pointed out to him, he states that he did not think it was necessary to go into his private affairs, especially his first marriage. Having to rely mainly on his statements, it is very doubtful if even now he has furnished the true facts.

***

Mr. Zangwill was the chief speaker at a dinner last week to celebrate the Fiftieth Birthday of Dr. Jochelman.

Jewish Chronicle,
27 February 1920

In proposing the health of Dr. Jochelman, Mr. Zangwill said:

I do not know when I have occupied a chair with more pleasure than on the present occasion. The only alloy in my pleasure is the reflection that Dr. Jochelman, whom we are met to honour, is fifty years old, and that I am even older. It is hard to believe that this fiery young man has really scored his half century. But despite Einstein, Time goes its implacable way, and all we can do is to celebrate the fact that few men have crammed more unselfish activity into fifty years than our distinguished guest. (Cheers.)

I have known him since the so-called Uganda movement in Zionism, ever active, ever eloquent, and, what is much rarer, ever luminous. Luminosity is indeed his central characteristic. Not mere brilliance – for fireworks are brilliant – but the luminosity of a lighthouse, of a light that guides. And just as he fascinated me when I first met him somewhere in Europe, so I knew his clear brain and resolute will would fascinate any committee which had the good sense to put him on it; and I am not in the least surprised that, though a comparative newcomer in London, he has already become indispensable in every committee, whether in the West End or the East End. He is, indeed, the man who makes both ends meet.

My only complaint is that Dr. Jochelman does far too much. For his heart, large as it is, is also weak. There was a time when his friends feared complete collapse, and they

still tremble. As their representative I would beg him to celebrate his fiftieth birthday by a little relaxation of his too copious activities – activities so numerous that it tires me even to think of them. For many years I have had the privilege of working with him, nominally as his President, but perhaps more truly as his puppet, the slave of his will to Territorialism. (Laughter.)

It only remains for me to ask you to drink long life to Dr Jochelman, and I would like to couple with the toast, his gifted, charming and devoted life companion, Mrs Jochelman. (Loud cheers.)

Chapter 36

Daily Herald,
20 July 1933
London Jewry stops work to-day. Thursday is the best day of the week for street traders and market-men. It is also the principal day of the week for slaughtering cattle. Stalls will be vacant to-day. No cattle will be slaughtered. Yiddish-speaking Jews will have to go without their own evening paper.

Western Gazette
In Stepney, Whitechapel, and other thickly-populated districts, long rows of shops and business premises were deserted.

Sheffield Independent
Every shop not Gentile-owned was closed.

Jewish Chronicle
Nearly every Jewish shop in the East End exhibited in the windows the following notice. 'National Jewish Day of Mourning and Protest. This establishment will be closed on July 20th as a mark of protest against Hitlerism. Join the Jewish Procession to Hyde Park.'

David Jochelman
The ascension to power by Hitler is marked in Germany by a series of government decrees calculated to humiliate its Jewish subjects. After nearly five months the persecution still continues unabated. Jewish Men and Women of All Classes! We call upon you to participate in this National Demonstration which will take place on July 20th. The civilised world must be awakened to the magnitude of this colossal tragedy.

Daily Herald
The main contingent of the procession will gather at Stepney Green at two o'clock. 'We expect that there will be 30,000 Jews there,' Dr. David Jochelman, President of

the Jewish Protest Committee, told the 'Daily Herald' last night. 'Another 20,000 will join us at Hyde Park.' The big procession will leave Stepney Green, and will reach Hyde Park by way of Whitechapel, Old-street, Seymour-street, and Edgware-road.

London Jews Hold Anti-Nazi Parade. 20,000 March From East End to Hyde Park in British Jewry's Biggest Rally. *New York Times*

Immediately prior to going to Press, yesterday morning, we received a telephone message from a Jewish Chronicle representative at Stepney Green, where the procession was assembling. Although, said the Jewish Chronicle man, an hour remains before the procession is due to move off, already thousands of Jews, young and old, are lined up. By the look of things I estimate that the procession will extend to about a mile and-a-half. Despite the humid and showery weather, not by any means the most desirable for a long route-march, the demonstrators are in good spirits and are anticipating the great parade with determination and enthusiasm. *Jewish Chronicle*

As I am speaking the weather is clearing up and, as if to cheer the procession, there is brilliant sunshine. Six thousand Jewish ex-Servicemen are on parade, wearing their war decorations, and many of them showing clearly the wounds they received in the Great War when fighting in the British Army – men with one arm, faces scarred and bearing testimony to the treatment of plastic surgery. The ex-soldiers' banner declares '1914 we defended Freedom against the Huns; 1933 we must defend Jews against Hitler's atrocities'. A large number of banners have reference to the Boycott. One of them reads: 'Be Loyal to the Boycott and avoid German Goods.'

All Jewish shops are shut and the atmosphere of resolute and dignified unanimity throughout the area is deeply impressive. As I am 'phoning this message, the numbers are increasing rapidly. A detachment of mounted police, as well as a large force of foot police, are on duty. Dr. Jochelman tells me the demonstration has exceeded all expectations.

Jewish Chronicle The long trek to Hyde Park left Stepney Green precisely at two o'clock, according to schedule time, to the ringing cheers of a dense crowd which had lined the pavements. The procession extended to a mile and a half in length, marching for the most part four abreast, and included many women. There were several octogenarian Rabbis in the march.

New York Times Bearded old men trudged bravely along the ranks, sometimes with their families, children and grandchildren marching alongside them.

B'nai B'rith Messenger Huge crowds, far outnumbering the marchers, lined the route of the procession and cheered all sections of the parade which took three and a half hours to pass. Scores of automobiles bore placards and boycott slogans were roared out through megaphones by hundreds of the demonstrators.

Sheffield Independent The leaders carried Union Jacks, and, among the inscriptions on the banners were:– 'Restore the Rights of Jews in Germany'; 'Protect the World Against Hitler'; 'Hitler is Violating the Laws of Man and God'; 'Down With Hitler and a New War will be Avoided'.

Jewish Chronicle The British public is well known to be undemonstrative and to watch with reserve processions and demonstrations, but there were numerous cases where sympathy was shown by spectators. 'Good luck, boys!' was a frequent call from Gentile onlookers. The crowds who lined the six-mile route were unmistakably impressed – were most favourably and profoundly impressed – by the sight of this seemingly endless stream of quietly marching human

beings. Non-Jewish men and women brought from their homes buckets and jugs with drinking water as well as oranges to assuage the thirst of those who were finding the march under a particularly hot sun a trying ordeal. An impressed Gentile remarked, 'Hitler's ears should be burning.'

The sun beat down on the marchers for most of the time, and many of the men preferred to walk in shirt-sleeves, carrying their jackets. The head of the procession did not reach the park till nearly 5 o'clock. Their arrival was awaited by an immense crowd. The procession took almost an hour to pass the gates, and when all the march-ers were inside the park a substantial part of the Jewish population of London must have been present. *The Times*

The average London resident, though vaguely aware that Jews form a large part of the population of such dis-tricts as Whitechapel, Shoreditch, Stepney, and Bethnal Green, with a better-to-do section in West Hampstead, seldom sees them in the mass. *Scotsman*

B'nai B'rith
Messenger

Speakers addressed the huge throng from several platforms set up through the park, decorated with bunting in the white and blue of the Zionist flag and with the five-pointed Jewish star. The speakers included Dr. David Jochelman, chief organizer of the demonstration.

Jewish Chronicle

Dr. Jochelman said that the aim of the demonstration was to tell the liberal and fair-minded English people the real truth about the position of the Jews in Germany. The people whose motto was 'Britain never, never, never shall be slaves,' would be able to appreciate what he meant when he said that the Hitler inquisitors had made a whole nation of 600,000 Jews, the overwhelming majority of whom had been born, and whose ancestors had lived, in Germany for nearly 2,000 years, into slaves, into worse than slaves. The Jews in Germany were continually being persecuted and humiliated in a way that no civilised human being in the twentieth century could bear without a protest of burning indignation. Dr Jochelman in conclusion appealed to all fair-minded British people to unite with them and fight together against the enemy of the Jews, against the enemy of liberty and of civilisation.

'The news of this great gathering, and all that it signifies, will travel round the world,' declared Dr. Jochelman, pointing to the whirring cine-cameras on the sound-film vans and the batteries of Press photographers.

Daily Herald

The procession and the scene in Hyde Park made an interesting film when shown among the news items in the Cinema Theatres. In the East End theatres Dr. Jochelman was loudly applauded.

Jewish Chronicle

Nazi Arrests Reply to Jewish Parade. While thousands of Jews marched through London yesterday, three hundred of their co-religionists were being herded through the streets of Nuremburg by storm troopers, under arrest. Rounded up by Nazis, they were taken to barracks. What happened to them after the barracks gates closed behind them is a mystery, for no word was allowed to reach the public. The previous night, a meeting of Jews at the Synagogue was dissolved, and arrests were made. Most of the persons arrested were shopkeepers.

Sheffield Independent, 21 July 1933

This unhappy outbreak of Jew-baiting in Germany will pass, and even be forgotten.

Sunday Mirror

Chapter 37

Mimi

I was born in 1935, in Mapesbury Road, in the corner room on the first floor. In those days, there wasn't another Naomi. My dad just wanted a nice Jewish name. I hated it as a child, because wherever I went people would say, 'Where did you get that name? How do you pronounce it? How do you spell it? Nyomi? Neomi? Niomi?'

I couldn't say Naomi, so I said Mimi. My dad called me Mickey, or Mishka, which means bear in Russian, because I was fat like a teddy bear.

When I was born, his surname was still Shlomovich legally. On my first passport, it says Benari, née Shlomovich. He said he hated the Russians so much, he didn't want a Russian name. When he left Russia he chose the name Benari, which means son of a lion in Hebrew. His first name was Yehuda, but he was always called Leva – the

Russian sound is Lyova. Lev is a Hebrew word for lion, as is Yehuda.

He left Russia when he was seventeen. He went to Warsaw for a while, where he had an uncle, he went on to Berlin, and moved on from there and landed up in Paris.

He studied Law and Arabic at the Sorbonne. He told me about his very first law class. They were all sent out to stand on a busy corner, and come back in half an hour and report what they'd seen. Everybody's version was different. And the professor said, 'That's your first lesson as a lawyer. You can't trust witnesses.'

My parents met in 1930. My dad was great friends with Fanny and Sonia's cousin, Victor. He went with Victor to a Zionist congress in Switzerland in 1930, and for some reason, Victor took my mum. She was twenty-one or twenty-two. She couldn't have cared less about Zionism, she just went along for the ride. They were having a meal, and she noticed my dad hadn't ordered any meat, because he had no money. So when he wasn't looking, she took a sausage off her plate and put it onto his. He always said, 'I was bought by a sausage.'

He was living in Paris, she was in London, and she'd go across by train to visit him. They were very romantic to start with. He bought her the *Rubaiyat of Omar Khayyam*. It's beautiful poetry. It was written in Persian, and he gave it to Mum in French, dedicated to her. I think he just thought she was so beautiful, and he never stopped thinking that.

He would tell stories of her scattiness. One day she arrived in Paris without her violin. He said, 'Where's your fiddle?' and she said, 'I don't know. Gone.'

They had a Jewish wedding in Paris in 1933, when Mum was twenty-five and Dad was twenty-seven. She had to walk around the groom seven times, in the Jewish tradition. She told me she thought it was very funny. Two years later I was born. They decided an English passport would be more useful to me than a French one, so she came over to England to have me, and then they went straight back to Paris.

We were just poor as church mice. They used to go to the cinema in turns, because they couldn't afford a babysitter. One of them would go for half, they'd come home in the interval, tell the other one what had happened, and then the other one would go and watch the second half.

My mum learnt the violin as a child, and she got her degree at the Royal Academy of Music. Afterwards she joined a girl band, and they used to play in cinemas during the silent movies. Then the talkies came in, and that put them out of work. She then played for a while in another girl's group. She loved playing. I once asked her, 'Why didn't you go on working?' And she said, 'I gave it up to have you.' For her, that was enough. She didn't do much during those years. Fanny did. She wrote a play, and she wrote a novel.

***

And the Stars Laughed is a first novel of unusual promise by Fanny Jocelyn, a young authoress who comes of a well-known Jewish family. She has chosen a subject which pervades the minds of all to-day, the passionate desire for peace. Somewhat boldly she has gone back to a period which she herself is too young to remember, the Great War – one is almost tempted to say the last one, not the present one.

Charles Landstone, *Jewish Chronicle*, 29 October 1937

Fanny Jocelyn conceals the identity of Miss Jochelman, daughter of the well-known worker on behalf of East European Jewry.

Jewish Chronicle

To David, Fairest critic, most loyal friend and, incidentally, My Father.

Fanny, *And the Stars Laughed*

The book has for the major part of its background the war. She attributes having chosen this subject to the influence of her early life. As a little girl in 1913 she lived in Russia. Just prior to the outbreak of war her father came to England and the family were separated. Miss Jocelyn can just remember the voyage to England which was most hazardous with the mines in the North Sea. With all the hundred books that have been written round the War, one feels that there is always room for another such as this. Vividly written, absorbing and real. The characters live.

Marylebone Mercury

Gerald Doncastle, a brilliant young writer, becomes engaged to the girl he loves just as the bells ring in the New Year, and Jean cries rapturously: 'I feel it's the greatest year the world has ever known.' It is at this youthful cry of hope and joy that the stars laugh so ironically, for the year in question is 1914.

Phyllis Bentley, *Yorkshire Post*

Fanny Jocelyn, known to many readers as part author of the unusual and striking play 'Come Out To Play', began working on this novel at the age of eighteen. It retains the chief qualities of extreme youth – warmth and

Marylebone Mercury

a passionate sincerity – which have remained in spite of several years of rewriting and judicious polishing. This passionate plea for peace has for its plot an enthralling story, swiftly and movingly told.

Phyllis Bentley,
Yorkshire Post

Miss Jocelyn writes one very revealing sentence. She says of her hero with approval: He had achieved the aim of every author's life. He had written a best-seller. Well, well! Miss Jocelyn will achieve that aim some day soon, I shouldn't wonder.

Chapter 38

No more gallant officer, no more charming and cultivated companion could have been imagined, than Vladimir Jabotinsky.

Ronald Storrs

At this time Jabotinsky has a larger personal and devoted following than any other Jew in Europe.

Jacob de Haas,
12 November 1934

The whippy little gray-haired, weather-beaten Jabotinsky will be put down in the post-mortem of Western civilization as one of its most fascinating personalities.

Edwin C. Hill

He was, when I first met him, in his middle forties, a man slightly under medium height who carried himself like a soldier and talked like a man of letters. He had a massive head with Slavonic features and displayed in his manners a strange, eighteenth-century courtesy. Part of his personal magnetism, which captivated his followers and opponents alike, was his voice: it made every language that he spoke – and he spoke eight to perfection – sound like Italian.

Arthur Koestler

Jabotinsky, the passionate Zionist, was utterly un-Jewish in manner, approach and deportment. He came from Odessa, but the inner life of Jewry had left no trace on him. He was rather ugly, immensely attractive, well spoken, generous; all of these qualities were, however, overlaid with a certain touch of the rather theatrically chivalresque, a certain queer and irrelevant knightliness, which was not at all Jewish.

Chaim Weizmann

David Ben-Gurion

There was in him complete internal spiritual freedom. He had nothing in him of the Galut Jew, and he was never embarrassed in the presence of a Gentile.

Pierre van Paassen

Vladimir Jabotinsky came from that intellectual milieu in Russian Jewry which had fully absorbed Russian civilization. When he first began to write his feuilletons and poetry in the Russian language, he was hailed by the critics of Petersburg and Moscow. The great Tolstoy himself welcomed in Jabotinsky 'a new writer of promise at last'. I was captivated by Jabotinsky's manner and deportment. There was an undeniable air of distinction about the man. He still had something of what I would call the old-world courtesy, a certain suavity, a certain urbanity, a certain charm and polish. His speech was plain, direct, unornamented, free from all faults of taste. He spoke with force and vigor, without the slightest trace of artificiality. Though he seldom spoke less than two hours or two hours and a half, he never rambled or went off on tangents.

I have heard many political speakers since, but no one who could cast a similar spell over his audience for three solid hours without ever resorting to cheap oratory. There was not a cliché in his speech; its power rested in its transparent lucidity and logical beauty.

Arthur Koestler

Listening to him speak was like attending a symphony concert.

Benzion Olsfanger

He has a 'different,' refreshing quality. When one hears him, one has the feeling of emerging from mossy thick-grown woods into green, sunlit fields offering far horizons. Jabotinsky is simplicity itself. Whatever he believes, he pronounces with the utmost earnestness and beauty. When he speaks, he stands upright and inflexible. He uses his voice only, modulating it according to the content. It is a forceful instrument.

Abraham Goldberg

There was a kind of spiritual radiance about his whole personality.

Kornei Chukovsky

In the ghettos of Eastern Europe he is already a tradition. As a spell-binder Jabotinsky is almost without rival. He is the only existing leader capable of supplying the flashing personality and keen insight required if anything is to be salvaged from the impending collapse of the Zionist adventure.

William B. Ziff

I do not think that Jabotinsky was exceeded by any man in the Zionist movement in physical and moral energy. He had no hobbies or pastimes. He was rarely even mildly joyous. He did not know and did not want to know what leisure was. Zionism was his sole passion. He literally burnt himself out by the intensity of his propagandistic endeavors: traveling without letup for years on end, speaking for hours at a stretch to large and small gatherings, dashing off newspaper articles on the corner

Pierre van Paassen

of coffee-house tables, scarcely taking off time to eat or sleep. He was always tense and in a hurry. He walked with clenched fists and a scowl on his face. With that bulldog jaw and those slightly protruding eyes behind a pair of thick glittering lenses, the brim of his hat pulled over his face like a helmet's visor, he conveyed the impression of something that for want of a better name may perhaps be described as ferocious grace.

Chaim Weizmann

His speeches at the early Congresses were provocative in tone but left no very distinct impression, so that one did not know, for instance, whether he was for Uganda or against. Many years afterwards, he left the Zionist Organization and, like Zangwill, founded his own. He is remembered as the founder of the Revisionist party.

Joseph Schechtman

The very term 'dictatorship' is by definition inapplicable to Jabotinsky's position in the Revisionist movement. Dictatorship presupposes the dictator's ability to impose his will by force or other irresistible means of pressure. No such means were at Jabotinsky's disposal. The only power he exerted over the masses of his followers was rooted in the deep, almost passionate affection they had for him. He commanded devotion of a fervor inspired by few public figures of our time. To many – possibly to the great majority – of his adherents, disciples, associates and friends he was not merely a thinker, a leader of, and fighter for, the Jewish people, but primarily their highly personal, emotional possession: each of them had his own intimate and captivating *romance* with the man Jabotinsky. To every one he was 'my Jabotinsky.'

***

Mimi

My dad was working then for Jabotinsky. Jabotinsky was from Ukraine – Dad had heard him talk there, and then followed him to Paris.

Jabotinsky sent him on a lecture tour to Poland in 1938. He went from village to village, and from town to town, saying, 'Get out while you can, don't you see what's coming?' And they didn't listen. Most people said, 'It won't happen here. I'm the only surgeon in this town,' or 'I'm the favourite opera singer. Don't worry, it won't happen to me.' That phrase always haunted him: it can't happen here. He felt that as a failure of his life, that he hadn't managed to persuade them to leave. He took matters to heart.

When he came home from Poland he brought me this funny suit – a fur hat, and a grey suede fur coat, and a fur muff. Somebody said to me in the street, 'What a beautiful coat you've got, where did you get it?' And I said, 'My daddy went to Poland to talk to Jews.'

Zionism has lost its spell over the Jewish soul. There are parties that have filled this gap with other things, things which may be good in themselves, but are not Zionism. Purely Zionist enthusiasm is in danger of disappearing. What we want now is to embark on a new and final experiment, but with different methods.

We Revisionists are a world-wide organization having grown up gradually through ten years of untiring effort, and now we have decided to place our machinery at the disposal of the anti-Hitler movement. The German anti-Jewish crusade is the most important and serious development in generations of our existence. If Hitler's regime is destined to stay, world Jewry is doomed.

Vladimir Jabotinsky

It is for three years that I have been calling on you, Jews of Poland, the glory of world Jewry, with an appeal. I have been ceaselessly warning you that the catastrophe is approaching. My hair has turned white and I have aged in these years, because you do not see the volcano which will soon begin to spew out its flames of extermination. I know: you do not see, because you are bothered and rushing about with everyday worries. Listen to my remarks at

Vladimir Jabotinsky, Warsaw, August 1938

the twelfth hour. May each one save his life while there is still time. And time is short.

Mass evacuation is the only remedy for the cancer of Jewish distress. It may be superhumanly difficult, it may be atrociously costly, but it is the only way to save Europe from being hustled into another catastrophe. The great advantage of the word 'evacuation' is its implied suggestion of organized orderliness. No other term conveys that important quality: 'emigration' has always meant a haphazard scramble; 'exodus' inevitably recalls the pursuing enemy host. 'Evacuation,' in modern times and under decent governments, has always been associated with forethought, careful planning, and decent accommodation at the end of the journey.

Do not think that I used this world lightly. For a long time I have been searching for a really appropriate term; I have pondered over it, I weighed it a thousand times, and I found no better, no more appropriate word. Several million Jews must, in the nearest future, evacuate the main centers of Eastern Europe and create in Palestine a national Jewish state.

We are facing an elemental calamity. We have got to save millions, many millions. I do not know whether it is a question of rehousing one third of the Jewish race, half of the Jewish race, or a quarter of the Jewish race; but it is a question of millions.

Destruction. Learn the word by heart, and God grant that I am mistaken.

Louis Lipsky   He never lived in the regular time of day. He had his own time. While we Zionists saw the clock at six, he saw it at twelve.

Chapter 39

Jabotinsky came over to England in 1938, when he realised there was going to be war. Dad was by this time his personal assistant, so where Jabotinsky was, he was. We came back at the same time.

Dad knew what was going on in Germany, and he knew it would come to France. The Germans could just march into France, which they did. England was safer because it was an island. And in England, he had Mum's family, and the house.

I don't think I have any memory of Grandpa David, except him being in bed. He spoiled me. Sonia and Fanny used to give me breakfast in the kitchen, and then they'd take me up to see him, and take up his breakfast. He had a very high bed. They would lift me up – it was quite a long way up – and I'd sit on his bed, and he'd feed me half his breakfast.

I remember Tamara taking me down to the corner where Mapesbury Road meets Exeter Road, and there she would teach me how to walk. She would walk with her feet turned out. She was trying to teach me, when I was three, how to walk like a lady.

Grandpa wasn't at Fanny's wedding to Hugh. Either he was in hospital at that time, or upstairs in bed, or he didn't really approve. I have a feeling that David was not happy with Fanny marrying a non-Jew, because he knew it meant the line of Judaism stopped there. He's not in the wedding photograph. It must be my dad taking the picture, because Tamara's restraining me, and I look as if I want to go and run to him.

Hugh   When the war broke out at the beginning of September 1939, my wife and I were on holiday. We had married five months before, and had had only a short honeymoon because we planned to take more holiday in September.

At the very beginning of our holiday, we heard a broadcast by Neville Chamberlain, the Prime Minister, telling us that we were at war with Germany. Immediately after he spoke, the sirens sounded for an air raid alert, and people rushed away from the beach to take shelter. It proved a false alarm.

***

Mimi   My dad used to take me to Oxford Circus sometimes. They had bunk beds in the Tube stations, all along the platforms. You could see people would be sleeping there later – they used to bag the same beds by leaving their blankets there. Sometimes they just lay on the platform.

We would go to the Movietone cinema. They had an hour-long programme that was news and Mickey Mouse, so we'd both get what we liked. Movietone news was the only way to actually see what was going on. You could read about the war, but if you wanted to see it, that was the only way. We saw soldiers on boats, getting off boats, marching here and there. It was all out of date, of course. I found it boring. I just wanted to watch Mickey Mouse.

Opposite the cinema was Jabotinsky's office, in Upper Regent Street. My dad took me there once, and introduced me. He said something like, 'Your honour, may I present my daughter.' Jabotinsky died in July 1940, so I would have been less than five. I remember being surprised. It's what you say when your daughter's grown up – you don't say it about a four-year-old. Jabotinsky came round from behind his desk, and bent down and shook my hand, and said, 'How do you do?' I said, 'Very well, thank you, and how is the movement getting on?'

I knew I was very honoured to be shaking the hand of this man. He was very charming. I had no idea what a movement was. Dad asked me afterwards, and I said, 'A kind of boat?'

I'd heard so much about him from my dad. He admired Jabotinsky so much. He never stopped talking about him, and emulating him. He quoted him every day of his life. He used to say, 'When you're eating chicken you must never use your fingers, unless it's a wing, and then you're allowed to.' That was what Jabotinsky's wife said, apparently. I think he adopted pretty well every one of Jabotinsky's ideas.

Jabotinsky's motto was 'Every individual is a king.' You've got to respect yourself. You have to dress properly, in a suit and a shirt – you can't just shlump around in any old clothes. You mustn't lean over your soup to get near it, you've got to sit upright and bring the spoon up to your mouth. You mustn't eat with your elbows out, you've got to bring them in to your sides. He wanted Jews to have self-respect. Having been the butt of anti-Semitism over all these centuries, he was trying to say, 'You're as good as anybody else. You're a king.' Dad tried to live up to that. He always wore a suit and tie. He wouldn't shlump around. He never ate garlic, because anti-Semites used to say the Jews smelt of garlic. Mum never had it in the house.

Vladimir Jabotinsky

The Jew wants to take his place among the foremost of all civilized peoples; wants to possess every bit of splendor and glory and greatness they possess.

Our starting point is to take the typical Yid of today and to imagine his diametrical opposite. Because the Yid is ugly, sickly, and lacks decorum, we shall endow the ideal image of the Hebrew with masculine beauty. The Yid is trodden upon and easily frightened and, therefore, the Hebrew ought to be proud and independent. The Yid is despised by all and, therefore, the Hebrew ought to charm all. The Yid has accepted submission and therefore the Hebrew ought to learn how to command. The Yid wants to conceal his identity from strangers and, therefore, the Hebrew should look the world in the eye and declare: 'I am a Hebrew.'

Only after removing the dust accumulated through two thousand years of exile, of *galut*, will the true, authentic Hebrew character reveal its glorious head. Only then shall we be able to say: This is a typical Hebrew, in every sense of the word.

***

Mimi

For the first few months of war, nothing happened. Everyone expected bombs and they didn't come. They called it the Phoney War. We used to go down into the cellar every night, just in case, but eventually we stopped doing it.

Hugh

Seven months went by with no fighting, then Germany overran Holland, Belgium and France. In June 1940 I was convalescing from an operation at Bournemouth. England was threatened with invasion, and I quite expected to wake up one morning to see German ships in Bournemouth Bay. Nothing happened then, but in August 1940, air raids on London started. My wife was about to have a baby. I took her one evening to the City of London maternity hospital. As I came away, a bomb fell quite close, and I jumped about a foot in the air. Soon there were air raids every night, but one got accustomed to the noise.

I was born in the City of London hospital, with bombs Michael dropping and buildings coming down. It was when the war really started. But obviously, I have no memory of that, aged nought.

The Phoney War went on for quite a while. We stayed Mimi until the bombing really started, and then Mum and I left London. We went to a village called Blisworth, where we stayed with a retired couple – Auntie Mary and Uncle Bert. They never had any kids. Uncle Bert used to take me to church every Sunday morning, and apparently I upset Grandpa, because I said, 'I love Jesus, and I will stick with him for the rest of my life.'

Dad stayed in London throughout the war. He always used to come and visit us at weekends. He joined the

Home Guard, because as a foreigner he wasn't allowed to be in the army, but he felt he had to show loyalty. He was dressed in the same uniform as the soldiers, made of tickly khaki wool. It was horrible material.

The idea was that if England were ever invaded, the Home Guard would hold them back. It didn't happen, but it could have done very easily. There was barbed wire on all the beaches, and pillboxes all the way along the coast – little huts with peepholes, which soldiers would hide in to see if we were being invaded. They stayed there for years after the war. I saw posters all over the place: 'Careless talk costs lives.' 'Walls have ears.'

But the trouble was the Home Guard was made up of people who for some reason had not joined the Army – usually because they were too old, or frail. I know they did a lot of marching up and down, and they probably learnt how to shoot, but I don't think they would have been very effectual had we really been invaded.

As a foreigner, my dad usually wasn't allowed to drive a car or ride a bicycle, but because he was in the

Home Guard, they gave him a Jeep. I got the impression he thought it was all a bit of a joke. In London he was lobbying MPs, telling them what was happening to the Jews, and nobody took any notice. It was a relief for him to come down into the countryside and play at being a soldier.

I was the only one who was lucky enough to get five years of peace before the war. One minute there was just me, then the next minute there was Judy. By the time she came along, Mum insisted she had to have a Jewish name that was acceptable in England, so they chose Judith.

Chapter 40

Jewish Chronicle,
11 July 1941 Immediately before this issue closed for press we learnt with regret of the death on Wednesday of Dr. David Jochelman, at the age of 73. The funeral is to-day (Friday) at the Willesden Jewish Cemetery, at 3 o'clock.

New York Times London, July 10 – Dr. David Jochelman died today at the age of 73. Mr. Jochelman was for many years a close associate of Israel Zangwill in the leadership of the Jewish Territorial Organization. He was one of the best known figures among Jews in the East End of London and his name was a household word in Jewish homes throughout Eastern Europe.

Mimi I was five when Grandpa died. He came back to his religion at the end, as people do. He asked my dad to say 'Kaddish' for him – the prayer for the dead. I knew that at some point he had abandoned his ultra-Orthodoxy. As a young man he was a Hasid, with a fur hat and side curls. He rejected all that, divorced his wife, went to Switzerland to study philosophy, and there he met Tamara. I knew he'd gone to the first Zionist congress. And that's all I knew.

Jewish Chronicle Dr Jochelman, who was born in Postavy, near Vilna, studied at the Yeshiva from the age of 11, and at one time it was his ambition to become a Rabbi. In 1900 he went to Berne, to study at the University. He was a delegate to several Zionist Congresses, and at the 'Uganda' Congress he was one of keenest advocates of the acceptance of the Uganda offer. It has been recorded, on behalf of Israel Zangwill himself, that but for Jochelman's enthusiasm and insistence, Zangwill might never have decided to break away and form the Ito (Jewish Territorial Organisation). Throughout his career, Dr. Jochelman was a stormy petrel, again and again demanding and organising a bolder Jewish stand than that of the more cautious leaders of Anglo-Jewry.

A touching little tribute was paid by Mrs Zangwill to Dr. Jochelman at the funeral. Israel Zangwill used to wear at all the big meetings of the Ito a yellow rose in his button-hole, saying that the Ito would take the Jews' yellow badge of shame and servitude and turn it into an emblem of honour. Mrs. Zangwill, therefore, when she attended the funeral had a wreath of yellow roses sent, to pay a tribute to Dr. Jochelman in memory of the Organisation.

Dr. Jochelman felt that the near future would bring a fresh outbreak of pogroms in Eastern Europe. His fears became a reality. Jewish pogroms have not ceased, ever widening in extent and deepening in horror. The pogroms of to-day are pogroms 'according to plan', pogroms of organised starvation, pogroms of enforced evacuation, pogroms of physical torture carried on behind the barbed wire of the concentration camp. The last time I saw him – it was before the war – he told me sadly, and I agreed, that never had an Itoland been so much needed. 'If only your husband were with us,' he said. 'If only I were well.' His voice had an accent of despair.

Edith Zangwill

Mrs. Zangwill recalled how her late husband and Dr. Jochelman had worked together for several years in furtherance of the same cause. There was, she said, so close a co-operation between them and so high an admiration which each felt for the other, that their lives became interlocked. The widow, daughters and sons-in-law attended the funeral.

Jewish Chronicle

Rabbi Samuel
Daiches He had a fund of deep and abiding Jewishness. He was a fine Hebrew scholar. His Hebrew diction was as fresh as if he had left only yesterday the Vilna 'Klaus'.

***

Michael Dave was born on the third of January 1942. He was eighteen months younger than me, and he was angelic-looking. He had blue eyes, and black curly hair. Fanny said I was jealous of him. Lolly was born eleven months later.

Lolly I was born at home on the ninth of October '43. In those days you tended to be born at home. Whenever I imagine being born, I can see myself, which of course I couldn't have done, in a little room with a big dark wardrobe. I can picture it in my head. My name on my birth certificate is Helen, which is Yelena, which boils down to Lolya, which boils down to Lolly. I gradually became aware that I was named after my grandmother's sister, Yelena, who was known as Lolya. I was named after a Russian aunt, and I was quite proud of being able to tell people this.

Michael My parents stayed in London for a bit of time, and then they decided that it would be much safer to go to the country. We moved to a village called Wilstead, which had one street running through it and nothing else. It was surrounded by fields.

We lived in the old Vicarage at the bottom of the village. My mother cycled up and down the village, with me in front of her. She had a black bicycle with a child seat on the front, so she could encase me with her arms. I can remember the feel of her knees coming up and hitting me in the back as she cycled along. My father was at Bletchley Park. — Lolly

Because of my age, I was not called up. I volunteered for the Fire Service and spent many nights on telephone duty, eating a lot of biscuits between calls. At last I joined the Navy in November 1942, but I was never to go to sea. I was sent on an eight-month course in London University to learn Japanese, and at the end of the course, was sent to the big intelligence centre at Bletchley, a hundred miles from the sea. The centre received intercepted enemy wireless messages, which had to be decoded and translated, so that we could find out what the enemy was doing. For example, one might learn where a German submarine was going to come to the surface, and British destroyers could be sent to the spot. — Hugh

I knew nothing of it. He never mentioned it, because he'd signed the Official Secrets Act. The joke within the family was that he was a sailor who never went to sea, and we never questioned it further than that. — Lolly

***

One minute there was just me, then the next minute there was Judy, and then there was Dan. — Mimi

My father wanted my mother to have an abortion. He said, 'There's no money, I don't have a job, and we can't — Judy

have another child.' He never mentioned the pregnancy, the whole time she was pregnant.

Mimi

I can understand why he didn't want yet another child. He always felt he couldn't afford any more kids. Mum had to argue to have Judy, then Dan was just too much for him. We really were so poor.

Dan was the nearest thing to David. David got Grandpa David's name because he was born just before Dan. He got there first, and Lolly too. Fanny was lucky – they just happened to die before her children were born. I think Mum felt very sore about this.

***

Michael

My mum was always sort of in love with her cousin Victor.

Lolly

Mummy used to tell me that Victor was in love with her, and had proposed to her. She was very fond of him.

Michael

He was a rather dashing, gallant figure, and he was killed almost with the last bullet of the war. I think my mother never really recovered. She always said it was such an unfair thing to happen, with six years of war over. Vic was born in March 1945.

Vicky was named after Victor.   Lolly

Fanny had four children under five at one point.   Mimi

Chapter 41

Mimi   We came back to London when I was nine, because the Blitz seemed to have stopped. People thought that was it. We had the whole of 22 Mapesbury Road to ourselves, which was nice. And then the rockets started.

I was always sure the bombs would drop somewhere else. But I'd hear them coming: *jjjjjjjj*. Then they'd stop, and we'd all count the seconds. I sat there wondering, until I heard the bang. And as soon as I heard the bang, I thought: 'Ok, it's not me.' I was just totally convinced it would never be me, it would be somebody else.

Judy   The house across the road got hit one night, and our windows broke. Mum came rushing into our rooms to see if we were alright, and Dan sat up in bed, and said: 'Oh, what a lovely bang!' as the house across the road got demolished.

Mimi   There was glass all over the cot. Judy said to me, 'Why would Mum have put a cot near the window with a baby in it?' But she was like that. Scatty. There was so much bombing that I'd walk down the street and I could see into people's houses. It was like a doll's house, without the front wall. I'd see all the furniture, and the wallpaper, and everything, just as it was. Every now and then I'd see a hole – a nothing. Just a pile of rubble. Boys used to go and clamber over them, and they were told not to, because something could still fall down a bit more.

I remember going to school and there was a family there in their dressing gowns. Their house had had a direct hit. They'd been in the Anderson shelter in the garden. The headmistress said, 'Will you please all ask your mums for any clothes, or saucepans, or whatever they can spare.' We knew all the bombing was coming from Hitler. At school we drew him on the leather soles of our shoes so we could walk all over him.

***

We had the Morrison shelter in the kitchen. We three slept under there, and Mum and Dad would sleep next to it, on a mattress. When the air raid warning came, they crept in with us. _{Mimi}

It was like a huge table tennis table, with very thick legs, made of iron. Supposedly, if a bomb fell, it wouldn't crush you under this table. _{Judy}

We were always ill because we didn't eat properly. Nothing was imported. We never had bananas, or oranges. I was always having coughs and colds. America used to send concentrated orange juice, and cod liver oil, and powdered eggs. We would go down to the town hall to collect all this stuff. _{Mimi}

Chocolates were rationed. We used to get a Mars bar, and Mum would cut it into thin slices, and it would last for quite a while. We'd get a slice each, after dinner. I got quite hooked on cough sweets, because they weren't rationed.

You couldn't get ice cream in the shops, and I loved ice cream – but there were still restaurants that served it. Once Dad took me to a restaurant with round tables and white tablecloths. I had a coffee ice cream, and he had a black coffee. It must have been very expensive.

When I used to go to the cinema with Mum and Dad towards the end of the war, there'd be a little notice underneath the film: 'An air raid has just started.' In the early days people would all get up and rush home, and then later on they didn't. They just stayed. You can get used to anything.

Hugh   At the end of the war, I was sent with a mixed service party of British and Americans to South Germany and Austria to look for the records of German intelligence. We went by Jeep. I was in Paris on VE night, the night of the German surrender in Europe. We went across Germany and saw many devastated cities. I thought it would take a lifetime to rebuild them, but I was wrong. Then we stayed for a fortnight in Berchtesgaden, a little town in South Germany, where the Nazi leaders had country homes. One of them was Hitler's, or rather, two. He had a house on ground level and one on the mountain above called the Eagle's Nest – a lift connected them. The one on the ground had been hit by a bomb. The tiles from the bathroom were scattered about. I picked one up, and still have it, though it looks like any other tile.

Mimi   At the end of the war, we were told, 'There's peace,' and then the news came on. And I remember saying to Mum, 'How can there be news when the war's over? What is there to talk about?'

Michael   My father and mother came back to Mapesbury Road in late 1945 with four children, all aged five to nought, who had been born during the war. And there was this family already living there, who we didn't know at all: three children, Mimi, Judy, and Dan, and their parents, Sonia and Leva, and my grandmother, Tamara. So we became quite a party.

Joan Snow to   I went round to Sonia's this evening for a little while
Len Snow,   and saw Hugh, Fanny and their family. Little Lolly is a
25 December 1945   beautiful child – a head of bright golden curls and she's fat and big and toddles around lisping delightfully and using all the wrong words in the right places. Little Victor is a handsome child and full of giggles and fun. Michael

is growing into a grand little chap. Dan has turned into the roughest little devil and fights everyone, without any regard as to whether they warrant his aggression. Little Judy just goes on quietly growing up into the most beautiful little girl, sunny-tempered, the prettiest of the whole bunch with her big dark shiny eyes and her dark wavy hair and dainty little ways. Hugh wishes me to send you his love – nice chap Hugh . . . Quiet and young-looking and so good-natured. Fanny has got rather thin and worn-looking but is otherwise full of personality.

Chapter 42

Judy   We all grew up together in this big house.

Michael   It was a bit of a madhouse. There were always people up and down the stairs, and in the garden, and playing ping-pong. Always things happening, almost always my mother in a rush to do something or other.

Judy   Fanny was always putting on plays for us. She'd be the director and we'd be the actors.

Mimi   All the kids had to take part, and probably the odd adult – anybody she could rope in. I can't think who we performed for.

Lolly   My mother would tell us stories in the bath. She told us about a monkey that had a very, very long tail

and wouldn't get out of the bath. Suddenly the plug was taken out, and the water started going round and round and round, and the monkey went down the drain. There was a world down there, and it had to be pulled out by its tail.

I think all the Cockerell kids wished that my mum was their mum, whereas we all wished that Fanny was our mum. Sonia was caring and loving, and if you fell over she comforted you, whereas Fanny used to go to the park and play cricket with the kids.

Mimi

My mother never really took us anywhere, but Fanny would take all of us. We would go swimming, and we'd go to circuses, and we'd go to Hampstead Heath, and we'd go on picnics. She had all this endless energy. My mother never did any of that. Fanny did it. Because that's how they mothered – together.

Judy

Fanny always used to lose children when she went shopping. Her kids used to trail along behind her. Once she lost David by mistake, and he was picked up by the police, and taken to the police station, and given cocoa and biscuits. He decided this was rather nice, so every time they went out he'd manage to get lost.

Mimi

By a certain point she became friendly with all the policemen there.

Judy

David Fireman was my best friend – a Jewish boy with a twin brother. We were once talking about Jewish refugees who had kept their accents. He lived in Edgware, where there were lots of refugees with thick accents to the end of their lives. He said to me that my mum had a Russian accent. I didn't believe him. I said, 'No, she hasn't.' And he said, 'Yes, she has – obviously she has.' She had read English at University College, London. She used to

Michael

say, 'I came to England aged eight, I didn't speak a word of English, and yet there I was, twelve years later, getting a degree in English.'

Lolly   When she and Sonia arrived here, they used to go to the park and rush up to other children, and want to join in their games. They were shunned, and my mother could never understand why. Perhaps it was because they were speaking in a foreign accent. My mother learnt English very quickly, and could speak it almost as well as a native. Auntie Sonie, on the other hand, always had quite a strong accent, even though she was two years younger.

***

Michael   Fanny was always thinking that she needed to save money, so she bought a second-hand Chevrolet. It was extremely cheap, because the steering wheel was on the wrong side. It meant that when she was driving along, she was pretty oblivious to oncoming traffic. It was dangerous, but it saved money. She would get hooted lots of times in the course of a drive. We would count the number of hoots, and have private bets.

A lot of people were terrified of driving with her, and Lolly wouldn't do it. But on the other hand, she was always driving people all over the place, people who couldn't drive, and they just had to grit their teeth and put up with it.

You didn't have to have a driving test until 1935, and Michael she'd got her licence before 1935. She worked on the basis that whatever she did, the drivers around her would understand what she had meant, even if she was turning left with her right indicator out.

She didn't actually take much notice of anybody else Lolly on the road. She would have a lot of people shaking their fists at her. But she was oblivious, really. Her attitude to driving was that everybody else makes stupid mistakes, and they need to get out the way.

There was a song we'd often sing called 'The Quarter- Michael master's Store'. It had been sung by soldiers during the war. I remember composing a new line, just as we turned out of Mapesbury Road, onto Willesden Lane, and had to swerve out of the way of a lorry. 'It was Mummy, Mummy, who made us all say lummy, in the car, in the car.' 'Blimey' means 'God blind me', 'lummy' means 'Lord love me.' It's what you would say if you got too near the edge of a cliff and nearly fell off.

She knocked down a policeman, and apologised, and Mimi invited him over to tea, and he came. She had an accident on a main road in the middle lane: she suddenly wanted to turn to left, so she cut across, and a lorry went into her. There was a court case, and she won, because he'd gone into her. It was quite nerve-wracking to be driven by her.

She was extremely volatile. She was always blowing Lolly up, and she was always having rows with people, particularly us, but she never shouted at my dad.

Mimi   They were totally different. Fanny was mad. She was
wild. Hugh was always very reserved and very, I thought,
English. I don't know how it worked. He was so meticulous, and so respectable. He'd come back from work, and
instead of finding his supper ready, the place was in a
mess, the kids were running everywhere, there wasn't any
food in the house, and he'd just disappear into his study.

Lolly   My mother never thought of herself as beautiful. She
was brought up to believe Auntie Sonie was the beautiful
one, and she was the clever one. She didn't really wear
makeup. Her dress sense could be summed up in one word:
Crimplene. Crimplene was a rather horrific man-made
fibre, a crumpled type of material that was quite popular
in those days. She had no dress sense, and no vanity.

Judy   My mother was the opposite of Fanny. Together they
made one person.

Mimi   There were eighteen months between them, but they
were like Siamese twins.

Michael   They signed off their letters 'FanSon'. You could never
tell who wrote them. Sonia was very calm, slightly scatty,
slightly surreal in terms of the things she would say.

Lolly   Auntie Sonie was very mild, and easily trodden upon.
My mother would never have been trodden upon by
anybody.

Michael   We didn't really know Leva very much. He was nice,
but he felt much more foreign than anyone else in the
family.

Judy   My father spoke seven languages, with a thick Russian
accent.

Lolly   I adored uncle Leva, because he made a terrific fuss
of me. I was this little fat girl with golden curls, and he
used to call me his 'hupka', which means Russian peasant

297

girl. He used to tease me, and pinch my cheek. He was thin, wiry, usually had a very good colour because he liked being in the open air. He dressed formally. He was virtually a chain smoker, he had very deep-green eyes, thinning dark hair, a hollow face, and bags of restless energy. He could be very curt with his family, and particularly with Sonia. Later on, I could see he was a tense man, a very frustrated man. But I didn't recognise that as a small child.

He used to always come home and try to tell Mum all the problems the Revisionist Movement had been having, which was in opposition to all the other Zionists at the time. She wasn't interested. She cared about the kids, and she cared about her music. I don't think she had thoughts about anything else. As soon as I was old enough to understand, he started talking to me instead. *Mimi*

***

The Morrison shelter was the kitchen table for years. Neither Sonia nor Fanny could ever cook. *Mimi*

My mother was the most awful cook. Really awful. She and Fanny. I think Fanny was worse. *Judy*

There was always a smell of burning around. She used to burn frozen peas. The telephone would ring, and she'd go off and forget. It was always our fault – we were so used to food burning that we didn't notice the smell any more. We always used to have a roast on Sunday that my mother would overcook like mad. We might comment if something was very burnt, and then she would always say, 'It's just a little brown round the edges.' She was a bad cook, but quite a confident cook. *Lolly*

Once she was making chocolate pudding. She needed flour, and she didn't have any flour, so she used potatoes. She argued that potatoes were starch, and flour was *Michael* starch. Chocolate potato pudding was the most disgusting thing that we ever had – every mouthful would be littered with chunks. She thought cooking took a great deal of time, and she was always rushing to do something else.

Lolly   If she could make things go quicker, she would. She would put anything and everything in her pressure cooker, and it was forever exploding. One year she put the Christmas pudding in the pressure cooker, and forgot about it, and it blew up. She went round the kitchen, taking the lumps off the walls, and saying, 'Well, it still tastes nice.' So we all went round the kitchen, taking lumps off the walls and putting them back into the pressure cooker. A couple of days after Christmas, she would say, 'Hugh, I've got a wonderful idea. Let's have a New Year's Eve party.' She would say it every single year, as though it was a totally new concept. All their friends would come. It was just something that you did on New Year's Eve – you went to Hugh and Fanny's party.

She used to make holishkes. They looked like Cornish pasties, but they were a mixture of cabbage and onion, fried up and then encased in pastry. She twisted the top of them and painted them with milk so that they were shiny and golden. Everybody expected them: 'we'll go to Fanny's party, and have one of her cabbage pies.' They were lovely, but they weren't for us. They were for her guests.

Mimi   Fanny and mum used to share the cooking, in theory, except it didn't quite work out that way. When it was Fanny's turn, she was so busy with other things, she'd forget. We'd come down for supper and there wasn't any, so Mum landed up cooking for everybody.

She was quite thrilled by tins, because they were a reasonably new invention. She thought, 'This is the miracle of the modern age.' She cooked Heinz tomato soup, oxtail soup, mushroom soup. Once she had visitors, and they said, 'Sonia, what lovely soup, how did you make it?' She said, 'It was a tin of oxtail, and a tin of mushroom, and I just mixed them.' She really was not a very imaginative cook. My dad used to cook borscht, gefilte fish balls, chopped herring with vinegar and onions, chopped liver. Mum never learnt how to do any of it.

Sonia was doing all the work, all the meals, all the washing up, and Fanny was floating around, doing her thing. She'd send her children off to school with colds and temperatures, and they'd get sent back. If she had a sore throat, she just wouldn't get up in the morning. She had four children to get ready. So my mother was always there, getting them dressed, and getting them ready for school, and making sure they had coats on. My father got really annoyed. **Judy**

My dad put his foot down. He said to Sonia, 'You're looking after those children as well as your own – it's not right. Why don't we separate? We live upstairs, and the Cockerells live downstairs.' And so we separated. **Mimi**

We became two separate households. It was a lot neater upstairs, and it was a lot more disciplined. I think the atmosphere was a lot quieter. Downstairs was chaos, and deeply messy. **Lolly**

We'd have our supper in the evening, and then Dan and I would go downstairs, and they'd still be eating. Fanny would sit and read to us. She read all the classics. *The Prince and the Pauper*, and *David Copperfield*. She'd sit with all the mess on the table, and nothing cleaned up, and spilt food, and she'd just read. It was such fun. We loved it. Most of the action was downstairs. **Judy**

My grandmother chose to be in our section of the house, rather than upstairs. **Lolly**

They gave Grandma the choice which family she wanted to live with. She chose to live with Fanny, which **Mimi** makes sense. She'd lived with them when they were evacuated. After Grandpa died, and Fanny was having all these children, and not coping, she went to help her with the kids, darning their socks. I suppose Fanny's need was greater. She chose to live with Fanny, and do all Fanny's work. But it's understandable. Mum never asked her for anything. She just gave up.

Lolly   She became virtually bedridden as she got iller and iller. Her bed was in the corner of the room, and she had a cabinet by the side of her bed full of bottles of medicine. There was a fireplace in her room, and we used to sit in front of her fire in the winter.

Michael   We thought she was very wise. She seemed wise, because she was so fantastically old. We would often go and see her in her room, and sometimes she would teach us a bit of Russian. She taught me a Russian nursery rhyme: 'Bozhya korovka, ty leti na niebo, tam tvoi detki

kushayut kotletki.' Which means, 'Ladybird, ladybird, fly away home, your house is on fire, and your children are up in heaven eating cutlets.' That's really the only Russian I ever learnt.

Chapter 43

Annie Bach,
14 October 1944 My dear, darling sister Tamara, my dear nieces Fannie and Sonie, their husbands and children. I am waiting for the happy day to have at last news from you, to know that you are all well and to be able to communicate with you. After years of sufferings and misery, we are at last liberated. England and America came to our rescue and delivered us. The Providence was good to me and saved me from the hands of the criminal Germans. My only desire is now to have news from you. I would like to go back to Paris and be nearer to you but for the moment there are no trains. My address: Pension Florida, 11 Avenue des Orangers, Nice. I am waiting for a message from you. Yours, Annie.

Michael   Annie had been in the south of France, and was sheltered from the Nazis through much of the war.

Judy   A family hid her up in an attic. And then after the war she came to England. We all had to go up and see her every day.

Lolly   She wore thick pebble-type glasses, she had very bad eyesight, which got worse and worse. She was bird-like – very thin and withered-looking.

Judy   She lived on her own in the room going up to the attic. She had a little gas ring in the corner where she'd cook her food.

Mimi   There was a sink, and a cooker, and a single bed which stuck out into the room, and next to it a bedside table, with a radio.

All day she listened to music.   Judy

She would sit in her armchair, very close to her radio.   Lolly
She loved classical music. You'd knock on the door, and
she would be there, sitting and listening.

I remember I went up once and I said, 'Why aren't you   Mimi
listening to the radio?' She said, 'It's Beethoven's ninth.
I've heard it so many times before.'

Auntie Annie always used to say, in her thick accent: Lolly
'Tamara is a saint'. She was my grandmother's protector.
That was her role in life. She was always telling us to keep
our voices down. If we were making too much noise,
which we did, all the time, she would shoo us away, and
tell us not to plague Grandma. Auntie Annie was called
Hansa – that was her Russian name.

Fanny insisted on anglicising everybody's names. Her   Mimi
name was Hansa, it wasn't Annie. I don't think she asked
Hansa if she minded, she just wanted to anglicise it. It
was as if Fanny didn't want anything alien or different
in the family. I always felt she was trying very hard to be
more English than the English. We called her Hansa, and
Fanny's kids called her Annie. Maybe Judy gave in to it,
but I didn't.

The whole household, apart from my father, spoke   Lolly
Russian. My mother and Auntie Sonie and my grandmother and Auntie Annie would sit around the dining
table. They each had a glass in a silver case with a little
handle, and they would have tea with lemon. They'd be
laughing and talking in Russian, and then we would come
in and then they would revert to English.

They wouldn't teach us Russian, which we were all   Judy
quite upset about. It was a language they could talk in
front of us and we wouldn't understand.

Michael	We thought that was rather unfair. We accepted it, but we thought it was cheating a bit.
Judy	We picked up bits and pieces.
Lolly	I only picked up the odd word. 'Nichevo': not at all. 'Ochen kharasho'. 'Na zdorovie'. I don't even know what they mean.
Mimi	My dad once managed to get hold of some vinyl records of Russian folk songs, and they invited Fanny and Hugh up to our sitting room to listen to them. We all sat on upright chairs, around the anthracite stove, and Dad played these songs. There was one called 'Chupchik', which means a lock of hair. Mum was whooping with delight, and Uncle Hugh just sat there, looking at her in amazement. Mum said, 'What's the matter? Don't you like it?' He said, 'Um – no.' And she said, 'Hugh, you haven't got a Russian soul.'

Chapter 44

In the summer of 1950 I went down to the New York
Public Library on Fifth Avenue. It's enormous. It has great
long tables with lamps at every place where you can sit
and read, and it has all sorts of things in it. Somebody
had told me there were phone books there, so I walked
in and asked. I went to the telephone directory section,
where they had a whole lot of phone books from all over
the world. I took out the London section, under J, and I
looked up the address, and there it was – 22 Mapesbury
Road. I wrote a letter. I said who I was, and was anybody
there. I knew my grandfather was dead, so I addressed it
to the house. I got a letter back. They knew I existed. And
within a few months I received an open ticket to come to
England.

I was stunned by the ticket. I didn't ask for it – it wouldn't have occurred to me to ask for something like that. They didn't owe me anything, I just wanted to get in touch with my father's relatives. But it seemed like a good idea at the time, and so I thought, 'Well, I'm gonna go.'

I think my mother was surprised. She didn't like the fact that I had, she felt, gone behind her back to find my relatives, but she got over it. I set sail in December of 1950. I was twenty, almost twenty-one. I had no intention of staying, I had no intention of not staying, I never thought one way or another. I just went.

I packed and went down to the wharf and got on the ship. When we started to sail the band struck up, and we stood on the deck and waved goodbye. It was just marvelous. They played us off, and we went right out into the Atlantic.

Oh God, it was exciting. That I will never forget. On the ship you meet all these lovely officers, standing around, and then you find your cabin, and put your things away, and you see what's there, and what other people are doing, and you settle down into the voyage. Then the ship runs into a storm, and half the people are incapacitated in their cabins, and they're throwing up all over the place, and you, who do not get seasick, are happy as a clam, running up and down the beautiful great big staircases, and eating heartily with the very few people who can manage to make it to the dining room. I loved it. The food was English, so it wasn't very good, but my mother had warned me the English can't cook.

Those who were still up would play games in the evening. They had horse races with wooden horses, which you could bet on – I was starting to learn English money, so I had fun. It was December, so people mostly stayed inside various parlors. You could walk out on deck, but not many people did because it was too cold. I walked out on the deck every day, over and over. They had deckchairs with blankets, and you could sit there if you wanted. I wasn't much of a sitter in those days, so I just walked, read, talked to people. December over the Atlantic is gray. I stood watching the ocean every now and then, but mainly, you've seen one ocean, you've seen them all.

A few days before Christmas, we docked at Liverpool. I got off the ship and went through Customs, and I got on the train to London.

My first impression of London was Mapesbury Road, and it was at night. Nothing seems to faze me. If you grow up in New York, you have so many varied experiences that, really, things don't startle you. But I was taken aback somewhat when I went to 22 Mapesbury Road.

It was a huge house on the corner, with a very unkempt yard. I remember walking into the hallway. It overwhelmed me. All I knew was my mother's family – it wasn't until I went over that I found this huge house, full of all these strangers, and I was related to almost all of them. These were my relatives, but I knew nothing about them, and they knew nothing about me.

I remember Fanny taking me in to see Tamara. She was lying in bed, and she threw her hands up and said, 'There is your grandfather.' That's what she said. There he is, right there. And he was.

Over Tamara's bed was a huge portrait of my grandfather – this gloomy, sort of foreboding portrait. He's coming out of darkness. I noticed he had this heavy hair, and he was familiar to me.

I had seen my grandfather in a hospital in Berlin. My father got a Guggenheim fellowship in 1931 and he went to Germany to study the theatre, and we went too, my mother and I. He was being operated on for kidney disease. It seems to me odd that a two-year-old would have a strong memory like that. He must have been a very commanding presence. Still in my head now, I can turn to that page and see him in the hospital bed. I was with my mother and my father, and he was lying in bed, propped up with pillows. He was a large man with black hair, and a mustache, and his hair was thick and dark. When I saw the painting I realized how much he and my father looked alike. I saw the son in the father.

Michael   Emjo Basshe arrived from America at about ten o'clock in the evening. We'd all gone to bed, and Fanny brought her into our room where we were sleeping, so that Emjo could see us all, and I woke up. I remember looking at her, and being surprised by these red spectacles that went up at the corners. That was the only thing I could remember when I woke up the next morning – the red spectacles.

Mimi   This wonderful cousin of ours suddenly turned up. Emjo Basshe. Double S. She was just so eccentric. She was full of energy, and full of life, and so sure of herself. The accent didn't bother us. We loved her. She used to wear a tight skirt with buttons all down the front, and she would hike it up and stand with her back to the fireplace to warm her behind, which was apparently what Southern women used to do. We knew Grandpa David had divorced his first wife. We didn't learn about Emmanuel until Emjo came over. But she didn't say much about him, and we didn't ask.

Lolly   I remember her handing out things she brought us from America. Chewing gum, maple syrup, chocolate. She had this American accent, which we found quite fascinating, because we only knew it from films.

Jo   I wore bangs in those days, which was not the fashion in England. Fanny made fun of it, because in England grown women didn't wear bangs at that time. She said only little girls wore bangs – she called it a fringe. I had worn my hair like that for years. I just tucked it away. It was something that wasn't done, but that was alright, I never cared one way or another.

She had corresponded with my mum, and she had Michael
that typical American handwriting. We were used to
seeing her name on the air mail letters. I remember thinking, 'Emjo. What a strange name for a person to have.' But
I knew that all Americans were a bit funny.

I had changed my name six or eight times by the time Jo
I went to England. I can't even remember all of them.
Emily, Emily-Anne, Rebecca. I ran through a whole lot of
names. I was never called by Emjo. Not because I didn't
like the name, or my father – I adored my father – but
because I didn't like people saying, 'Where did that come
from? How do you spell it? And how do you pronounce
it?' I got tired of that. The first morning I was there, Fanny
said I would be called Jo. She just decided that Jo was a
better name than Emjo, or than any other name, and I
didn't give her any objection. I didn't have any. I've been
Jo ever since.

I had no idea of how long I was going to stay. I never
planned anything. Tamara had sent me an open ticket, so
I could go home any time I wanted. I slept in the living
room for a couple of nights, and then I was moved onto
the second floor, and Mimi and I shared a room. I lived
at Mapesbury Road for about a year.

I got used to it pretty quick. Sonia and Fanny yelling at
each other, seven children racing up and down the stairs,
the general chaos – it was not the normal English family.
It was not that sedate. It was kind of wild at times, but I
liked it.

The two women ran everything. Hugh was at work
all day. Really it was the two women, and the children.
Michael was a nice kid, he really was. He was very bright,
you could see he would go far – but he was a little boy.
Really, a twenty-year-old woman is not going to associate
with a twelve-year-old boy very much. Vicky was so cute.
He was five. At dinnertime he would slide into his seat,

and just before his rear end got onto the chair, he would say 'What's for pud?' He and Lolly looked like twins. They were both blond, so was Michael. David was the only dark one. David always looked very vague. He had big gray eyes, and he had trouble with them – he was nearsighted, or farsighted. Judy was just lovely. She was so pretty, and so lively. And Mimi of course was closer to my age. I was sort of in awe of her being a ballet dancer.

Dan was excited about everything. He got worked up about all sorts of things. Sonia always said, 'Hit him, Jo! Hit him!' Obviously I didn't hit him, because I wasn't going to hit a little boy. But she couldn't manage him. He had two very calm, much older sisters. Judy was a very good student, Mimi was a very devoted dancer. He really ran wild.

It was a lively household, with this spectre sitting in her bedroom, Tamara. Not a ghost, but sort of like a character from a Victorian novel. The whole house seemed very Victorian, and she seemed like something out of the past. It was her heavy accent, and 'There is your grandfather.' I never knew her to get out of bed. She must have gotten out at some time, but she ruled as a matriarch from the bed.

I was sort of afraid of her. I don't think she liked me. I didn't feel any desire to be close to her, and I didn't feel any wish from her to be close to me. I was from Grandfather's first family, and she couldn't have felt very warm toward me. She was very nice to me, so I really shouldn't have felt that way, but I did. She didn't encourage me to ask questions, or talk. I never knew what to say to her. I probably should have sat down and said, 'Tell me about Grandfather', but I never thought of doing that.

She struck me as more Russian than Jewish. She didn't look Jewish – of course, some people do, some people don't – but she just struck me as something out of a Tolstoy or Dostoevsky novel. She was in her nightclothes.

She didn't wear a nightcap, but I wouldn't have been surprised if she had.

Sonia was a sweet lady – very different from Fanny. I loved Fanny, but I'd never say Fanny was sweet. Sonia was. She always struck me as vague, somewhat lackadaisical. She floated through life, occasionally picking up her violin and playing something. Musicians are slightly away with the fairies. They hear things we don't hear. She would play the Hatikva, the Israeli national anthem, because that's what Dan liked. It's such a sad tune. It's a minor key, and so is sort of mournful.

They looked nothing alike. Sonia was taller, and she had finer features, and an aquiline nose. Fanny said her nose was a potato, and Sonia's was a beak, and that I had the best nose in the family. But they both looked very Jewish. Auntie Sonia looked Sephardic. Sephardics tend to be taller – they've had better food over the centuries. Frankly, they're better-looking: more upper class, more aristocratic-looking than the Ashkenazis. The Ashkenazis are short and stocky, and generally slightly homely. Fanny was more Ashkenazi. Her looks came from liveliness, rather than from elegance or beauty. She was a bit on the plain side, but very animated, and very strong-minded, much more so than Sonia.

Fanny was totally immersed in being English. It wasn't anything I could put my finger on, but it was a sort of 'we'. 'We English.' She was English through and through, whereas Sonia was definitely foreign. Sonia loved Yiddish – she said it was so rich and wonderful. Fanny never expressed an opinion that I heard. Fanny had married a thorough Englishman, and Sonia had married a cosmopolitan Jew. Fundamentally, their lives were different.

I started working within a couple of weeks – Fanny got me a job teaching at a school in the East End. They were desperate for teachers after the war, and nobody wanted to teach in the East End. I had no experience, but they took anybody. It was pretty shabby. I asked Fanny and Sonia to give me extra clothes if they had any, because the kids were poorly dressed. There were a bunch of very bright Jewish boys I really liked. The schoolroom didn't have a flat floor – it went up, like a balcony in a theatre, so that everybody could see, which was really not a bad idea. We had a fire burning in the classroom because there was no central heating.

I think the whole family was somewhat eccentric, but Fanny was really a character in many ways. She wrote me a letter before I had left New York, and she signed it 'Your affectionate half-aunt Fanny.' She was sorry that my last name was not Jochelman, because she wanted to show around her niece, Miss Jochelman.

Fanny wanted to teach me as much as possible about English life. She got me tickets for the pantomime, because she knew we didn't have them in the States. I loved it. There were a lot of words I had to learn, mainly about money. English money was in those days very difficult: shillings and pence, and twenty shillings, and twelve pence to a shilling, and a half a crown. When I went to buy something I would just hold out a handful of money, and the shopkeeper would pick out what they wanted. It took me months before I was happy with the money.

Before I got there, England was a place in my head. I'd grown up on English children's books. My mother was an Anglophile – she was always very attached to England, partly because of the literature. If it was a British book, my mother would get it for me. She felt they were the best. I had read *Wind in the Willows*, and all the Beatrix Potter books, the A. A. Milne books, *Alice in Wonderland*, *Alice Through the Looking Glass*. Everything jumbled together to make England.

The first week I was there, I made a beeline for the theatre. I went to a huge number of shows. In England the theatre was so cheap – my God, you sat in the orchestra for three and six. The most expensive was seven and six, which equated to about a dollar. I would see anything, everything. It was so cheap, and it was so good. I used to go on my own to Saturday matinees. It was heaven.

I walked all over London. I went to the Tower of London, I went to the National Gallery. Westminster Abbey was stunning. It's a vast cemetery, which is kind of horrifying, but I loved it. We don't have anything like it. In the US there are a few eighteenth-century things, like Mount Vernon and Monticello, but that's about as old as we get. You have St Patrick's Cathedral in New York, which is a gothic fake. It's nice to have it, but it doesn't compare to Westminster Abbey.

London was sort of gray, but it was fascinating. I really had rose-coloured glasses. There was so much theatre, and there were so many old buildings. It may have been drab to them, but it sure wasn't drab to me.

***

I'd eat pretty much anything until I met English cooking. I had never had bad food in my life – I'd had either Jewish food or Southern food – but boy, Fanny's cooking was terrible. Things were boiled, and everything was white, absolutely white. Boiled potatoes and white sauce, and boiled tongue, which is not something I really care about. Plain white fish, with white potatoes and cauliflower. She had her own ways, and I would never have interfered. I couldn't have helped anyway – I didn't know what the hell she was doing. Nobody I ever knew could cook that badly. It was a pity, because she obviously hated it.

Fanny struck me as sort of harried – she never really seemed to get a hold of things. She had too many children, and a house, and a sick mother. She tried very hard, to be organized, and clean, and cook, but Fanny was the most atrocious housekeeper you ever met, and she couldn't cook worth a damn. Not everybody is cut out to be a 'balabusta', and she in particular was not. Even though she was a good mother, she would have been better off having only two children, getting out of the house and becoming a career woman, as we used to call them. She didn't have the life she should have had.

Uncle Hugh went down every day to the City in his bowler hat. Somehow it was very odd to see this very proper Englishman in this slightly mad house of Eastern European Jews. Hugh was the slightly alien presence – this tall, statuesque man didn't really belong. He wasn't there in the daytime, and when he was there, he wasn't really there. At dinner he sat at one end of the table and Fanny sat at the other, and the children in the middle, all eating this strange mixture that Fanny had prepared, and Vicky asking what was for pud as he slid into his chair. I can see why, because the food was so bad that he was only interested in dessert. The kids talked a lot, and every once in a while Hugh would make a wry observation. He would say things like, 'Do you think we should give that to the deserving poor?' I had never heard that expression before, and I've never forgotten it.

He almost wasn't there. He seemed happy, in his rather stolid British way, but what he was doing, marrying into a Jewish family, and having this huge number of kids all around him, I will never know.

Life in England in 1950 was very different from New York. It was weird coming from America to a country which had barely survived the war. There were still bits of the war everywhere, like after an earthquake – it doesn't end when it ends. I remember going to have lunch with Hugh. He took me down to where he worked, and showed me around the City. The City was where the financial area

315

was, and the Nazis had bombed that extensively during the Blitz.

All the bomb residue was still all over the place. They had carted off the rubble, but they hadn't rebuilt. There were great gaping holes here and there. Sometimes there was grass growing, or little trees. It was five years after the war – England was still very badly off.

We didn't suffer in the US. War in America meant rationing: canned goods, coffee, butter, meat. They announced you could only buy three pairs of shoes a year. I remember rather resenting it, but there was a war on. That was what people would say. 'Don't you know there's a war on?'

My mother went down and got these ugly gray books full of little stamps that you pulled apart when you bought something. Our rationing was not as bad as it was in England, by a long shot, because we grow almost all our own food. I think bananas were missing, but we had oranges and lemons, and all sorts of things. England didn't. Fanny had already got ration books for me, before I even arrived.

I remember hearing broadcasts from Britain during the war. There was so much static it was difficult to hear them sometimes. It was one particular broadcaster, Edward R. Murrow – he would broadcast from England, but it was sort of chancy, full of funny noises.

I almost remember every single day of the bombing of London. It's still very clear in my mind. A whole year that Hitler tried to bring Britain to its knees and didn't. My mother did remind me, 'You have cousins in England.' She wondered what was happening to them, but she fretted about all of England. She was very pro-England. Everybody was pro-English in the war. Not only were we anti-German, but the spectacle of England being bombed like that was absolutely horrifying.

Chuchill was enormously admired in America. He was one of the Big Three: Stalin, Churchill and Roosevelt – or, I should say, Roosevelt, Churchill and Stalin. There were photographs of them in people's living rooms. Everybody had the famous picture of the three of them sitting next to each other at Yalta. They were the saviors of the world. Churchill of course tried desperately to get us into the war – he knew England couldn't survive without the US. England had been a great nation, and they didn't know that they were no longer a great nation. They could not defend themselves, and Churchill knew that. Roosevelt wanted to get us in, and he did as much as he could, but Congress wouldn't let him. Those were very dark days. Germany had taken over all of Europe.

I was in Washington DC all through the war. My mother said it was too hot in North Carolina – she said it was 105 in the shade – and so we got on a bus and we left. She remarried a year after my father died, and my stepfather got a job in the government. We moved to Washington in 1940.

My high school years were taken up with the war. It was a constant presence. There were people in uniform all over the place. My mother was an air raid warden, and we had air raid drills in school. One day we were at a restaurant, and the manager came over and said there was a message for my stepfather, so he walked off to the telephone. He came back, and he said, 'The Japanese have bombed Pearl Harbor.' And the next day we were at war. 'A date that will live in infamy,' as FDR said, and I heard him say it.

'Let's remember Pearl Harbor as we go to meet the foe, let's remember Pearl Harbor as we did the Alamo.' It was a popular song, and we sang it in school. 'We will always remember how they died for Liberty. Let's remember Pearl Harbor, and go on to victory.'

FDR died in April '45. It was so close to the end of the war. I remember going into the classroom the next day, and my teacher, Miss Hemington, who was a typical schoolmarm of the twenties with a bun at her back, wrote on the blackboard, 'Now he too belongs to the ages.'

Chapter 45

Jo   We had Passover in Fanny's dining room. It was somewhat chaotic and rather odd, as everything was in that
household.

Mimi   The Morrison shelter was all beautifully laid. We put
our best clothes on. It was like a party.

Jo   Here you have Uncle Hugh sitting with a bowler hat
on his head at one end of the Passover table, and Fanny
fussing at the other. Fussing over the food, and fussing
over this and that, and telling everybody what to do. That
was Fanny. She ran things.

Michael   She was in her normal, rather harassed state.

Jo   Leva was there, only for a few days. He was in the
middle, paying very little attention – my feeling is he was
utterly indifferent to the whole thing. He didn't seem to
take it seriously.

Mimi   The traditional way is that a man leads the whole
thing, but my dad knew absolutely nothing about
Judaism. He was brought up without it, so it was never
part of his life. So Passover was run by Fanny, even
though she didn't know very much either. When Grandpa
David was alive, and I was about three or four, I remember looking into the dining room and seeing a long
table with a white tablecloth, and cushions on his chair.
That's all I remember. But I was too young to be invited.
Passover was the one thing that Fanny still hung on to,
for some reason.

I became an atheist when my father died, because I just couldn't fathom a God who would do that to a child. But I never was what you'd call a true believer. I really had very little religion to discard. After that I tried to be religious a few times – it never worked. I became an Anglican when I was thirteen. A girlfriend, Cynthia, and I, decided, I do not know why, to get baptized. So we did. My mother didn't like it, but she threw us a party. I left that after six months.

And I tried being Jewish for a year. I kept kosher, but it's a bit of a pain because you can't have bacon for breakfast. I went to synagogue a couple of times, but I couldn't follow the service, I didn't know what was going on. It was just alien to me. A church is home. I can manage church – although it bores the hell out of me – but I didn't feel at home in a synagogue. It's not as exciting, the music is not as interesting or as easy to follow, or easy to join in, as Christian hymns. The services are sort of boring, and they're in a language which is impenetrable. I find the Christian services boring enough, but the Jewish services were just deadly. I wanted to feel something, but it didn't work.

I didn't know anybody who was ultra-Orthodox. There's a whole section of Brooklyn in which you find yourself in Poland in the eighteenth century. The men wear old clothes and hats and 'paes' – the curls down the side of the head. The women wear long dresses, and they cover their hair unless they drive men to distraction, and they have huge numbers of children. Living in this narrow eighteenth-century world, and thinking only of God, is really so depriving. The world is a very rich place, and I couldn't believe in a God who would require that of people.

You can be a Jew and yet you don't have to follow the rules. Some of my friends kept the Sabbath, some of them didn't. Some of them did not mix 'fleisch' and 'milsch', some did. And some went to synagogue once a year, some went every week. Most of my boyfriends were Jewish, most of my friends were Jewish. They never counted me as half Jewish. I was Jewish. I'm half, I'm baptized, but I feel Jewish. No matter what you become, if you are born a Jew, you are always a Jew.

My father shed it all. He married a 'shiksa'. He was buried in a Christian cemetery. I don't remember if he ever ate pork, and that's sort of the final test. He held on to the music – Russian music. I don't remember any Yiddish or Hebrew songs.

My mother once said something very peculiar: she deliberately chose someone who was Jewish for my father. I have never understood what the hell she meant by that. She married him because she fell in love with him, I suppose, but I got the idea that she was very pleased that this had been my inheritance, as it were. My ancestry. I didn't ask her any more, but I just remember her saying that. It stayed in my mind.

My religiosity lasted six months. I couldn't fool myself, so I gave it up. If there is a God, and he's all powerful, he certainly is a rat. What kind of a miserable God does the horrible things that go on in the world? That's the only reason you have heaven: so many people have had rotten lives. I can't see living forever in the clouds with angels. There may be something, who knows. I doubt it. But I don't care.

I just dropped the whole thing. Really, religion makes no sense to me. I can understand people in dire straits, but where was God in Auschwitz, as they say. It's a good question. Where was God in Auschwitz? If the Jews are the chosen people of God, he has a hell of a lousy way of showing it.

I had never been at a Seder before, but I knew the story because it's Old Testament, and all Southern children, and children of Southern mothers, know the Old

Testament. I grew up on Bible stories. My mother used to sing 'Pharaoh's army got drownded.' It's a spiritual. Black people related to the Jews in coming out of Egypt, being freed from slavery. 'Oh Mary, don't you weep, don't you moan, God's going to call you and you're going home.' But that's not religion. Religion is going and being miserable for two hours on Sunday morning, listening to a man standing up there telling you all sorts of things you're not interested in, and boring you out of your mind. My mother didn't care for religion, but she certainly thought you should know the Bible.

We had gefilte fish, which I absolutely loved, Lolly homemade by Auntie Annie or Tamara, and radishes, and pickled herrings all chopped up, and matzo, and chopped-up chicken liver.

There was a big ritual plate. We ate bitter herbs to Mimi remind us of the bitterness of life when we were slaves, and 'charoset', a paste made of wine and nuts and apples and dates, to remind us of the mortar we had to use when we were building the pyramids. Boiled egg in salt water, to remind us of the tears our ancestors shed when they were slaves. When *we* were slaves, you're supposed to say. You can't say what happened to them – it happened to us. We ate those, and then we ate a five-course meal. The last sentence in the Passover ceremony is 'Next year in Jerusalem.' Most people say it, and they don't mean it.

We did mean it then. Because Sonia and her family Jo were going to Jerusalem.

Chapter 46

Lilian Winstanley,
4 July 1946   It is quite impossible to define what a nation really is. There are all degrees of nationality, so that nations are not clearly defined individuals like men and women. At present the principle of nationality is making endless trouble in the world, and all sorts of people are claiming to be 'sacred' because they are nations. One of the worst cases is that of Palestine.

Wyndham Deedes   The Jews, the eleven or twelve million of them throughout the world, possess very nearly all those things which go to the making of a nation: a long history; tragedies shared in common; hopes, ideals, and a religion. They also feel they have a land which is theirs, although they do not yet possess it. This is the one thing which lacks to complete totality of nationhood. Just as an individual has a right to express his own personality and make his contribution, so has a nation. But in order to do this a nation must have some theatre or stage upon which to play its part.

Frederick Morgan   No one who has been close to the war and who has seen the results of Nazi bestiality at its worst can fail to be sympathetic to the aspirations of the surviving remnants of European Jewry.

Jewish Chronicle   The Jewish life, as it used to be lived, has been torn to tatters.

Aaron Wright   For the great majority of them there is no hope and no future in Europe.

323

Is it fair to expect them to rebuild their shattered lives Thomas Horder among the tombstones of their fellows? Uprooted and homeless, where in liberated or conquered Europe are they to feel secure?

There can scarcely be a limit to the reparation owed The Times by the civilized world to a people so grievously wronged. Yet it is clear that the claims of conscience cannot be discharged by a process which creates new wrongs in remedying the old.

The principal difficulty is that Palestine is already the Nevill Barbour homeland of another people.

Had the situation of Palestine been as clear and as The Times simple as it appears to the enthusiastic Zionist, the country would long have ceased to constitute one of the storm centres of the Middle East. Palestine has always been counted a portion of the Arab world. The Arabs at present living in Palestine dread and abhor the prospect of being reduced to a minority community in a country they have always regarded as their own.

No case can possibly be made out for one race stealing Carey Lord the territory of another race, whether or not it claims the right to do so on the grounds that once upon a time – say two thousand years ago – some of their forebears were citizens of Palestine.

The strongest sentiment need not be allowed to brush Nottingham Journal aside the sentiments of all other people, and the march of history through 2,000 years.

If Hitler had put forward as his claim to Czechoslo- Truth vakia a former German occupancy of that land brought to an end 1,700 years ago the howl of derision can be imagined. It is precisely on this insubstantial claim that Zionism bases its demand for Palestine.

Henry Norman Smith   It must, they say, be Palestine, 'for historical reasons'. Red Indians might, with equal energy, demand the title deeds of all Manhattan! That more than a thousand years have passed since the Dispersal is nothing to Zionists. That 360,000 Arabs, whose ancestors peopled the land for centuries, should now be driven out, merely brings a shrug to the shoulders of the comfortable British or American Zionist, who blandly reminds you of what his compatriots endured at Hitler's hands. Two wrongs do not make a right.

Dundee Courier   The Nazi empire of slavery and murder is no more. It was Hitler's boast that he would eliminate every Jew from Europe; must they still quit the Continent now that their fiendish enemy has been destroyed?

The Times   The most useful thing that can be done now is to relieve the lot of Jewish displaced persons by opening to them countries other than Palestine. This would go far to allay the spirit of desperation in Jewry.

Winston Churchill   No one can imagine that there is room in Palestine for the great masses of Jews who wish to leave Europe, or that they could be absorbed in any period which it is now useful to contemplate.

325

No power on earth will give Palestine the expansive- John Squire
ness of a concertina, or will squeeze a quart of population
into a pint-pot of territory. Even if every non-Jew in Palestine were to vanish tomorrow there would still be no
room in the country for all the Jews. Had the zealots been
willing to establish their Jewish state in a possible place,
they had their chance long ago. Kenya, before it had been
settled, was offered by a British Government: Herzl was
inclined to it; but the devotees of Zion would not listen.
Even now there might be tracts for settlement available.

Is it too much to expect that world-wide sympathy *Thomas Comyn-Platt*
should be followed by practical evidence? A solution
might well be arrived at by every country in Europe – and
America too – agreeing to accept a given quota. The suggestion may not appeal to either Jew or Gentile, but at any
rate it is fairer than that the Arabs should be compelled to
shoulder the entire burden.

If the United States were to open a corner of its vast *The Times*
empty spaces to the Jews, many of them would go there
gladly, rather than to Palestine. If the British and French
Empires, the huge untenanted lands of Soviet Russia, the
under-populated pampas of South America were opened
to the Jews, the response would be immediate and large.
The Jews have formed a valued and enriching element
in the populations of Europe and America too long for
world opinion to regard their segregation in Palestine as
the sole hope of rebuilding their shattered lives.

There is still a place for them in Europe. It would be a *Daily Mail*
tragic thing for the world if it came to be thought that the
old Continent could offer them no hope and no future.

Let us then cease trying to cram millions of Jews into *Maude Royden Shaw*
an intensely hostile little country, about as big as Wales,
and let us count up the mileage of the British Common-
wealth, the U.S.A., and the U.S.S.R. for a change.

Harold Reinhart The Christian nations of the world should vie with each other in offering asylum to the relatively few Jewish survivors of the Hitler terror.

Charles Graves We have to face the plain truth, however unpleasant it may be, that none of the nations wants these Jewish refugees.

The Times There is little doubt that Zionism receives strong support from those who do not give a fig where the homeless Jews go so long as they go somewhere else.

Aberdeen Press and Journal, 2 July 1946 Perhaps it is just as well to state here that the British people have responsibilities in Palestine – to Arabs as well as to Jews. Their duty, laid upon them by mandate, is to promote the peaceful welfare of Palestine in the interests of all the inhabitants.

Scotsman The most unquenchable optimist would not maintain that Britain's Mandate over Palestine has been a conspicuous success.

John Hall British rule came to a Palestine of primitive conditions. Its 750,000 inhabitants were disease-ridden and poor in a land that was poverty-stricken, undeveloped, and prey to raiding nomads from the desert borders. We taught them husbandry, made loans, and nurtured the Palestine of today, with its good roads, fruitful farms, and show-places like Tel-Aviv.

Evening Standard A whole generation of administrators, judges, civil servants, doctors, technicians, have given their best to Palestine, not for recognition or fortune, but in the great British tradition of service.

Sunday Mirror The Mandate, dating from the First World War, favoured 'the establishment in Palestine of a National Home for the Jewish people'. The Mandate also said that the rights of non-Jews must be protected.

From that day to this, the bottomless ambiguity of these balanced sentiments has been the curse and blight of the Palestine question.

J. L. Garvin

If the Mandate was ever workable at the outset it certainly ceased to be so from the moment when Hitler's persecution of the Jews in Europe sent them surging into Palestine at a rate and in numbers which threw the whole Arab World into confusion and dismay.

Quintin Hogg

In 1939 the British Government decided to allow 75,000 more Jews into Palestine and then to stop immigration.

Daily Mail

Britain was attacked by the Jews for not allowing sufficient to enter and condemned by the Arabs for allowing too many.

Halifax Evening Courier

Arabs and Jews unite in their detestation of British rule.

Quintin Hogg

When we undertook the mandate, we became trustees for the inhabitants until such time as they could govern themselves. We are now faced on the one hand with an Arab demand for immediate independence, and on the other with a Zionist demand for a Jewish State.

Edward Spears

The two sides are irreconcilable, and well Britain knows it. British administration has been enlightened, conciliatory, and impartial, but to no purpose. In such an atmosphere any attempt to force a solution favourable to one side would set the Middle East aflame. If that happened, Britain would be blamed.

Daily Mail

Above all things, by hook or crook, we must make an end of this vile moral dilemma.

J. L. Garvin

A question larger than that of Palestine is whether Britain, even in this age, is to continue to act as the policeman of the world, and whether her fighting Forces are

Daily Mail

to be embroiled in every quarrel remote from their own shores.

Quintin Hogg

What right have we to be in Palestine at all? Are we there to protect our interest? But what interest are we protecting by making ourselves hated by Arab and Jew alike? Why should we stay on for the sake of keeping peace between two communities who do not want it kept?

Gloucester Citizen,
22 July 1946

British Military H.Q. Blown Up. Five floors of the King David Hotel in Jerusalem were blown up to-day by a heavy explosion which rocked the centre of the city. The explosion is attributed to Jewish terrorists.

Daily Telegraph

The limit of endurance so far as Britain is concerned has been reached. We British do not like failing, and here we have failed. But the failure is not our fault, and undoubtedly public opinion is solidly against continuing an odious and thankless task.

The Times,
2 August 1946

Mr. Churchill came into the Palestine debate in the House of Commons today with a strong criticism of the Government.

Daily Mail

Mr. Winston Churchill, with a bulldog tenacity in the tradition of his best war-time speeches, charged the Government to evacuate Palestine.

Winston Churchill

The handling of Palestinian affairs, up to this particular minute, has been a complete failure; it has gone from bad to worse, and one does not feel that there is any grip of the matter which is going to succeed. The one rightful, reasonable, simple, and compulsive lever which we hold is a sincere readiness to resign the mission, to lay our Mandate at the feet of the United Nations organisation and thereafter to evacuate the country with which we have no connection or tradition.

Three decades of embittered controversy have reached another stage with the British Government's declaration yesterday that it intends to abandon Palestine.

Henry Brandon, 28 September 1947

Britain, as a ruling Power, has never before been associated with so sorry a welter of bad blood, bad memories and bad prospects as marks the ending of this mandate.

Evening Standard

For those who remember how the Mandate began, there is something inexpressibly painful in the manner of its ending. It is distressing to see Britain, for the first time in modern history, abandoning, with no clear provision for the future, a territory for which she has been responsible.

Leonard J. Stein

After 27 years of unselfish labour, Britain has at last laid down the mandate in Palestine, and so ends another chapter in the nation's history of useful contribution to the wellbeing of international affairs. It is unlikely that there will be any votes of thanks, or any real recognition or appreciation of the cost to us, in lives and money, that has been involved in maintaining a smooth and efficient administration there. But there can be no doubt about the relief that is felt that our responsibility has ended at last. Our men have laboured long and hard; they leave with every reason for pride and none for shame.

Hull Daily Mail

History will call the mandate an honourable chapter in our story.

Sunday Times

Farewell to Zion. The long-suffering people of Britain have now washed their hands of Palestine.

Truth

What will happen when British troops leave Palestine twelve days hence? No one can tell.

Belfast Telegraph

The Jews will have to stand on their own feet. Their geographical position is not enviable. On three sides they are hemmed in by Arabian States - Egypt in the south,

Coventry Evening Telegraph

Syria in the north, Transjordan in the east, Saudi-Arabia in the south-east. In the west they have an outlet to the sea. If they cannot come to an understanding with the Arabs, they will have to fight it out.

The Times There is now no hope that Britain will be able to transfer authority in orderly fashion. Civil administration is paralysed; Government offices and commercial establishments have almost ceased to function; postal and telephone services are suspended.

Herbert Sidebotham When British authority ceases, some other authority must be there – to control the police, the education services, the health services, the agricultural services, or what you will. These are not threads which can be let drop for a few weeks or months and then picked up again. Someone must be there to hold them all the time.

The Times. Many Jews now feel that their destiny, and, perhaps, the final answer for Palestine, lies in their hands alone.

***

L. S. Amery, 14 May 1948 In a few hours we shall have formally abandoned the last remnant of responsibility for Palestine.

J. L. Hays As the Union Jack on the roof of our Government's House in Jerusalem was lowered, as a solitary piper played a lament, and Britain's 30 years' reign in Palestine ended, so the first Jewish State in 1,878 years was born.

Shields Daily News Jews Proclaim 'New Israel' As We Quit Today.

Yorkshire Evening Post Jews in Tel Aviv this afternoon proclaimed the birth of the Jewish State of Israel – eight hours before the end of the mandate.

Manchester Guardian The simple ceremony was held at 4 p.m. in Tel Aviv's museum – a small, square building holding probably less than three hundred. Mr. Ben-Gurion delivered the

331

proclamation standing beneath a large portrait of Dr. Theodore Herzl, founder of Zionism, between two white-and-blue banners with the Star of David, which is the emblem of the new State.

The hall was packed from wall to wall. It was still, and the heat was intense. Movie cameramen and newspaper photographers from other countries added to the mounting temperature with their arc-lamps and flash-bulbs. There were so many newspapermen and reporters that they seemed to fill the hall. Why not? The peoples of Europe and America were turning their eyes at this moment to the tiny corner in which the pages of the Bible were being re-enacted and the vision of its prophecies being fulfilled. Exactly at four o'clock Ben-Gurion rose, rapped the gavel on the table and the gathering rose to its feet. Spontaneously they began to sing the 'Hatikvah' anthem, not according to plan. It was to have been played by the Philharmonic Orchestra, concealed on the upper floor, but the singing preceded the music.

Zeev Sharef

Ben-Gurion said: 'The Land of Israel was the birth-place of the Jewish people. Here their spiritual, religious and national identity was formed. Exiled from Israel the Jewish people remained faithful to it in all the countries of their dispersion, never ceasing to pray and hope for their return. The First Zionist Congress proclaimed the right of the Jewish people to national revival in their own country.'

After reading the ten paragraphs of the preamble, he paused for a moment, and then in a raised voice continued: 'Accordingly we are met together in solemn assembly today, the day of the termination of the British Mandate for Palestine; and by virtue of the natural and historic right of the Jewish people. We hereby proclaim the establishment of the Jewish State in Palestine, to be called the State of Israel.'

As he pronounced these words the entire audience rose to its feet and burst into prolonged hand-clapping. All were seized by ineffable joy, their faces irradiated. The full impact of what had been done came home to those present – the significance of the creation of the State. The ceremony was symbolical but none of the tangible symbols was performed: no foreign flags were lowered nor was the national flag hauled up, no volleys or salvos in salute, no marching troops, no oratory. This was modesty almost to the point of diffidence – yet the reading of the dry legal jargon gave perfect expression to the quality, the breadth, the sweep, the nobility of the vision unfolded in that hall.

'Hatikvah' was struck up by the orchestra; and, the music resounding from above, it seemed as if the heavens had opened and were pouring out a song of joy on the rebirth of the nation. The audience stood motionless, transfixed, listening to the poignant melody coming from nowhere, as it were – and as the violins sobbed away the last note the Chairman declared: 'The State of Israel is established. This meeting is adjourned.' The barriers fell, restraint disappeared, the tears of rejoicing streamed copiously.

Outside the hall thousands had gathered from all parts of the city. They broke through the cordons and all semblance of order vanished as they milled with ushers and guards. Round after round of applause rolled out as the public figures left the building. The streets of Tel Aviv were filled with crowds which had been listening raptly to the proceedings broadcast over public address systems. Suddenly the city was seized by spontaneous festivity. What loomed in the future, nebulous as a dream, now became transposed into the present.

Jewish Chronicle   Jews all over the world, in the great cities of Europe, America, South Africa, and, above all, in the D.P. camps in Germany, Austria, and Italy, are overjoyed at the proclamation of the establishment of the new Jewish State, Israel. Polish Jewry greeted the proclamation with the utmost joy. Thanksgiving services were held in the Warsaw, Cracow, Lublin and Lodz synagogues. Thirty thousand Paris Jews met on Wednesday evening at the Velodrome D'Hiver to celebrate. In Czechoslovakia, mass meetings were called in all Jewish centres when the news was received. Extraordinary scenes marked the celebration in Johannesburg. Several thousand young men and women, carrying banners and torches, marched through the main streets. Crowds of young Jews continued singing and dancing until late at night.

American Jews were overjoyed. Large crowds of Jews celebrated in Times-square until the early hours, singing the Zionist national anthem and waving Zionist flags. The new national flag of Israel was hoisted beside the Stars and Stripes.

Leicester Evening Mail

Tomorrow, a new chapter will open in the age-old story of this significant strip of territory at the eastern end of the Mediterranean sea.

Jewish Chronicle

Immigration begins. First unrestricted immigration to the new Jewish State of Israel began to-day, ten hours after the creation of the State. The steamer Theti, the first to reach Tel Aviv since the lifting of the British blockade at midnight, disembarked 491 Jews, who were wildly cheered.

Sunderland Daily Echo, 15 May 1948

The Jewish people have kept their appointment with history. The Jewish State, the dream of twenty centuries of homeless wandering, is to-day a reality.

Abba Hillel Silver

Can it be true? A Jewish State? Is it not really a dream? Today is May the 15th – an historic day if ever there were one; not only for the Jews but also for humanity at large. For us Jews this day brings to a close a long and bitter

Shlomo Zalman Shragai

chapter and opens up a new and brighter era. Today the Jewish people becomes an equal member among the family of nations. From now onwards, whoever so desires may return home.

***

Civil & Military Gazette, 20 October 1949

While the founding of the state of Israel helped to give new life to many thousands of Jewish refugees in Europe, it created a new problem.

Manchester Evening News, 25 March 1949

For six months a host of 800,000 strong has been trudging, starving and dying, across the sands of the Middle East.

Civil & Military Gazette

Arab women and children are streaming along Palestine's roads towards the frontiers of Syria, Transjordan, Lebanon.

"THERE, YESTERDAY, WERE WE"

They came out of the barren hills above Jordan, out of the drab deserts of Southern Palestine; out of the orange-groves about Jaffa, and out of the towns in the strip from Acre to Tel Aviv.

Coventry Evening Telegraph

In most of the country, villages stand deserted or have been razed to the ground by Jews.

Sunday Mirror

The problem is heavily complicated by the official Jewish decision that they will not permit Arab refugees to return to their homes. The intention is to 'requisition' Arab property for the use of Jewish refugees from Europe. In this way it will be possible for the Israeli government greatly to increase the speed of immigration.

Scotsman

The once all-Arab cities of Jaffa, Ramleh, and Acre are now filling up with new Jewish immigrants.

J. L. Hays

It is one of the most tragic ironies of modern times that the establishment of a home for the Jews, who have suffered so much, should have involved great misery for so many helpless Arabs.

London Daily News

Jews should understand better than anybody what it means to be a refugee: and that they should remain passive in face of the tragedy ought to be unthinkable.

Victor Gollancz, *The Times*

Bewildered and beaten, the Palestine Arabs are asking: "Where can we go? What can we do?" And, frequently, "When can we go home, go back to Palestine?"

J. L. Hays

Chapter 47

Jo   I remember Hugh saying to me something about Zionism, and Israel, and how much did I know, and I really knew very little. Israel was important in New York, but not as important as it was at 22 Mapesbury. And he said, 'Well, you'll find out.'

Michael   It had always been said that one day they would go and live in Israel.

Mimi   We knew as soon as we could go, we would be going. When my dad proposed, he said to my mum, 'I want to go to Israel as soon as I can – will you come with me?' And she said yes. So we always knew. Fanny was terribly upset. Her whole attitude was against it. My mum was very much in her shadow – she did everything Fanny said if she possibly could. But first of all, she had promised Dad, secondly, she could not stand the cold, and the thought of going to a hot country was just wonderful. She never really was a Zionist. She only went for the weather.

Michael   England was very cold in those days after the war. In the winter of 1946 to '47, there were huge snowdrifts and power cuts.

Mimi   Most people didn't have central heating. We did – but it didn't work. Because of a bomb nearby, the pipes had burst, so the house was freezing.

Lolly   I shared a bedroom with my three brothers. Quite often the bathroom upstairs would spring a leak, so there were buckets around the room. You'd go to sleep, absolutely freezing, with this *drip*, *drip*, *drip* into these horrible buckets. We got chilblains on our feet, on our hands, everywhere. Your feet swell up, your hands swell up, and go red, and go purple, and sometimes they can burst a bit. It's agony. We all used to get them. The boys used to get them on their ears, because of their short hair.

I used to freeze to death. I had to have my clothes at   Mimi
the end of the bed, and I'd get dressed under the blankets before I got up. It was really icy cold. Sonia always suffered. She was always wrapped up. Nobody dressed nicely in those days – you couldn't. She wore thick beige stockings, and bloomers which covered the top of the stockings, and a skirt down to just below her knees, and some sort of pullover, at least one vest underneath, if not two, and a cardigan. I saw her sweeping the floor wearing her outdoor coat and her gloves, and a scarf around her ears.

I remember when she went to Israel, she said, 'Oh,   Jo
thank God. I'll be warm for the first time in my life.'

Dad left in '49, about eighteen months before us. As   Mimi
soon as he was able to go, he went.

He came to find us a house, but I don't think he   Judy
needed a year and half for that.

It is said that he had a couple of flirtations. More than   Mimi
that – affairs, I suppose. With beautiful women, always beautiful women. He wrote all the time. He was looking for a house, and a job. There were camps for immigrants – just tent cities. Some people stayed there as long as five or six years. He knew he wasn't going to take Mum to live in one of these tents in a camp, so he had to wait. He got a bit of money in advance from Tamara, because she'd said she was going to leave Sonia and Fanny half each, and managed to get hold of a flat. Mum had to pack up

all by herself. We took everything. We didn't have any nice furniture – I can't believe we took it with us, but we did.

Judy   We were very excited, because we were buying new things, and packing.

Jo   It had been planned for so long. It took months and months for everything to be packed up and sent. Israel had nothing, so they were taking everything with them. All sorts of furniture went – only the table remained there. I shared a room with Mimi, and everything was taken out. It was very stark. We only had two beds, that was it. I remember Dan being very excited, jumping all around all the time. Dan was absolutely devoted to the idea of Israel, and constantly reminding everybody they were going. He was a ferocious Zionist, all four feet of him. He got so angry if anybody said Palestine, and didn't say Israel. Of course, his sisters kind of teased him. He wanted to go so badly. I think he was looking forward to going much more than anybody else.

Tamara was very unhappy about it, because I think Auntie Sonie was her favorite. Fanny was somewhat prickly and difficult, and Sonia was easygoing. She was gentler, she was more reserved, she didn't put herself forward. I had a certain feeling that Fanny and I were more alike. Fanny at one time made some recognition that Tamara would be very unhappy about Sonia leaving, and Fanny being the one who remained. Fanny didn't want them to go either. But they were going.

Lolly   When it happened it was like a bolt from the blue. One day they were there, and the next day they were gone.

Jo   They were intending to go for so long, and packing, and talking about it, and then it happened. There was a real hole when they left, for everybody. It was kind of empty. I'm sure Fanny missed Sonia desperately. It must have been terrible for her, but she wasn't one to complain.

She didn't wear her heart on her sleeve. She just bustled along. My memory is full of Fanny bustling.

We had to take a train from Victoria to Dover, with all our luggage, and then take a boat across the Channel, which took about two hours, and was terribly stormy. _{Judy}

It was hectic. Mum could hardly cope. She just found it all too much. We'd sent everything we could, but we had an awful lot of baggage. Somebody had given her some cut-glass bowls – they'd all broken when we got to Paris. _{Mimi}

We got on a train to Marseilles, and that took a night and a day. Then we were on the boat from Marseilles to Haifa for five days. _{Judy}

The boat journey was beautiful – we sat in the sun on the deck all day. We arrived at Haifa port. Haifa is built on the hills, so a boat is the best place to see it from. It goes from sea level into mountain, with buildings all the way up. Dad was there to meet us. _{Mimi}

My father met us in Haifa, and he was so excited. The next day we had a car take us to Jerusalem. We were so happy to all be together again. _{Judy}

There was only one road up to Jerusalem in those days. It was a little narrow road, and it wove backwards and forwards. All the mountains were bare, because there were no trees yet. It's flat for a while, and then it starts to climb, and you just saw all the different hills – every time we turned the corner there was another hill. I loved Jerusalem from the moment I saw it. It just pulls at your heartstrings. It's such a beautiful city, because it's built on seven hills. Up, and down. There's something about it: it's full of life, full of energy. The light seems to be different there. It's the sunlight, it's the colour of the buildings. There was a law you had to build only in Jerusalem stone, _{Mimi}

which is kind of pinky yellow. When I used to go shopping with Judy, every time we turned a corner there was another picture postcard. It was absolutely glorious. On a Friday afternoon, as it gets towards Shabbat, and all the shops start shutting and the buses stop running, there's a kind of a peaceful, lovely atmosphere. You just feel it.

Judy Everything was just so strange. I remember the guy would come in a donkey and cart and sell ice to people. You'd hear him yelling. We had brought a fridge from England, but nobody had fridges – they had iceboxes. At the top you put this huge chunk of ice, and it lasts a day. There were three little main streets, and the buses were all rickety old things. Nobody I knew had a car.

Mimi There were little tiny shops. There weren't many paved roads. If you got off the main road, Jaffa Street, mainly you were walking on dirt tracks.

I saw an awful lot of people with numbers on their arms. I remember once I was on a bus, sitting near the front. In those days the buses didn't have many seats, so everybody was strap hanging, and I just saw arm after arm.

Judy They had radio programmes of people looking for each other for years afterwards. They would call out names and say, last seen wherever they were last seen in Europe, and thought to have come to Israel, and people would find each other, or they wouldn't.

When we got to Israel, we didn't really know anything about the Holocaust, and most of those first years were spent learning about it. We knew people who had just come out of the camps, and were trying to live some sort of normal life again. That was the focus.

It wasn't until later that I realised we weren't really kept adrift of what was going on: that the Arabs were being thrown out of their homes, and thrown out of their country. The whole atmosphere was that children were children, and we didn't have to know about all these grown-up things. It just wasn't part of our lives.

I remember seeing derelict houses that had been abandoned – I didn't think, then, about what it meant. I was eleven years old, I'd just come to this strange country, and I was learning another language. I never gave them much thought.

Leva believed that the land was ours, was Jewish. He thought the State of Israel belonged to Israel. As I got older I began to see things in a different light. I don't know who has claim to this land, I don't think anybody really knows. But it's obvious that the Palestinians didn't leave, they were thrown out. Who would want to leave their home?

***

In the early days we heard a lot of Yiddish and German. It was actually Jabotinsky who really pushed for Hebrew to be the language people spoke – you don't need Yiddish if you're going to build a new people, and a new country. Dad had a friend who used to come round and teach us. It's a reconstruction of the ancient Hebrew of the Bible: originally it was carved into stone, so almost all the lines are straight, and the letters denote what they're talking about. The letter 'shin', which means 'tooth', has a line along the bottom, and three lines going up, so it looks like a few upper teeth. The first letter of the word for door is 'delet', and it looks like the open door of a tent. I found it fascinating.

My dad felt he'd come home. He was asked to be the director of the Jabotinsky Institute, so he carried on the work of researching Jabotinsky and saving his ideas. He kept the same level of admiration for Jabotinsky until the day he died.

It was only later that he became disillusioned. He was desperately disappointed that Israel didn't turn out the way he thought it would. The whole of his generation were disappointed. They were willing to give up everything in order to build a country, and a lot of people who were there couldn't have cared less about building up the country. That upset him. Some people who had escaped the Nazis were not running to, they were running from.

My friend's mother had come from Germany. She never learnt Hebrew at all – she only spoke German. Some German Jews resented having to leave Germany. They knew that Hitler hated what he called the garlic-smelling Jews from Eastern Europe, but they were not like that. They felt they were real Germans. They had their own shops and their own newspaper, and they just didn't want to be there.

He thought they would become idealistic, but they didn't. Those early Zionists all had their own dreams of what this perfect country was going to be, and obviously they were just dreams.

My mum made friends. She went to Hebrew classes, and she found other musicians. They used to play quartets together in each other's houses. She missed Fanny terribly – we all knew that.

The rationing in England was just beginning to end, and she was back in it again. It was the last thing she needed, having just escaped from it. When we went to the grocer, we had to take the jar for our honey, and they would give us a chunk of butter wrapped in newspaper. She used to insist on buying Corn Flakes – they were imported, and they were terribly expensive. Israelis don't eat Corn Flakes for breakfast, but she didn't want to change.

My mother had a terrible time in the beginning when we moved. All her life here, she always used to talk about 'At home'. I'd say, 'Mum, where's home?' and she'd say, 'Oh, home – in England. Home.'

Judy

I suppose when Judy and Mimi and Dan and Leva and Sonie went off to Israel and we were left in England, we all thought, nice for them to try it, but they'll be back soon. We sort of felt that. It won't be too long before they'll be back.

Michael

It was all just so exciting that we were moving, and I don't think I really felt that we were leaving them, until it

Judy

344

actually happened. I didn't really think about it – didn't stop to think, this is the end of being with the Cockerells.

Michael   These were our cousins, our friends, people whom we'd grown up with. They must come back.

Judy   It was all so new. It wasn't until later on that I realised what we'd lost, really.

Michael   We couldn't really believe it was going to be for very long, because they belonged with us in Mapesbury Road, not in this exotic place called Israel. So they'd be back. We knew they'd be back.

Afterword

Mapesbury Road has one remaining occupant: my Uncle Dave. He uses a few of the rooms, and the rest of the house is uninhabited. What was once Tamara's bedroom is now filled with the detritus of the twentieth century: old furniture piled halfway to the ceiling, fat notebooks filled with Fanny's adolescent short stories, envelopes wadded with black-and-white photographs never put into frames or albums, Russian picture books presumably read to Fanny and Sonia as children. At the far end of the room, only accessible by navigating a landscape of obstacles, is Hugh's desk. Its drawers are filled with his carefully type-written notes, the staples rusted and the paper yellowed. His glasses are in the top drawer, still in their case. He died in 1995, six years after Fanny, and left the house to Dave in his will.

Sonia and Leva never came back to Mapesbury Road. Mimi returned in her twenties to become a ballet dancer, got married, had a daughter and has lived in London ever since, but she never stopped thinking of Israel as her home. Dan died in 2016. Judy married the son of Holocaust survivors, and they lived together in Tel Aviv until his death in 2023. She has three children and eight grandchildren. Since 2018 I have visited Judy's family regularly: I have had my first Passover and my first Hanukkah with them, I have watched them light candles and say prayers before Shabbat dinner, and I have listened to them joke and argue in rapid Hebrew. Despite their warmth I always feel like an outsider, like their lives are alien to mine. I am always aware of a road that forked

347

when Sonia left for Israel and Fanny stayed in England, or perhaps earlier, when Fanny married an Englishman and Sonia married a Russian Jew, creating two paths that have been inching further and further apart ever since.

Jo went back to New York in 1953, after two years in London. She won a place at Columbia University, where she met her husband, Colin. Jo became a teacher and Colin became a university professor. Before I started the book I had no idea of her existence, or of her father's. I encountered Emjo a few months into my research – a playwright who died in 1939, and whose surname had originally been Jochelman. I wondered if he might be a distant relative, and I asked my dad if he had heard of him. 'I remember Emjo Basshe,' he said, to my surprise. 'But she didn't die in 1939. She came to Mapesbury Road in 1950, when she must have been about twenty.' The mystery confounded us both – Emjo Basshe didn't quite seem a common enough name to belong to two people by coincidence. Not long after, I was looking through some papers scanned by a distant cousin, Sue Dorman, and I came across a single page of a letter written by Jo. The first page was missing, so I had no idea who it was written to, but it solved the mystery. 'My father changed his name, taking the "Em" from Emmanuel and the "Jo" from Jochelman, and then adopted his grandmother's name, Hode Basshe. I was given the identical name. I have a signature of his in which he writes, after his name, the Roman numeral "I".'

Sue told me that Emjo II had shortened her name to Jo, was now eighty-nine and lived in Canada. Jo did not do email, but Colin did. In late 2019 I got in touch with him, and received a reply a few days later. 'Dear Rachel, No need to apologize for your 'out-of-the-blue' email. We were delighted to hear from you. Jo immediately said, 'Oh, she must be Michael's daughter. Tell her I'll write to her.' If you have any specific questions don't wait, just send them.'

By this time I had a long list of questions for Jo: about her father, about David Jochelmann, and about her visit to Mapesbury Road. We exchanged a few emails through Colin's account, and I sent over a photo of her I had found among Fanny's possessions in the detritus-filled room at Mapesbury Road. I asked if I could come and visit her. 'You are welcome to come to Canada,' she wrote back, 'but frankly, I think we, and especially you, might be better off phoning. We are old and I am no longer the girl in the picture – I will be 90 in February.' She gave me her land-line, and on a Sunday morning in January 2020 I called the number. I was inexplicably nervous as I listened to the dial tone.

'Hello?' The voice sounded too young to belong to an 89-year-old.

'Hi,' I said. 'Is that – is that by any chance Jo?'

'Who's this?'

I knew I had the wrong number.

'It's Rachel Cockerell.'

'Rachel! Hi! Colin, it's Rachel on the phone!'

'If this is a bad time I can call you back another day,' I said.

'No, no, this is perfect. I'm sitting in my armchair, I've got a cat on my lap, well, I did until just a second ago when he jumped off, it's snowing outside, everyone's trying to shovel the snow from their front yards and their driveways. So this is perfect.'

It was the start of nearly two years of weekly recorded conversations, and hundreds of pages of transcripts, out of which Jo's section of the book emerged.

***

If someone had told me, when I started this book, that the first half would be taken over by a long-dead, long-forgotten author, to whom I bore no relation, I would have been a little resistant. But Israel Zangwill won a place in my heart, perhaps more than any other character. It may have been because I felt a kinship with him: I too, have 'long arms, long legs, long fingers, and exceedingly long hair'. I, too, am negligent of my apparel, and pieces of paper are often falling out of my pockets. But it was also because Zangwill came alive most vividly for me.

There were so many small but delightful descriptions of him I had to cut: 'Five minutes spent in observing the author would bring to the mind of the spectator at least one deduction – that he is fond of comfort,' a *Washington Times* journalist wrote in 1899. 'During the conversation of yester-evening he confined himself to a chair of the loungiest sort, occasionally stretching himself far beyond its boundaries and not infrequently throwing either one or both legs over its arms.'

'He strays about Paris in the middle of the street, rather than on the sidewalk, in constant danger of being run down by the omnipresent Parisian coacher,' wrote an American journalist travelling in Europe in the 1890s. 'Anyone but Zangwill would be run down. I think some guardian angel must guide his footsteps from under the noses of rearing cab-horses, landing him unruffled among his anxious friends upon the sidewalk. On the other hand, if there is anything over which one could possibly stumble Zangwill is sure to do so. We were waiting for him one day, when we heard an ominous rumble and banging in the hall. One of our party promptly exclaimed, 'Israel must be coming. Something's falling downstairs.'

I once heard an interview with Olia Hercules, the Ukrainian chef and author, in which she talked about the instability of the past. 'In my family, storytelling was extremely important,' she said. 'We would sit on this long table, and everyone would cook, and these stories would come out – of course, a lot of the stories were connected to the Second World War. The adults talked about it all the time. It was very much at the forefront of our conversation. My family are such amazing storytellers, I can almost picture it. And sometimes it feels like a false memory, almost.'

I have spent three years listening to stories about Zangwill told to me by the dead. Some of them have almost crossed the border between imagination and memory: the dinner in Vienna at the close of the nineteenth century when Herzl served Zangwill a whole crab, the day of Zangwill's wedding to Edith in the spring of 1903, the night in 1908 when *The Melting Pot* premiered in Washington.

'Was he one of the immortals? – one of the score or so of our contemporaries whose names will be remembered centuries hence? I think so,' wrote Frederic Whyte in 1931. So far, Whyte's prediction has been wrong. Zangwill was once the most famous Jew in the world, and yet he has disappeared almost without a trace. It may be because he more or less abandoned his career as a novelist for the Jewish cause. 'If Zangwill had continued to write fiction – and had continued to write it with the same many-sided genius that he showed in the last ten years of the 19th century – there cannot be much doubt that his literary reputation would have stood immensely higher than it does today,' wrote Robert Lynd after Zangwill died in 1926 at the age of sixty-two, in relative obscurity. I wonder if, at the end of his life, he felt the sacrifice of his legacy had been worth it. He did not live to see the founding of a Jewish State, and the ITO fell drastically short of his hopes. I am sure the stress and disappointment of Territorialism contributed to his early death.

And yet I have to be grateful for how things unfolded. In 1913 Jacob Schiff wrote a letter to Zangwill about David Jochelmann. It was soon after David's trip to the US, where he had met Schiff in New York and travelled on to Galveston. 'He told me in New York that he has decided to go to America with his family,' Schiff wrote. A year later, Zangwill wrote to David, 'Your future belongs to England.'

I think back to what Shmarya Levin wrote about Herzl's funeral. 'In my imagination, I saw the unresting chain of events that had led to this moment: Kishineff–Uganda, Uganda–Herzl.' These chain links, and the ones that followed, shaped the fate of my family. Without the ITO, and the Galveston Plan, and the way it all crumbled, Zangwill would never have met my great-grandfather, worked with him, and persuaded him to move his family to London as the First World War broke out. 'He confessed to me once that he had wasted half his life on Zionism,' Zangwill's friend Jerome K. Jerome wrote in 1925. I have Zangwill's half-wasted life to thank for my existence.

Acknowledgements

In late 2021, as the US Government lifted the Covid-19 travel ban, I embarked on a research trip to archives in Cincinnati, Carbondale, Ann Arbor, Austin, Galveston, Princeton and New York. I'm so grateful to all the archivists who ungrudgingly carried out my endless requests for boxes and folders stored in the deepest recesses of their vaults.

A few particular highlights: finding letters written by David Jochelmann in Kyiv in 1908 and marvelling at the strangeness of reading them in Ohio in 2021. Visiting Princeton University's Firestone Library, where I knew a folder entitled 'Emjo Basshe' awaited me in Otto Kahn's archive. I feared it would only contain a few scraps of paper, and instead found a thick wedge of typewritten letters: Emjo's originals to Kahn interleaved with carbon copies of Kahn's replies, each one meticulously stamped with a date by a diligent secretary a hundred years ago. In the Firestone Library I experienced the sensation of eavesdropping more uncannily than at any other point on my trip. Meeting the late Jimmy Kessler, Rabbi of Galveston for 32 years, and his wife Shelley Nussenblatt, a descendant of Galveston immigrants. Jimmy and Shelley took me for fish tacos on Galveston Beach, and we talked about assimilation and the Melting Pot over the sound of crashing waves.

Thank you to those who hosted me during my trip: Kelly Finkel in Austin, Lisa Belshaw in Princeton, and Peter and Ellen Hoenig in New York. Peter grew up in London, next door to 22 Mapesbury Road, and painted a vivid picture of the house and its inhabitants from an outsider's perspective.

To Anne Fletcher, Professor of Theater at Southern Illinois University, for the post-library sushi in Carbondale, over which we discussed Emjo and the other New Playwrights as if they were mutual friends. To Jessamyn Ressler-Maerlender and her family, for the Shabbat dinner at their house in Ann Arbor, where I got my first real-life glimpse of American Judaism.

To the late David Hoffman, whom I cold-called from England in early 2021 after finding his name online. Instead of hanging up, David told me about his grandmother, Sarah Bernstein, who immigrated to Galveston in 1913, aged 19. Later, David sent me a taped interview with Sarah as an old woman. It was the first and only time I heard the distinctive Russian-Texan accent of the Galveston immigrant. I spent a perfect weekend with David and his wife Binnie at their ranch near Austin, riding horses across fields dotted with mesquite trees.

The papers of Zangwill and the Galveston Movement have somewhat ironically ended up in the Central Zionist Archives in Jerusalem, which I visited in 2022. I'm so grateful to Giora Katz for all his help there.

My two research trips were incredibly useful, but I wrote most of this book lying on my sofa in London. I was astonished to learn how much historical material is available online, for free. My most treasured discovery was Fulton History, a website with over 50 million pages of US newspapers dating back to 1795, each one diligently scanned and uploaded by Tom Tryniski of Fulton, New York. Also invaluable were Chronicling America, The Internet Archive, Portal to Texas History, HathiTrust, and the National Library of Israel's Newspaper Collection. 'You have to have so much primary source material that you are drowning, you think you can never get through it all,' says the historian Candice Millard. I was never happier than stumbling upon a database I had never heard of, typing in the name 'Zangwill', and clicking on the first of 2,000 results.

Thank you to the academics and specialists who have been so generous with their time and expertise, responding to my cold emails with detailed answers to all my questions and several unsolicited attachments. I sometimes felt as though the people in this book existed only in my head, and it was thrilling to be able to talk to others who knew them just as well as I did. As one historian wrote to me, 'I think there are fewer than a half-dozen of us who love Zangwill.' Our conversations also gave me the pleasant sensation of being the great-granddaughter of a minor celebrity. Another historian, after pressing me about my connection to the Galveston movement, said, 'Now, Jochelmann. I didn't realize that's who you're descended from. Very Big Deal!' To David Faiman, Adam Rovner, Meri-Jane Rochelson, and in particular to Bryan Edward Stone.

To the former inhabitants of Mapesbury Road who agreed to be interviewed for this book: Judy Segal, Mimi Benari, Lolly Seager and Michael Cockerell. To Judy's daughters, Karni Govreen Segal and Shelli Segal-Shaked, who treated me as a part of their (immediate) family on all my visits to Tel Aviv. To Sue Dorman, the real family genealogist.

Thank you to my agent, Sabhbh Curran, for believing in *Melting Point* from the beginning, and for her wisdom and humour throughout. To my editor, Phil Connor, for his warmth and equanimity, his insightful edits, and for gently suggesting I remove my 764 uses of 'said' and 471 uses of 'wrote', and consider presenting the sources in another way. To my copyeditor, Mark Handsley, and my proofreader, Robert Shore, for reading the manuscript with such care and attention. To Wilf Dickie who took on the perhaps somewhat daunting task of typesetting this book, and created something so elegant. To Caroline Young, designer of my wonderful cover. To Joe Thomas, the finest publicity director I could have hoped for. Thank you also to Areen Ali, Louise Rothwell, and the rest of the team at Headline Wildfire.

To Lucy and John Dos Passos Coggin, daughter and grandson of John Dos Passos, for their permission to quote from Dos Passos's writing. To Caroline Zangwill and Patty Holland-Branch, Zangwill's granddaughters (both extremely youthful for people whose grandfather was born in 1864), for their memories and stories. To Virginia Ogilvy for her reminiscences of her grandfather, Otto Kahn. To Emma Soames for her help with the Churchill material.

To Davie Lou Solka, Linda Goff, Vickie Vogel and Sheldon Lippman at the New Mexico Jewish Historical Society, for letting me speak at their 2021 conference, and to Bette Evans, Jan Hart, Harry Harelik and the late David Hoffman, all descendants of Galveston immigrants, whose panel I very much gatecrashed. To Larry Stein and Elaine Stein for the photograph of 19 immigrants (and many photobombers) aboard a Galveston-bound ship in 1913, among them Elaine's mother Belle, the frowning toddler in the middle row. To David Matlow, owner of the world's largest private Herzl collection, for the scanned page of Egon Zweig's notebook in which he tallied the Uganda vote at the Sixth Zionist Congress.

To Tom Tyson, Flora Fraser, Amelia Webb, Karen Lowther, Eliza Levien and Alice Cockerell, for reading the manuscript and giving so much good advice. To Claudia Cockerell, and to Jonah Freud, for suggesting I shift the sources into the margins. To Lamorna Ash for obligingly discussing every detail of every stage of this book. To Bridget and Philip Beck, under whose roof some of it was written.

To Isobel Cockerell, my most trusted reader and editor. Thank you for reading the manuscript, annotating almost every line, making many cuts, and occasionally leaving gratifying comments such as 'Where do you bloody find these descriptions'.

To my parents, Anna Lloyd and Michael Cockerell, both documentary makers, whose strong opinions on the correct and incorrect ways of telling a story have seeped into this book. Special thanks to the former for reading my first draft. Much of it was boring, repetitive, and filled with gaping holes, but after an hour-long phone conversation I began to see how it might be improved. And thanks to the latter, for providing the subject matter, and for the words of sympathy while I tried to reduce the manuscript from 120,000 to 90,000 words: 'Editing feels at first like cutting off your fingernails, then like cutting off your fingers, then your hands, and finally your arms.'

My way into this story was through chance encounters with books that mentioned David Jochelmann. The chief among those was Bernard Marinbach's *Galveston: Ellis Island of the West*, published in 1983 and widely considered the gold standard in the (albeit rather narrow) field of Galveston scholarship. I felt Marinbach's invisible presence throughout the writing process: I imagined him disapproving of my amateurishness, pointing out each of my glaring omissions. Eventually I summoned up the courage to get in touch with him, and emailed him my manuscript. When I was in Jerusalem he invited me for coffee on his balcony. The stern figure of my imagination turned out to be a benevolent New Yorker in his seventies, who emigrated to Israel as a young man and retained his heavy Brooklyn accent. He said, to my surprise and relief, that he liked the way I had told the story, and he didn't mind my glaring omissions. Thank you, Bernie – without your book mine would not exist, and I would never have known about David Jochelmann, Zangwill, the two Emjo Basshes, or anyone else.

Which brings me to my final thanks. Just before my US trip I stopped off in Canada, where I met Jo and Colin for the first time face-to-face. They came to collect me at the train station. Colin was as I expected him to be: tall and lanky, with a sprightliness reminiscent of a Quentin Blake illustration. Jo was almost a foot shorter than Colin, and wore, to my slight surprise, a purple t-shirt, purple shorts, and white tennis shoes. She had the immaculate posture imparted on her in the 1930s by Doris, and the same hooded eyes as Fanny and Emjo. I stayed with them for a week, and met their friends, Domenic Marsella, Tom Dilworth and Kai Hildebrandt, who knew me as 'cousin Rachel from the Sunday phone calls'.

Thank you, Jo, for the innumerable hours of conversation, for your razor-sharp memory, for making me laugh and teaching me so much, and for letting me tell the story of you and your father.

Selected Bibliography

ARCHIVES

Annie Russell papers, Manuscripts and Archives Division, New York Public Library, Astor, Lenox and Tilden Foundations.

Billy Rose Theatre Division, New York Public Library for the Performing Arts, Astor, Lenox and Tilden Foundations.

Central Zionist Archives, Jerusalem.

Jacob Rader Marcus Center of the American Jewish Archives, Cincinnati.

National Archives, Kew.

Otto H. Kahn Papers, Manuscripts Division, Department of Special Collections, Princeton University Library.

Special Collections Research Center, Morris Library, Southern Illinois University, Carbondale.

Special Collections Research Center, University of Michigan Library, Ann Arbor.

PUBLISHED SOURCES

Adler, Cyrus, ed., *Jacob H. Schiff; His Life and Letters*, 2 vols, New York: Doubleday, Doran, 1928.

Alroey, Gur, *Zionism without Zion: The Jewish Territorial Organization and Its Conflict with the Zionist Organization*, Detroit: Wayne State University Press, 2016.

Bein, Alex, *Theodore Herzl: A Biography*, New York: Atheneum, 1962.

de Haas, Jacob, *Theodor Herzl: A Biographical Study*, 2 vols, Chicago: The Leonard Company, 1927.

Elon, Amos, *Herzl*, New York: Holt, Rinehart and Winston, 1975.

Fletcher, Anne, *Rediscovering Mordecai Gorelik: Scene Design and American Theatre*, Carbondale: SIU Press, 2009.

Gurwitz, Alexander Z., *Memories of Two Generations: A Yiddish Life in Russia and Texas*, ed. Bryan Edward Stone, trans. Rabbi Amram Prero, Tuscaloosa: The University of Alabama Press, 2016.

Horowitz, Brian, and Leon Katsis, eds, *Vladimir Jabotinsky's Story of My Life*, Detroit: Wayne State University Press, 2015.

Knox, George A., and Herbert M. Stahl, *Dos Passos and 'The Revolting Playwrights'*, Copenhagen: Munksgaard, 1964.

Leftwich, Joseph, *Israel Zangwill*, New York: T. Yoseloff, 1957.

Levin, Shmarya, *The Arena*, New York: Arno Press, 1975.

Ludington, Townsend, ed., *The Fourteenth Chronicle: Letters and Diaries of John Dos Passos*, Boston: Gambit, 1973.

Marinbach, Bernard, *Galveston: Ellis Island of the West*, Albany: SUNY Press, 1983.

Nahon, Shlomo Umberto, ed., *The Jubilee of the First Zionist Congress: 1897–1947*, Jerusalem: Executive of the Zionist Organisation, 1947.

Patai, Raphael, ed., *The Complete Diaries of Theodor Herzl*, vols 1–4, New York: Herzl Press and Thomas Yoseloff, 1960.

Pawel, Ernst, *The Labyrinth of Exile: A Life of Theodor Herzl*, New York: Farrar, Straus & Giroux, 1989.

Rochelson, Meri-Jane, *A Jew in the Public Arena: The Career of Israel Zangwill*, Detroit: Wayne State University Press, 2008.

Rosenberger, Erwin, *Herzl As I Remember Him*, New York: Herzl Press, 1959.

Rovner, Adam, *In the Shadow of Zion: Promised Lands Before Israel*, New York: NYU Press, 2014.

Schechtman, Joseph B., *The Vladimir Jabotinsky Story*, New York: T. Yoseloff, 1956.

Simon, Maurice, ed., *Speeches, Articles and Letters of Israel Zangwill*, London: The Soncino Press, 1937.

Waldman, Morris D., *Nor by Power*, New York: International Universities Press, 1953.

Weisbord, Robert G., *African Zion: The Attempt to Establish a Jewish Colony in the East Africa Protectorate, 1903–1905*, Philadelphia: The Jewish Publication Society of America, 1968.

Weisgal, Meyer Wolfe, ed., *Theodor Herzl: A Memorial*, New York: New Palestine, 1929.

Weizmann, Chaim, *Trial and Error*, London: Hamish Hamilton, 1949.

Zipperstein, Steven J., *Pogrom: Kishinev and the Tilt of History*, New York: Liveright Publishing, 2018.

Zweig, Stefan, *The World of Yesterday*, London: Cassel and Company Ltd, 1943.

Notes

Abbreviations

NYT *New York Times*
JC *Jewish Chronicle*

Where full publishing details are given in the Selected Bibliography, they are not repeated here.

Preface

The question was: Jill Owens, 'Powell's Interview: George Saunders, Author of "Lincoln in the Bardo"', 6 Feb 2017, https://powells.com/post/interviews/powells-interview-george-saunders-author-of-lincoln-in-the-bardo accessed 3/4/2020

The past felt fissile: Robert Macfarlane, *The Old Ways*, London: Penguin, 2013, 325.

the pieces of a pattern: Emily St. John Mandel, *Station Eleven*, London: Picador, 2015, 181.

I think how little: W. G. Sebald, *Austerlitz*, trans. Anthea Bell, New York: The Modern Library, 2001, 24.

the rush and roar: John Howard Lawson, 'On "Processional"', *NYT*, 1 Feb 1925, 152.

And though he is: Laura Cumming, *On Chapel Sands*, London: Chatto & Windus, 2019, 273.

PART ONE

Chapter 1

A year ago: quoted in 'Leader of the Zionist Movement', *Chicago Daily Tribune*, 17 Jul 1901, 16.

In appearance: Ray Frank, 'A Zionist Meeting in London', *American Hebrew*, 21 Oct 1898, 739.

Those who see him: quoted in 'The Gathering of the Yellow Roses', *Dublin Daily Express*, 25 Aug 1903, 6.

An artist might paint: Julius Haber, 'Cyrus Sulzberger's View of Theodor Herzl', *Jewish Floridian*, 8 Apr 1960, 9.

He looks like kings: Cyrus L. Sulzberger, 'An American's View of the Congress', *American Hebrew*, 11 Sep 1903, 527.

Without posing: Jacob de Haas, 'Theodor Herzl: A Brief Sketch of His Life', *Maccabaean* 7, no. 3, Sep 1904, 139–40.

I still remember: quoted in 'Excerpts from the Correspondence between Theodor Herzl and Arthur Schnitzler, 1892–1895', trans. Joel Carmichael, *Midstream* 6, no. 1, winter 1960, 48.

I remember a meeting: quoted in Israel Cohen, *Theodor Herzl, Founder of Political Zionism*, New York: T. Yoseloff, 1959, 52.

I regard him: Jacob de Haas, *Theodor Herzl: A Biographical Study*, 2:258.

Herzl made a colossal: Brian Horowitz and Leonid Katsis, eds, *Vladimir Jabotinsky's Story of My Life*, Detroit: Wayne State University Press, 2015, 23.

Dr. Herzl has practised: 'Advent of the New Moses', *Pall Mall Gazette*, 29 Jul 1897, 7.

He had become: Stefan Zweig, *The World of Yesterday*, 101.

His readers were: Zweig, 'The King of the Jews', in Raphael Patai, ed., *Herzl Yearbook, Vol. 3: Herzl Centennial Issue*, New York: Herzl Press, 1960, 110–12.

For some time: Raphael Patai, ed., *The Complete Diaries of Theodor Herzl*, 1:3.

I wrote walking: Theodor Herzl, 'Experiences and Moods: An Autobiographic Sketch', in Meyer Wolfe Weisgal, ed., *Theodor Herzl, A Memorial*, 183–4. See also 'Theodor Herzl: An Autobiography', *JC*, 14 Jan 1898, 20.

As the century: Zweig, 'King of the Jews', *Herzl Centennial Issue*, 110.

I can still remember: Zweig, *World of Yesterday*, 103.

In Vienna, he caught: Erwin Rosenberger, *Herzl As I Remember Him*, New York: Herzl Press, 1959, 75.

When he entered: Zweig, 'King of the Jews', *Herzl Centennial Issue*, 110.

Dr. Beck, my: Patai, ed., *Complete Diaries*, 1:316.

Acquaintances ask me: ibid., 1:301.

Vienna, where he thought: Zweig, *World of Yesterday*, 104.

Theodor Herzl came into: Shmarya Levin, *The Arena*, 129.

The personality of Herzl: Chaim Weizmann, 'Fifty Years of Zionism', in Shlomo Umberto Nahon, ed., *Jubilee of the First Zionist Congress*, 10–11.

Recent movements: 'Palestine for the Jews', *Utica Sunday Journal*, 23 Jul 1901, 14.

That one watchword: 'Zionist Congress', *Jersey City News*, 30 Aug 1897, 1.

If the project reaches: 'News Notes', *Middlesex Gazette*, 28 Aug 1897, 2.

Until about thirty: 'The Jews' Return to Palestine', *Pall Mall Gazette*, 10 Aug 1897, 7.

It has always been: 'Movement of the Zionists', *Wichita Daily Eagle*, 13 Aug 1899, 12.

We are face to face: 'A Dream of a Jewish State', *JC*, 17 Jan 1896, 14–15.

It will be interesting: 'The "New Zion" Movement: Dream of Patriotic Jews', *Elmira Morning Telegram*, 25 Jul 1897.

The entire: 'Can the Jews Buy Palestine?', *New York Sun*, 30 Mar 1902, 32.

The climate of Palestine: '"New Zion" Movement', *Elmira Morning Telegram*.

Herzl has realized: Julius Uprimny, 'Dr. Herzl–Intime', *Maccabaean* 3, no. 3, 132–3.

The campaign's centre: Patai, ed., *Complete Diaries*, 1:276.

I was the first: quoted in *Judaean Addresses; Selected*, New York: Block Pub. Co., 1927, 3:95.

I have the most vivid: Louis Zangwill, 'Herzl Invades England: How the Unknown Leader Came to Israel Zangwill with His Idea', in Weisgal, ed., *Herzl: A Memorial*, 41.

He was a man: Israel Zangwill, 'Zionism and Territorialism', *Fortnightly Review* 86, no. 520, Apr 1910, 645.

Our conversation: Patai, ed., *Complete Diaries*, 1:276.

A black-bearded stranger: 'Memorial Meeting at the Great Assembly Hall', *JC*, 15 Jul 1904, 11.

Chapter 2

There is a new writer: 'Our Handbook', *The Referee*, 7 Jun 1891, 2.

When, about five: 'What They Read: I. Zangwill', *Vogue*, 2 Apr 1896, 249–50.

Walk down: quoted in 'I. Zangwill', *The Jewish South*, 5 Mar 1897, 4.

Mr Zangwill possesses: 'Literary Notes', *Grand Ledge Independent*, 18 Sep 1896, 2.

The very archetype: Noel Y. Harte, 'Israel Zangwill Chats of Zion and Art', *New York Herald*, 6 Nov 1904, M3.

The dramatist is: 'Zangwill on Dreyfus', *Washington Times*, 11 Sep 1899, 2.

He looks as if: 'Zangwill in his Den', *New York Press*, 23 Feb 1896, 6.

Zangwill was the very: Hayden Church, 'Interesting Pen Picture of Zangwill', *New York Press*, 1 Feb 1914, 4.

He was always a little: Reuben Brainin, 'Israel Zangwill – Twelve Years After', *American Hebrew*, 14 May 1909, 28.

He was probably: quoted in Joseph Leftwich, *Israel Zangwill*, 110.

Walking the streets: Hamlin Garland, 'I. Zangwill', Conservative Review 2, no. 2, Nov 1899, 408.

When I first met: quoted in 'Zangwill's Personality', *American Hebrew*, 1 Feb 1895, 381.

Mr. Zangwill lives: 'Zangwill: A Talk with Him in His London Home – as to America', *NYT*, 6 Jul 1901.

I well remember: Church, 'Interesting Pen Picture of Zangwill', *New York Press*, 4.

His library is barely: Isidore Harris, 'Mr. Israel Zangwill Interviewed', *Bookman* 13, no. 77, Feb 1898, 145–8.

Mr. Zangwill is manifestly: 'Footlights and Foyer', *Billboard*, 25 May 1901, 8.

He has a wonderful: 'Zangwill in His Den', *New York Press*, 6.

Of course everyone: G. B. Burgin, 'Israel Zangwill as I Know Him', *Critic* 42, no. 3, Mar 1903, 266.

His method of work: quoted in 'I. Zangwill', *Jewish South*, 4.

As the well-informed: 'Stage and Study', *Illustrated Buffalo Press*, 23 Oct 1898, 12.

It may be said: Emanu Elzas, 'Israel Zangwill', *The American Israelite*, 10 Oct 1895, 7.

Zangwill is the man: I. F. Marcosson, 'Zangwill Talks About the Ghetto Jew', *Louisville Courier-Journal*, 18 Sep 1898.

If you have: 'Cosy Corner Chat', *Gentlewoman*, 27 May 1893, 17.

The "Children of the Ghetto": 'Children of the Ghetto', *Reform Advocate*, 3 Dec 1892, 7.

We are glad: 'A Chat about Books', *Queen*, 24 Mar 1894, 28.

With the firm: Washington Gladden, 'Can Jews Be Christians?', *American Hebrew*, 4 Dec 1896, 132.

"Children of the Ghetto" has: 'Our London Letter', *Derby Daily Telegraph*, 16 Nov 1892, 2.

Few books have: 'Zangwill Here', *American Hebrew*, 2 Sep 1898, 507.

Zangwill will: 'Notes & Comments', *South Wales Daily Post*, 3 Oct 1894, 2.

After many: 'The Coming of Zangwill', *American Hebrew*, 26 Aug 1898, 478.

Israel Zangwill is: 'Zangwill', *New York Press*, 9 Aug 1899, 2.

It was an easy task: 'Zangwill Here', *American Hebrew*, 2 Sep 1898, 507.

I. Zangwill is not: Dexter Marshall, 'Our New York Letter: Zangwill and the Critics; His Play and His Personality; Zangwill Physically Considered', *Elmira Evening Gazette*, 26 Oct 1899, 4.

The first impression: 'Zangwill Here and Very Modest', *New York Journal*, 28 Aug 1898, 41.

His conversation: quoted in 'Zangwill's Personality', *American Hebrew*, 381.

His mind seems: 'Man of Epigrams', *Buffalo Press*, 26 Oct 1898, 8.

You feel yourself: quoted in 'Zangwill's Brilliant Success', *American Hebrew*, 422.

If he were ignorant: Theodore Dreiser, 'The Real Zangwill', in Yoshinobu Hakutani, ed., *Selected Magazine Articles of Theodore Dreiser*, New Jersey: Fairleigh Dickinson University Press, 1986, 68.

It was in the spring: Kellner, 'Herzl and Zangwill in Vienna', in Weisgal, ed., *Herzl: A Memorial*, 73.

Chapter 3

Since Dr. Theodore Herzl: 'What Zionism Means', *Brooklyn Daily Eagle*, 24 Jul 1897, 9.

And now: 'New Jerusalem', *Albany Times-Union*, 2 Aug 1897, 4.

On the train: Patai, ed., *Complete Diaries*, 2:575.

It was Herzl: quoted in Ernst Pawel, *Labyrinth of Exile*, 320.

He assumed the entire: Rosenberger, *Herzl As I Remember Him*, 63.

Most of the threads: Patai, ed., *Complete Diaries*, 2:575.

Stage-managing: quoted in Pawel, *Labyrinth of Exile*, 329–30.

The Zionist congress: 'Palestine, the New Zion', *Oswego Daily Times*, 3 Sep 1897, 2.

Every train brings: Patai, ed., *Complete Diaries*, 2:579.

Stirred by earnest: Berthold Feiwel, 'Around the Congress', in Nahon, ed., *Jubilee*, 92.

Writers and journalists: Israel Zangwill, *Dreamers of the Ghetto*, Philadelphia: The Jewish Publication Society of America, 1898, 431.

This parliament: 'Disgraceful Scenes at Basle Convention', *Syracuse Journal*, 27 Jul 1905, 1.

Prominent were: 'My Impressions of the Basle Congress', *JC*, 10 Sep 1897, 10.

Every street corner: 'The New Jerusalem Congress', *Pall Mall Gazette*, 30 Aug 1897, 6.

Everybody came to me: Patai, ed., *Complete Diaries*, 2:586.

Good humour: 'New Jerusalem Congress', *Pall Mall Gazette*, 6.

Never has such: 'The Religious World', *London Daily News*, 18 Aug 1900, 6.

Perhaps the streets: de Haas, *Theodor Herzl*, 1:170.

All possible languages: Feiwel, 'Around the Congress', in Nahon ed., *Jubilee*, 92.

With sunset: de Haas, 'Zionistic Reminiscences', *Maccabaean* 4, no. 5, May 1903, 269.

One of my: Patai, ed., *Complete Diaries*, 2:581.

The first time: Joseph Cowen, 'My Conversion to Zionism', in Weisgal, ed., *Herzl: A Memorial*, 104–6.

The entrance ticket: Feiwel, 'Around the Congress', in Nahon, ed., *Jubilee*, 92–3.

The opening session: quoted in 'The Zionist Congress: Dr. Herzl's Address', *American Hebrew*, 17 Sep 1897, 576.

The great hall: quoted in Nahon, ed., *Jubilee*, 64.

Buzz and buzz: de Haas, *Zionistic Reminiscences*, 269.

To say that: 'The Zionist Congress', *JC*, 3 Sep 1897, 10.

I was greeted: Patai, ed., *Complete Diaries*, 2:583–4.

No man perhaps: de Haas, *Zionistic Reminiscences*, 269.

His voice is: Zangwill, *Dreamers of the Ghetto*, 434–6.

Fellow Delegates: Nellie Straus, ed., *The Congress Addresses of Theodor Herzl*, New York: Federation of American Zionists, 1917, 5–9.

Loud cheers: 'The Zionist Congress', *JC*, 12.

For fifteen: quoted in Alex Bein, *Theodore Herzl: A Biography*, 231–2.

I shall never: Bernard Horwich, *My First Eighty Years*, Chicago: Argus Books, 1939, 239–40.

At the first: Kellner, 'Herzl and Zangwill in Vienna', in Weisgal, ed., *Herzl: A Memorial*, 73.

Zangwill began: de Haas, *Zionistic Reminiscences*, 272.

The Congress was: Rosa Sonneschein, 'The Zionist Congress', *American Jewess* 6, no. 1, Oct 1897, 20.

To understand: 'The Zionists', *London Daily News*, 2 Jan 1902, 5.

It seems that: Isaac Cohen, 'The Zionist Congress', *Sunderland Daily Echo*, 31 Aug 1903, 3.

Mostly all address: 'The Zionist Congress', *Yorkshire Post*, 30 Dec 1901, 5.

One out of: Cohen, 'The Zionist Congress', *Sunderland Daily Echo*, 27 Aug 1903, 3.

Once, while Nordau: Patai, ed., *Complete Diaries*, 2:586.

An historic: 'The Zionist Congress at Basle', *Pall Mall Gazette*, 3 Sep 1897, 7.

Amid an impressive: 'Herzl's Address', *American Hebrew*, 576.

It was a simple: 'The Zionist Congress at Basle', *Pall Mall Gazette*, 7.

To describe the fervid: 'Herzl's Address', *American Hebrew*, 576.

Israel Zangwill, who: 'Zionist Congress', *Pall Mall Gazette*, 7.

It was not a question: de Haas, *Zionistic Reminiscences*, 273.

The barely united: 'Zionist Congress', *Pall Mall Gazette*, 7.

The scene continued: de Haas, *Zionistic Reminiscences*, 273.

Chapter 4

Kishineff is a handsome: Michael Davitt, *Within the Pale: The True Story of Anti-Semitic Persecution in Russia*, New York: A.S. Barnes & Co., 1903, 158.

The Russian journals: 'Horrible Deeds in Kishinev', *American Hebrew*, 15 May 1903, 857.

The civilized: 'By Order of the Czar', *Hampshire Telegraph*, 23 May 1903, 6.

As fuller information: 'An Easter Outbreak', *St James's Gazette*, 1 May 1903, 4.

Reports grow hourly: 'Slaughter of Jews Appals the World', *New York Evening World*, 15 May 1903, 1.

The feeling against: 'The Kishineff Atrocities', *New York Independent*, 21 May 1903, 3.

A report was circulated: 'Awful Story Is Too True', *Lockport Journal*, 15 May 1901.

The Kishinev Jews: quoted in 'The Power of Russian Darkness', *American Hebrew*, 22 May 1903, 11.

The riots began: 'The Kishineff Outrages', *Evening Mail*, 14 Aug 1903, 5.

Street kiosks: 'The Jews in Russia', *Evening Standard*, 1 May 1903, 5.

Bands of half-drunk: 'Summary of the News', *Sheffield Daily Telegraph*, 19 May 1903, 5.

They ripped: 'The Russian Horror', *American Israelite*, 14 May 1903, 6.

We all went: 'Letter Received from Kishineff', *Rochester Democrat and Chronicle*, 31 May 1903, 20.

The interiors: 'The Kishineff Outrages', *Evening Mail*, 5.

The most awful: quoted in 'The Outrages at Kischineff', *JC*, 15 May 1903, 9.

The noise of: quoted in 'The Outrages on the Jews at Kischineff', *JC*, 8 May 1903, 7.

In the meanwhile: Isidore Singer, *Russia at the Bar of the American People*, New York: Funk & Wagnalls, 1904, 12.

All day the riot: 'Summary of the News', *Sheffield Daily Telegraph*, 5.

Early the next: quoted in 'The Outrages on the Jews at Kischineff', *JC*, 7.

I took refuge: 'Frightful Story of Jew Massacre', *Rochester Democrat and Chronicle*, 17 May 1903, 1.

Most of the victims: 'Russia's Internal Troubles', *Sheffield Daily Telegraph*, 1 May 1903, 5.

The men in: 'A Survivor from Kishenev', *New York Evening Post*, 27 May 1903, 3.

Many Jews: 'More Details of the Kishineff Massacre', *NYT*, 16 May 1903, 1.

At five: Singer, *Russia at the Bar of the American People*, 12.

The chief of police: 'A Survivor from Kishenev', *New York Evening Post*, 3.

It is bad enough: 'Now Probing the Massacre of Jews', *Syracuse Evening Herald*, 13 May 1903, 1.

Kishineff has been: 'Russian Jew Massacres', *Manchester Courier*, 12 May 1903, 7.

Last night the city: quoted in 'The Power of Russian Darkness', *American Hebrew*, 11.

The streets resemble: quoted in 'The Kishineff Massacre', *London Daily News*, 16 May 1903, 7.

Gloom and sorrow: quoted in 'The Power of Russian Darkness', *American Hebrew*, 11.

When I arrived: 'The Jews in Russia', *Evening Standard*, 1 May 1903, 5.

Thousands of pillaged: quoted in 'The Power of Russian Darkness', *American Hebrew*, 11.

A dispatch giving: 'Russians Refuse to Protect Jews', *Washington Times*, 18 May 1903, 1.

All of the readers: 'Relief for Russians', *Pokeepsie Evening Enterprise*, 18 May 1903, 5.

The outrages are: 'Editorial', *Ithaca Daily Journal*, 18 May 1903, 4.

The murderous: 'Anti-Semitism', *Shields Daily News*, 9 May 1903, 3.

The leopard: 'The Kischineff Tragedy', *The Jewish Exponent*, 8 May 1903, 4.

The outlook for: 'The Kishineff Massacre', *Belfast News-Letter*, 27 May 1903, 10.

No one can read: quoted in 'The Power of Russian Darkness', *American Hebrew*, 11.

Every American: Cyrus Adler, ed., *The Voice of America on Kishineff*, Philadelphia: The Jewish Publication Society of America, 1904, 124.

I need not: ibid., 472, 476.

What is the lesson: 'Eyes of Jews All Over the World Turned to Zion by the Kishineff Atrocities', *Brooklyn Daily Eagle*, 31 May 1903, 3.

Such persecution: 'The World-Wide Zionist Movement among Jews', 20 May 1903, 4.

It is possible 'Editorial', *Batavia Daily News*, 10 Jun 1903, 2.

The news from: 'Clock of Time Is Put Back by the Slaying of Jews in Kishenev, Russia, Says Zangwill to the Enquirer Readers', *Cincinnati Enquirer*, 16 May 1903, 1.

Kishinev is not: Patai, ed., *Complete Diaries*, 4:1501.

Chapter 5

One mark of: Winston S. Churchill, *Great Contemporaries*, London: Thornton Butterworth, 1937, 61, 72.

I am thinking: Patai, ed., *Complete Diaries*, 2:644.

Talked yesterday: ibid., 4:1360, 1363.

With Chamberlain: ibid., 4:1473.

The whole country: quoted in Adam Rovner, *In the Shadow of Zion*, 52–3.

If Dr. Herzl: quoted in Robert G. Weisbord, *African Zion*, 30.

My personal: quoted in Bein, *Herzl: A Biography*, 494.

By the time: 'My Morning Paper', *Sketch*, 26 Aug 1903, 20.

Five congresses: Isaac Cohen, 'Palestine for the Jews', *Sunderland Daily Echo*, 18 Aug 1903, 5.

How the movement: 'The Sixth Zionist Congress', *JC*, 21 Aug 1903, 16.

The attendance: 'The Zionist Congress', *Leeds Mercury*, 22 Aug 1903, 4.

A conservative: 'Sixth International Zionist Congress', *American Hebrew*, 28 Aug 1903, 463.

As on past occasions: 'Our London Letter', *Manchester Courier*, 29 Jun 1903, 6.

The delegates began: Abram Lipsky, 'Sixth International Zionist Congress', *American Hebrew*, 4 Sep 1903, 495.

Basel was strewn: Leon Zolotkoff, 'For a New Zion in East Africa', *Chicago Tribune*, 13 Sep 1903, 2.

Three days before: Gotthard Deutsch, 'Zionism: Notes about the Sixth Congress', *American Israelite*, 10 Sep 1903, 4.

Those who were: 'The Zionist Congress', *Manchester Guardian*, 1 Sep 1903, 12.

The Sixth Zionist: Lipsky, 'Sixth Congress', *American Hebrew*, 495.

80–100 delegates: Deutsch, 'Notes', *American Israelite*, 4.

Basle has grown: 'A Survey', *JC*, 4 Sep 1903, 13. 6

It was an impatient: Levin, *The Arena*, 255.

A little after: Cohen, 'Zionist Congress', *Sunderland Daily Echo*, 3.

Wave after wave: 'The Zionist Congress', *Manchester Guardian*, 12.

He did not wait: Lipsky, 'Sixth Congress', *American Hebrew*, 495.

Fellow delegates: Straus, ed., *Congress Addresses*, 32–8.

The offer took: 'The Zionist Congress', *Tablet*, 29 Aug 1903, 3.

I was sitting: Shmarya Levin, *Forward from Exile: The Autobiography of Shmarya Levin*, Philadelphia: Jewish Publication Society of America, 1967, 80.

The effect: Chaim Weizmann, *Trial and Error*, 111.

When the map: Levin, *The Arena*, 258.

The first word: Zolotkoff, 'For a New Zion', *Chicago Tribune*, 2.

When a young: A. H. Reich, 'In Memoriam', in Weisgal, ed., *Herzl: A Memorial*, 122.

No one was mistaken: Weizmann, *Trial and Error*, 113.

After his speech: Martin Buber, 'The Man and the Cause', in *Herzl: A Memorial*, 23.

The congress was: Cohen, 'Zionist Congress', *Sunderland Daily Echo*, 26 Aug 1903, 3.

For days the work: 'Zionist Congress', *Daily Telegraph*, 31 Aug 1903, 5.

Although England: Cohen, 'Zionist Congress', *Sunderland Daily Echo*, 3.

Israel has been: quoted in ibid.

Dr Herzl called: Cohen, 'The Zionist Congress', 29 Aug 1903, 3.

Dr. Nordau stood: Zolotkoff, 'For a New Zion', *Chicago Tribune*, 2.

Before attaining: 'Dr Herzl's Speech', *JC*, 28 Aug 1903, supplement, iii.

Max Nordau is: Sulzberger, 'An American's View of the Congress', *American Hebrew*, 527.

The tide began: Lipsky, 'Sixth International Zionist Congress', *American Hebrew*, 11 Sep 1903, 529.

The most important: 'Eighth Sitting – Wednesday Afternoon', *JC*, 4 Sep 1903, 12.

Everywhere there was: quoted in Gur Alroey, *Zionism without Zion*, 28.

At five o'clock: Sulzberger, 'An American's View', *American Hebrew*, 527.

The effect: Weizmann, *Trial and Error*, 115.

Ja, nein: quoted in Alroey, *Zionism without Zion*, 28.

The names of: Weizmann, 'Reminiscences', in Arthur Hertzberg, ed., *The Zionist Idea*, New York: Harper & Row, 1966, 578–83.

The resolution passed: Lipsky, 'Sixth Congress', *American Hebrew*, 529.

The No-Sayers: Levin, *The Arena*, 257.

When the result: Weizmann, *Trial and Error*, 116.

Curiously imagining: 'Mr Zangwill on the East African Scheme', *JC*, 11 Sep 1903, 10–11.

Hats, handkerchiefs: Sulzberger, 'An American's View', *American Hebrew*, 527.

As a protest: 'Zionist Congress', *Manchester Guardian*, 12.

The scene was: Lipsky, 'Sixth Congress', *American Hebrew*, 529.

I was one: Horowitz and Katsis, eds, *Vladimir Jabotinsky's Story of My Life*, 69.

It was the Russian: 'Zionism's Fidelity to Zionism', *Jewish Exponent*, 4 Sep 1903, 4.

The very delegates: Israel Zangwill, 'Zionism and Territorialism', *Fortnightly Review*, 649.

These people have: quoted in Weisbord, *African Zion*, 147.

The last night: Levin, *The Arena*, 258.

As we sat: Weizmann, *Trial and Error*, 116.

It was precisely: quoted in Horowitz, *Vladimir Jabotinsky's Russian Years, 1900–1925,* Bloomington: Indiana University Press, 2020, 35.

He was received: Weizmann, *Trial and Error*, 116–17.

The war against Herzl: Levin, *The Arena*, 259.

Over two thousand: Lipsky, 'Sixth Congress', *American Hebrew*, 495.

At half past: 'The Zionist Congress: The Final Sitting', *JC*, 3 Sep 1897, 14.

The closing of: Lipsky, 'Sixth Congress', *American Hebrew*, 529.

This has been: 'Dr. Herzl's Closing Speech', *JC*, 4 Sep 1903, 13.

When Herzl said: Lipsky, 'Sixth Congress', *American Hebrew*, 495.

It seems to me: quoted in Shmuel Katz, *Lone Wolf: A Biography of Vladimir (Ze'ev) Jabotinsky*, New York: Barricade Books, 1996, 1:53.

He uttered the words: Levin, *The Arena*, 259.

Dr. Herzl restored: 'Herzl's Closing Speech', *JC*, 13.

President Herzl's: Zolotkoff, 'For a New Zion', *Chicago Tribune*, 2.

The scene went on, 'Herzl's Closing Speech', *JC*, 13.

Dr. Herzl immediately: Lipsky, 'Sixth Congress', *American Hebrew*, 529.

Theodor Herzl left: 'The Leader', *JC*, 4 Sep 1903, 14.

The Sixth Congress: Patai, ed., *Complete Diaries*, 4:1547–8.

Chapter 6

England Offers Jews: 'England Offers Jews a Country', *Chicago Tribune*, 24 Aug 1903, 2.

The English Government: 'Editorial', *Birmingham Daily Gazette*, 7 Sep 1903, 4.

The sensational: quoted in 'Back to Zion', *Peterhead Sentinel*, 7 Nov 1903, 6.

It is a noble: 'Zionist Congress', *Daily Telegraph*, 31 Aug 1903, 5.

In no other nation: 'Editorial', *Manchester Evening News*, 1 Sep 1903, 2.

British East Africa is: 'The New Zion', *Newcastle Daily Chronicle*, 7 Sep 1903, 9.

It is not too much: Roger P. Barnum, 'England's Plan to Forward the Zionist Movement', *Topeka State Journal*, 5 Oct 1903, 8.

A crowded meeting: 'Zangwill on the East African Scheme', *JC*, 10.

British east Africa has: 'England Offers Jews a Country', *Chicago Tribune*, 2.

The proffered territory: Barnum, 'England's Plan', *Topeka State Journal*, 8.

This plateau: 'Our London Correspondence', *Manchester Guardian*, 7 Dec 1904, 6.

Here we have: 'Sir Charles Eliot on East Africa and the Zionist Colony', *JC*, 24 Mar 1905, 12.

The country is of noble: Sir Harry Johnston, *The Uganda Protectorate*, 23–30.

The green forest: Edward Julian, 'Wealth of Uganda', *Barton County Democrat*, 10 Jan 1902, 6.

Although the territory: Barnum, 'England's Plan', *Topeka State Journal*, 8.

Excursionists will see: Johnston, *Uganda Protectorate*, London: Hutchinson & Co, 1904, 34.

The native trouble: 'Eliot on East Africa', *JC*, 12.

The country which: 'Zionists' Promised Land', *New York Daily News*, 7 Oct 1903, 4.

The two iron streaks: Winston S. Churchill, *My African Journey*, Toronto: William Briggs, 1909, 3, 8.

It is not improbable: 'Zionists' Promised Land', *New York Daily News*, 4.

Under the stimulus: 'England Offers Jews a Country', *Chicago Tribune*, 2.

The experiment: 'The New Zion', *Western Morning News*, 28 Aug 1903, 8.

Zionism passes: 'Zionist Congress', *Daily Telegraph*, 5.

Naturally the offer: 'Editorial', *Manchester Evening News*, 2.

Would it be profitable: Julius I. Goldstein, 'Not Uganda but Palestine for the Jews', *New York Sun*, 14 Sep 1903, 4.

We can understand: 'Zionism without Zion', *JC*, 28 Aug 1903, 15.

It is said: 'Zionists' Promised Land', *New York Daily News*, 4.

We have received: 'The Zionists and East Africa', *The Times*, 29 Aug 1903, 7.

A white population: 'The Zionists', *Northampton Mercury*, 28 Aug 1903, 5.

I think that it: quoted in 'Jewish African Colony', *Westminster Gazette*, 4 Sep 1903, 6.

The result would: Lucien Wolf, 'Lord Lansdowne and the Zionists', *The Times*, 28 Aug 1903, 5.

Is it to be: Arnold White, 'Is It to Be "Jewganda?"', *Daily Express*, 4 Sep 1903, 4.

The aspirations: 'Editorial', *The Times*, 7 Sep 1903, 7.

Chapter 7

Israel Zangwill to Marry: 'Israel Zangwill to Marry', *NYT*, 29 Oct 1903, 1.

The friends of: 'London Letter', *Western Daily Press*, 2 Nov 1903, 6.

A sensation: 'Chit-Chat', *Shields Daily Gazette*, 30 Oct 1903, 2.

Zangwill's betrothal: 'Reflections on Intermarriage', *New York Evening Telegram*, 11 Apr 1903, 3.

Miss Ayrton's tastes: 'Our London Letter', *Aberdeen Press*, 3 Nov 1903, 5.

The bride has: 'News of Two Capitals', *New-York Daily Tribune*, 29 Nov 1903, 4.

Miss Ayrton also: 'Zangwill's Bride-to-be', *Washington Post*, 8 Nov 1903, ES5.

Early to-day: 'Fashionable Marriages', *Westminster Gazette*, 26 Nov 1903, 12.

After the ceremony: 'Mr. Zangwill's Marriage', *Daily Mirror*, 27 Nov 1903, 5.

Professor and Mrs: 'Bridegroom's Original Present to His Bride', *Yorkshire Evening Post*, 27 Nov 1903, 4.

The presents were: 'Zangwill's Marriage', *Daily Mirror*, 5.

The presents could: 'Fashionable Marriages', *Evening Standard*, 27 Nov 1903, 8.

The clever author: 'Fashion and Gossip', *Elgin Courant*, 4 Dec 1903, 6.

The bride was quite: 'A Mirror of Modes', *London Daily News*, 30 Nov 1903, 12.

Miss Ayrton is: 'Zion Wedding', *Daily Express*, 27 Nov 1903, 5.

Beautiful, tall: Florence Brooks, 'Zangwill Talks About East African Zion', *NYT*, 23 Oct 1904, 28.

Her soft voice: H. P. Zangwill Horn, 'The Magic Mirror: Portrait of the Zangwill Family',

Jewish Monthly 5, no. 4, Jul 1951, 213–17.

She has black eyes: 'Israel Zangwill's Future Wife, Miss Edith Ayrton, Is a Chemist, a Gifted Young Authoress, a Beauty As Well, and a Gentile', *New York Sunday Telegraph*, 1 Nov 1903, 4.

Seeing this delightfully: Harte, 'Zangwill Chats of Zion and Art', *New York Herald*, M3.

The new Mrs. Zangwill: 'Girls' Gossip', *Truth*, 3 Dec 1903, 52.

Although Miss Ayrton: 'Zangwill's Bride-to-be', *Washington Post*, ES5

Mr. Zangwill made: 'The Jews and East Africa: Interview with Mr. Zangwill', *Manchester Guardian*, 22 Jun 1904, 5.

Chapter 8

Ever since: 'Dr. Herzl's Illness', *Jewish Exponent*, 3 Jun 1904, 4.

My physicians: Patai, ed., *Complete Diaries*, 4:1623–4.

I don't know: Rosenberger, *Herzl As I Remember Him*, 167

Theodor Herzl came: quoted in Pawel, *Labyrinth of Exile*, 522–3.

I was called: de Haas, *Theodor Herzl*, 2:242–9.

In a beautiful spot: 'The Late Dr. Herzl', *JC*, 10.

A strange day: quoted in Pawel, *Labyrinth of Exile*, 31.

The library: 'Late Herzl', *JC*, 10.

The coffin lay: Rosenberger, *Herzl As I Remember Him*, 240.

In front of: quoted in 'Late Herzl', *JC*, 10.

The vast gathering: ibid.

I walked: Rosenberger, *Herzl As I Remember Him*, 241.

The bulk: quoted in 'Late Herzl', *JC*, 10.

The procession was: Zweig, *World of Yesterday*, 91.

Cheek by jowl: 'Late Herzl', *JC*, 10.

The dark mass: quoted in Amos Elon, *Herzl*, 402.

The greatest procession: Levin, *The Arena*, 259.

We were now: 'Herzl's Funeral', *American Hebrew*, 22 Jul 1904, 252.

Herzl's body: 'Late Herzl', *JC*, 10.

For him it was: quoted in Pawel, *Labyrinth of Exile*, 530.

He died at: quoted in Leon Simon, 'Herzl and Ahad Ha-am', in Weisgal, ed., *Herzl: A Memorial*, 89–91.

We sat at midnight: "'High Tragedy": Israel Zangwill's Tribute to Herzl', *Jewish Exponent*, 2 Sep 1904, 7.

Chapter 9

Zionist Movement: 'Zionist Movement without a Leader', *Syracuse Journal*, 2 Dec 2 1904, 10.

One wonders: quoted in 'The Zionist Congress', *Northern Whig*, 4 Aug 1905, 8.

The future: 'The Head of the Zionist Movement', *Leeds Mercury*, 9 Jul 1904, 6.

It is, of course: 'The Dead Leader', *American Hebrew*, 8 Jul 1904, 200.

Some favor: 'Without a Leader', *Syracuse Journal*, 10.

Since the death: 'Israel Zangwill, Dreamer of the Ghetto', *Washington Evening Star*, 28 Jan 1905, 7.

There has been: 'Dinner to Mr. and Mrs. I. Zangwill', *JC*, 7 Apr 1905, 12.

Mr. Zangwill sails: 'Mr. Zangwill Sails for New York', *NYT*, 13 Oct 1904, 6.

Israel Zangwill, author: 'Zangwill's Zionism', *New-York Daily Tribune*, 12 Dec 1904, 6.

On previous visits: 'Zangwill's Visit', *Jewish Exponent*, 21 Oct 1904, 4.

Israel Zangwill, with 'Israel Zangwill's Mission', *New York Sun*, 20 Oct 1904, 6.

We have in sight: quoted in 'Zangwill, Zionism and Judaism', *American Hebrew*, 11 Nov 1904, 694.

Mr. Zangwill has: Frank G. Carpenter, 'Jews Plan to Build New Zion in East Africa', *Atlanta Constitution*, 27 Nov 1904, F7.

Walking to and fro: Brooks, 'Zangwill Talks About East African Zion', *NYT*, 28.

Any territory: Zangwill, 'Zionism and East Africa', *Menorah* 37, no. 6, Dec 1904, 335.

A commission: 'Our London Correspondence', *Manchester Guardian*, 7 Dec 1904, 6.

It is announced: 'The Zionists and East Africa', *Leeds Mercury*, 17 Dec 1904, 16.

If their report: Cyrus C. Adams, 'The Home in Africa Offered by England to the Jews', *NYT*, 18 Dec 1904, 39.

Chapter 10

Even the torrid: 'Zion and East Africa', *Sketch*, 9 Aug 1905, 12.

The preparations: 'Rivalry of Factions Threatens Zionists', *Syracuse Journal*, 26 Jul 1905, 1.

Basel is transformed: 'Rivalry of Factions', *Syracuse Journal*, 1.

When I entered: 'The Seventh Zionist Congress', *JC*, 28 Jul 1905, 13.

The difficult question: 'Rivalry of Factions', *Syracuse Journal*, 1.

Next to the: 'The Zionist Congress at Basle', *American Israelite*, 27 Jul 1905, 7.

This morning: Maurice Leon, 'Hebrews of All the Nations Gather at Basle to Plan New Jewish State', *Cincinnati Enquirer*, 28 Jul 1905, 6.

The great congress: 'Jews Still Turn to Zion', *New York Sun*, 27 Aug 1905, 8.

With admirable oratory: Leon, 'Hebrews of All the Nations Gather', *Cincinnati Enquirer*, 6.

A request was made: Julius H. Greenstone, 'The Zionist Congress: Some Preliminary Incidents', *Jewish Exponent*, 11 Aug 1905, 6.

Then the great crowd: Leon, 'Hebrews of All the Nations Gather', *Cincinnati Enquirer*, 6.

When I asked: Zolotkoff, 'Zionists Greatly Miss Old Leader', *Chicago Tribune*, 20 Aug 1905, 13.

In the afternoon: 'Fatherland for Jew', *Washington Post*, 27 Aug 1905, B9.

Delegate Leopold: 'The Congress of Zionists', *Syracuse Daily Journal*, 28 Jul 1905, 1.

The commission had returned: Zolotkoff, 'Zionists Greatly Miss Old Leader', *Chicago Tribune*, 13.

Unfortunately for: 'A Great Aspiration', *Leeds Mercury*, 31 Jul 1905, 4.

Committee Sent to Africa: 'Zionists Report Against Offer of Uganda Colony', *Chicago Daily Tribune*, 29 Jul 1903, 3.

The formal debate: Greenstone, 'Zionist Congress', *Jewish Exponent*, 6.

A special sitting: Leon, 'Zionists Cling to Old Canaan', *Cincinnati Enquirer*, 31 Jul 1905, 5.

Nordau was in the chair: Deutsch, 'Dr. Deutsch Writes of Basle Congress', *American Israelite*, 17 Aug 1905, 7.

Israel Zangwill, who: 'Jews Still Turn to Zion', *New York Sun*, 8.

The debate lasted: Leon, 'Zionists Cling to Old Canaan', *Cincinnati Enquirer*, 5.

Six o'clock: 'The Seventh Congress', *JC*, 4 Aug 1905, 21.

The Congress was resumed: 'Zionist Congress', *Manchester Guardian*, 5 Aug 1905, 7.

Just after noon: 'Zangwill Explains His Attack on Nordau', *American Hebrew*, 6 Oct 1905, 518.

The committee presented: Leon, 'Zionists Cling to Old Canaan', *Cincinnati Enquirer*, 5.

Immediately upon: 'Congress of Zionists', *Syracuse Daily Journal*, 1.

I beg to move: 'Seventh Congress', *JC*, 19.

The congress was in: 'Congress of Zionists', *Syracuse Daily Journal*, 1.

Finally the question: Deutsch, 'Basle Congress', *American Israelite*, 7.

Speeches were now: Levin, *The Arena*, 282.

At the seventh Congress: Weizmann, 'Fifty Years of Zionism', in Nahon, ed., *Jubilee*, 13.

Zionists, in a Tumult: 'Zionists, in a Tumult, Reject British Offer', *NYT*, 31 Jul 1905, 4.

The Uganda Project: 'The Uganda Project Dropped', *Scotsman*, 31 Jul 1905, 8.

Scenes of extraordinary: 'Zion v. Uganda', *Pall Mall Gazette*, 31 Jul 1905, 2.

Even the most: 'Zion and East Africa', *Sketch*, 12.

From Basle: 'Notes and Comments', *Yorkshire Post*, 31 Jul 1905, 6.

The Zangwill party: 'The Zionist Congress', *New-York Tribune*, 3 Aug 1905, 6.

The victors restrained: 'Seventh Congress', *JC*, 21.

Zangwill was granted: Greenstone, 'Zionist Congress', *Jewish Exponent*, 6.

Mr. Zangwill himself: 'Zion v. Uganda', *Pall Mall Gazette*, 2.

Thirty delegates: 'Fatherland for Jew', *Washington Post*, B9.

A group, consisting: Levin, *The Arena*, 282.

From that time: 'Jews Still Turn to Zion', *New York Sun*, 8.

Zionists Split: 'Zionists Split', *Ithaca Daily News*, 2 Aug 1905, 1.

The Territorial: 'Basel Zionists Split in Twain', *Syracuse Journal*, 1 Aug 1905, 2.

Israel Zangwill, the noted: 'Zangwill Leader of Zion Secessionists', *Brooklyn Standard-Union*, 2 Aug 1905, 6.

Should there be: 'Zangwill's Manifesto', *American Hebrew*, 8 Sep 1905, 409.

The homing instinct: 'Zangwill Writes on Home for "Wandering Jew"', *Syracuse Journal*, 19 May 1906, 6.

The restriction: 'Mr. Zangwill's Manifesto', *JC*, 25 Aug 1905, 8.

Chapter 11

A race of some: 'Mr. Zangwill at Leeds', *JC*, 18 Jun 1909, 23–4.

Earth-hunger: 'Mr. Zangwill's Address', *JC*, 6 Mar 1908, 14.

ITOism does not: 'Itoism, Brilliant Address by Mr. Israel Zangwill: Territorialism as Practical Politics', 4 Apr 1913, 24.

There must exist: 'Zangwill at Leeds', *JC*, 25.

The Jews must leave: quoted in 'Zangwill Urges Jews to Quit Russian Soil', *NYT*, 10 Nov 1905, 2.

There lies: 'Zangwill's Address', *JC*, 6 Mar 1908, 14.

If we cannot: quoted in 'Jewish Autonomy', *Sunday Star*, 17 Jun 1906, 5.

Search for a New: 'Search for a New Judæa', *Globe*, 2 Apr 1909, 11.

As everyone knows: 'London Letter: Jewish Colonisation', *Manchester Courier*, 10 May 1909, 6.

Zangwill's New: 'Zangwill's New Palestine', *Chicago Tribune*, 28 Mar 1909, 2.

The Jewish Territorial: 'The Jews and Cyrenaica', *Morning Post*, 2 Apr 1909, 9.
The interior of: Zangwill, 'Zionism and Territorialism', *Fortnightly Review*, 651.
Cyrenaica is a great: 'An Unpromising Land', *Evening Standard*, 3 Apr 1909, 9.
Its most striking: 'The Jews and Cyrenaica', *Morning Post*, 9.
This beautiful: 'The Jewish World', *Daily Telegraph*, 27 Mar 1909, 5.
It would appear: 'Notes and Comments', *Yorkshire Post*, 27 Mar 1909, 8.
There are forests: 'Day by Day', *Irish News*, 5 Apr 1909, 7.
It is cooled: 'Summary of News', *Freeman's Journal*, 29 Mar 1909, 6.
In view of: 'The Inhabitants of Cyrenaica', *Staffordshire Sentinel*, 31 Mar 1910, 3.
Unexplored, almost: 'A Delectable Land', *Falkirk Herald*, 25 Oct 1911, 3.
It is possible: 'The Jewish World', *Daily Telegraph*, 5.
The report of: 'The Jews and Cyrenaica', *Morning Post*, 9.
Professor Gregory returned: Zangwill, 'Zionism and Territorialism',
    Fortnightly Review, 651.
An Unpromising Land: 'An Unpromising Land', *Evening Standard*, 9.
The report was far: 'To-day's Gossip: Barren Cyrenaica', *Sunderland Daily
    Echo*, 5 Oct 1911, 5.
Waterless Cyrenaica: 'Search for a New Judæa', *Globe*, 11.
Cyrenaica turns out: 'Zangwill and the Hesperides', *NYT*, 3 Apr 1909, 8.
Mr. Zangwill does: 'Zionist Scheme Fails', *London Daily News*, 2 Apr 1909, 7.
A few ancient vases: Zangwill, 'Zionism and Territorialism', *Fortnightly
    Review*, 652.
The disappointing: 'Our London Correspondence', *Manchester Guardian*,
    3 May 1909, 6.
Mesopotamia New Home: quoted in 'New Home for Jews', *Washington Post*,
    20 May 1909, 6.
For the refugee: 'Zangwill at Leeds', *JC*, 25.
Although the bulk: 'One Plan, One People: Speech Delivered by Mr. Zangwill',
    Jewish Exponent, 4 Jun 1909, 9.
Moreover, when: 'Zangwill at Leeds', *JC*, 26.
We are on the eve: 'From Our London Correspondent', *Liverpool Daily Post*,
    10 Jul 1909, 7.
It has transpired: quoted in Moshe Perlmann, 'Paul Haupt and the
    Mesopotamian Project, 1892–1914', *Publications of the American Jewish
    Historical Society* 47, no. 3, 1958, 171.
Australia is Zangwill's: 'Australia Is Zangwill's New Itoland', *Jewish Advocate*,
    5 Aug 1910, 1.
The irrepressible: 'Zangwill's Latest Folly: Wishes to Settle a Million Russian
    Jews in a Desert', *American Israelite*, 22 Sep 1910, 7.
The scheme is still: quoted in 'Zangwill Finds Itoland in Australia', *American
    Hebrew*, 12 Aug 1910, 373.
Some correspondence: 'Zangwill and an Australian Colony', *American
    Hebrew*, 21 Jun 1907, 179.

The **Canadian government:** 'No Colony Land Grants', *American Israelite*, 6 Sep 1906, 6.

The **Jewish Territorial:** 'Editorial', *Greenock Telegraph*, 23 Jan 1909, 6.

An attempt to get: quoted in 'The New Promised Land', *Lyttelton Times*, 7 Sep 1912, 11.

The **Zionist party:** 'Editorial', *New York Evening Post*, 16 Jun 1909, 2.

Chapter 12

Fifty-two William street: Morris D. Waldman, 'The Galveston Movement', *Jewish Social Service Quarterly* 4, no. 3, Mar 1928, 197–8.

Mr Schiff is a kindly: 'Wall Street Men', *Saturday Evening Post*, 22 Jun 1907, 17.

Mr. Schiff is to-day: 'Jacob Schiff the New Money King', *Philadelphia Press*, Jacob H. Schiff Papers, MS-456, American Jewish Archives.

His appearance: Morris D. Waldman, *Nor by Power*, 323.

The **promised land:** 'Mr. Schiff's Address', *American Hebrew*, 2 Aug 1907, 309.

This nation has: Jacob H. Schiff, 'Restriction or Regulation', *Troy Times*, 2 Nov 1907, 7.

Who would imagine: 'Diffuse Immigrants Says Jacob H. Schiff', *NYT*, 19 Jul 1909, 14.

The **Jew of the future:** 'Mr. Schiff on Jerusalem Conditions', *American Hebrew*, 8 May 1908, 10.

A well distributed: 'Diffuse Immigrants Says Schiff', *NYT*, 14.

The **Jew should not:** 'Zionism Utterly Condemned', *American Israelite*, 29 Aug 1907, 5.

As I stand: 'Mr. Schiff's Address', *American Hebrew*, 309 .

With God's help: Jacob H. Schiff, 'Technical Education among Jews', *Menorah* 3, no. 4, Jul 1887, 38.

New York City is: 'Big Wave of Jews Coming', *New-York Tribune*, 17 Dec 1905, 53.

In New York: 'Solving the Immigration Problem', *New York Press*, 30 Sep 1906, 8.

Few outside: 'Big Wave of Jews Coming', *New-York Tribune*, 53.

He finds many: 'Solving the Immigration Problem', *New York Press*, 8.

It is true: 'Jewish Immigrants Are Well Cared For Here', *New York Sun*, 7 Apr 1912, 10.

The **East Side had:** Waldman, *Nor by Power*, 309.

On the East side: Frederick Boyd Stevenson, 'New York's Ghetto', *Waterbury Democrat*, 9 Mar 1901, 3.

When I recall: Henry James, *The American Scene*, London: Chapman and Hall Ltd, 1907, 130–2.

To counteract 'Big Wave of Jews Coming', *New-York Tribune*, 53.

The country is large: 'Notes', *American Israelite*, 17 Apr 1913, 7.

Such men: 'Editorial', *Atlanta Constitution*, 6 Aug 1905, 4.

At the corner: 'Jewish Immigrants Are Well Cared For Here', *New York Sun*, 10.

He is a strange: David Bressler, 'The Removal Work', *Reform Advocate*, 25 Mar 1911, 203.

If the applicant: 'Relieving Congestion in Russian Jewish Quarter', *NYT*, 20 Jan 1907, 33.

A big furniture: 'Finding New Homes for East Side Residents', *New York Tribune*, 1 Nov 1903, 35.

During the past: 'Removal Work', *Jewish Exponent*, 3 May 1907, 4.

Those who are: Bressler, 'The Removal Work', *Reform Advocate*, 206.

Once the immigrant: Waldman, *Nor by Power*, 341.

To take the plunge: Bressler, 'The Removal Work', *Reform Advocate*, 1 Apr 1911, 242.

Schiff made clear: Waldman, *Nor by Power*, 341.

Chapter 13

Though the somewhat: Waldman, *Nor by Power*, 340–1.

It appears: Adler, ed., *Schiff; His Life and Letters*, 2:97–8.

Surely the carrying: quoted in Alroey, *Zionism without Zion*, 245.

I am firmly convinced: quoted in Zosa Szajkowski, 'Paul Nathan, Lucien Wolf, Jacob H. Schiff and the Jewish Revolutionary Movements in Eastern Europe 1903–1917', *Jewish Social Studies* 29, no. 1, 1967, 24.

The difficulty: quoted in Naomi W. Cohen, 'Jacob H. Schiff: A Study in American Jewish Leadership', Hanover, NH: Brandeis University Press, 1990, 165.

Zangwill compromised: Waldman, 'Galveston Movement', 200.

My opinion: quoted in Isaac M. Fein, 'Israel Zangwill and American Jewry', *American Jewish Historical Quarterly* 60, no. 1, 1970, 29.

The Industrial Removal Office: Adler, ed., *Schiff*, 2:98–9.

As the plan: Waldman, *Nor by Power*, 341.

Baltimore was rejected: Waldman, 'Galveston Movement', 200.

I advised against: Waldman, *Nor by Power*, 341.

I remember the thrill: Waldman, 'Galveston Movement', 201.

"Well,' said Mr Schiff: Waldman, *Nor by Power*, 342.

On November 7th: Waldman, 'Galveston Movement', 201.

There is something: Bill Nye, 'Nye's Texas Rambles', *Fairhaven Herald*, 10 May 1891, 6.

The scenery: 'A Texas Ranger', *Ottawa Free Trader*, 5 May 1883, 2.

Galveston is the prettiest: 'Letter from M. J. Moore', *Bolivar Breeze*, 2 Apr 1914, 2.

The streets are: 'A Southern Watering Place', *Paterson Evening News*, 23 Aug 1893, 7.

This is certainly 'Letter from Texas', *Jackson Daily Clarion*, 31 Jan 1867, 2.

Many of the streets: 'Letter from the Lone Star State', *Plattsburgh Republican*, 29 Dec 1897, 2.

This is: quoted in 'The City of Oleanders', *Londonderry Sifter*, 2 Apr 1885, 1.

On every side: 'To the Rio Grande and Beyond', *Weymouth Gazette*, 11 Feb 1876, 2.

It will soon be: 'Galveston Defies the Sea', *Eagle River Review*, 21 Jul 1905, 4.

The world knows: Edward Mott, 'Texan Truths', *Hammondsport Herald*, 11 Apr 1906, 2.

Many asserted: 'New Galveston', *Daily Argus*, 1 Sep 1905, 7.

A similar storm: William E. Curtis, 'To Save the City, Building a Great Wall around Galveston', *Washington Evening Star*, 5 Jul 1905, 12.

Frame residences: 'Galveston Almost Annihilated', *Liberty Southern Herald*, 14 Sep 1900, 2.

The storm swept: 'Trail of Tornado', *Maysville Evening Bulletin*, 12 Sep 1900, 1.

Every able bodied: 'The Galveston Horror', *Liberty Southern Herald*, 21 Sep 1900, 2.

A beautiful city: 'Galveston', *London Daily News*, 17 Sep 1900, 6.

The story of the: 'How the City of Galveston Is Being Rapidly Rebuilt', *Pittsburgh Daily Post*, 30 Nov 1902, 31.

At the cost: Mott, 'Texan Truths', *Hammondsport Herald*, 2.

Today, a new: John Quill, 'Under Six Flags: John Quill's Story of Wonderful Texas', *Daily Kennebec Journal*, 1 Nov 1905, 11.

Chapter 14

Ladies and Gentlemen: 'The ITO and Its New Activity: Israel Zangwill Speaks on the Distribution of Immigration in America', *American Hebrew*, 18 Jan 1907, 272.

Russian Jews: 'Russian Jews for Texas', *NYT*, 8 Jun 1907, 1.

ITOLAND, U.S.A.: 'ITOLAND, U.S.A.', *Daily Express*, 3 Aug 1908, 3.

Mr. Zangwill Favors: 'Political Items', *Auburn Citizen*, 22 Apr 1910, 4.

The latest attempt: 'Jewish Immigration', *Argus*, 6 Jan 1907, 4.

Jews leaving Europe: 'To Send Jews West', *Auburn Citizen*, 8 Mar 1907, 2.

Texas Colony: 'Texas Colony for Jews', *Columbia Republican*, 28 Dec 1906, 1.

Is America likely: 'Helping the Jew "Back to the Land"', *Chicago Livestock World*, 30 Aug 1907, 1.

There is not: 'To Send Them to Galveston', *Washington Evening Star*, 1 Jan 1907, 20.

Mr. Zangwill denied: 'Half a Million to Hebrew Colony', *New York Herald*, 31 Dec 1906, 9.

Though private rumours: 'Mr Schiff and the Galveston Scheme', *JC*, 27 Nov 1908, 12.

In private conversation: 'Our New York Letter', *Port Jervis Evening Gazette*, 26 Oct 1899, 4.

W. R. Wheeler: 'Dream of Jews Lost in America', *Chicago Sunday Tribune*, 27 Oct 1907, 4.

Mr. Alexander Harkavy: 'Euthanasia of Hebrews Here', *New York Herald*, 8 Jan 1907, 9.

Mr. Israel Zangwill appears: 'The Euthanasia of the Race: The New Jewry of New York', *American Hebrew*, 18 Jan 1907, 269.

Chapter 15

It was with a light: Waldman, 'Galveston Movement', 202.

Rabbi Henry Cohen: Waldman, *Nor by Power*, 342.

He was 'the Rabbi': Waldman, 'Galveston Movement', 203.

Galvestonians are proud: 'A Great Texan, A Great American – Dr. Henry Cohen', *Galveston Week*, 28 May 1898, 5.

You can pick up: Webb Waldron, 'The Busiest Man in Town', *Rotarian* 54, no. 2, Feb 1939, 38.

In all the state: Irve Tunick, 'An American Ballad', *Frontiers of Faith*, NBC Television, 15 May 1955, quoted in A. Stanley Dreyfus, ed., *Henry Cohen, Messenger of the Lord,* New York: Bloch, 1963, 77.

It is an experience: Jacob R. Marcus, 'Necrology: Henry Cohen', *Publication of the American Jewish Historical Society* 42, no. 4, Jun 1953, 455.

At his home: Bob Nesbitt, 'Dr. Cohen Says He Has No Time to Think of Retiring', *Galveston News*, 24 Apr 1938, 6.

Although born: 'Dual Anniversary of Rabbi Cohen, Temple Friday', *Galveston News*, 7, Henry Cohen Papers 79-0033, News Clips Honoring Cohen 1933–1943, Rosenberg Library.

Dr. Cohen, a classmate: Wilhelmina Beane, 'Treasure of Ancient Manuscripts, Books Owned by Galveston Rabbi', *Houston Press,* 19 Apr 1938, 1.

As boys: Henry Cohen, 'Israel Zangwill: An Appreciation' (manuscript) , Essays and Themes, Undated, Box 3M326, Henry Cohen Papers, Dolph Briscoe Center for American History, The University of Texas at Austin.

It was the day: Waldman, *Nor by Power*, 203.

Temple B'nai Israel: 'Columbus and the Jews', *Galveston Daily News*, 23 Oct 1892, 5.

The Galveston idea: Zangwill, 'The ITO to Land in North Africa', *American Hebrew*, 27 Dec 1907, 201.

The time came: Alexander Z. Gurwitz, *Memories of Two Generations: A Yiddish Life in Russia and Texas*, ed. Bryan Edward Stone, trans. Rabbi Amram Prero, Tuscaloosa: The University of Alabama Press, 269–74.

Colony of Hebrews: 'Colony of Hebrews Sailing for Texas', *Washington Times*, 8 Jun 1907, 5.

The steamer Cassel: 'Russian Jews for Texas', *NYT*, 1.

After spending a month: 'Just Landed: How "Future Citizens" Enter the United States at Galveston', *Houston Post*, 18 Sep 1909, 19.

The ship stopped: Gurwitz, *Memories*, 292.

In less time: 'Just Landed', *Houston Post*, 19.

Dressed in the: C. H. Abbot, 'To Jerusalem by Way of American Farms', *San Francisco Call*, 25 Aug 1907.

Nearly all: 'Jewish Immigrants', *B'nai B'rith Messenger*, 9 Aug 1907, 8.

To a stranger: 'Just Landed', *Houston Post*, 19.

We had to exit: Gurwitz, *Memories*, 292–3.

The immigrants, after: 'Jewish Immigrants', *B'nai B'rith Messenger*, 8.

Every preparation: Abbot, 'To Jerusalem', *San Francisco Call*.

Each one: quoted in Gary Dean Best, 'Jacob H. Schiff's Galveston Movement', *American Jewish Archives Journal* 30, no. 1, Apr 1978, 54.

The intelligence: Rabbi Henry Cohen, 'The Galveston Immigration Movement', *Jewish Herald*, 5 Feb 1909, 1.

Rabbi Cohen was: : 'Jewish Immigrants', *B'nai B'rith Messenger*, 8.

The examination: Cohen, 'Galveston Movement', *Jewish Herald*, 1.

I was busy: Waldman, *Nor by Power*, 344.

The spirit of: Abbot, 'To Jerusalem', *San Francisco Call*.

The first load: quoted in 'Immigration', *Galveston Daily News*, 17 Aug 1907, 2.

With the arrival: 'Arrive at Galveston', *Detroit Free Press*, 30 Jun 1907, 9.

As soon as: Gurwitz, *Memories*, 294–300.

Our first group: Cohen, 'Galveston Movement', *Jewish Herald*, 1.

There is always: 'Just Landed', *Houston Post*, 19.

All sorts: quoted in 'The Galveston Movement', *American Israelite*, 25 Jun 1908, 1.

There is scarcely: Zangwill, *A Land of Refuge*, London: Jewish Territorial Organization, 1907, 22.

Chapter 16

One of the most: 'Itoism, Zionism, and Things in General: An Interview for the JC with Mr. Israel Zangwill', *JC*, 12 Jun 1908, 16.

I shut my eyes: 'The Writing of Plays – by the Men Who Do It', *NYT*, 18 Oct 1908, 5.

Dear President Roosevelt: quoted in Aviva F. Taubenfeld, *Rough Writing: Ethnic Authorship in Theodore Roosevelt's America*, New York: NYU Press, 2008, 13.

The mighty tide: Theodore Roosevelt, *American Ideals: and Other Essays, Social and Political*, New York: Putnam, 1904, 65–9.

On board the steamer: 'Zangwill Here', *Billboard*, 10 Oct 1908, 6.

As a general: 'News of the Theaters', *Chicago Sunday Tribune*, 10 Jul 1904.

Several friends: 'Israel Zangwill in New York', *American Hebrew*, 25 Sep 1908, 505.

Mr. Zangwill was: 'Mr. Zangwill in Town', *Jewish Exponent*, 16 Oct 1908, 2.

There is still: Harte, 'Zangwill Chats of Zion and Art', *New York Herald*, M3.

His face has grown: Brainin, 'Zangwill – Twelve Years After', *American Hebrew*, 28.

Zangwill Melts: 'Zangwill Melts Us Up into Play', *Brooklyn Daily Star*, 5 Oct 1908, 2.

Tomorrow evening: 'At the Theaters', *Washington Post*, 4 Oct 1908, M6.

A great audience: 'The Melting Pot: Walker Whiteside Tells of the "Brewing" of the Great Play', *Rome Daily Sentinel*, 29 Dec 1909, 2–3.

The President sat: quoted in 'Zangwill's Play Produced', *Jewish Exponent*, 9 Oct 1908, 2.

President Roosevelt occupied: Simon Wolf, *The Presidents I Have Known from 1860–1918*, Washington DC: Byron S. Adams, 1918, 282.

Even Washington: quoted in 'Zangwill's Play Produced', *Jewish Exponent*, 2.

Mr Zangwill shows: 'God's Crucible', *Nation*, 31 Jan 1914, 739–40.

The hero: 'Mr. Zangwill's New Dramatic Gospel', *Current Literature* 45, no. 6, Dec 1908, 671–2.

David is rather: 'The Playgoer', *New York Tribune*, 17 Oct 1909, 6.

Walker Whiteside preserved: 'The Tragedy of Kishineff: Israel Zangwill's "Melting Pot"', *American Hebrew*, 10 Sep 1909, 467.

David Quixano has: '"The Melting Pot" by Mr. Zangwill', *NYT*, 25 Sep 1909, 22.

David loses: 'Player Folk', *New York Press*, 11 Aug 1909, 4.

The real crux: quoted in 'The Week in New York', *Billboard*, 18 Sep 1909, 6.

At the sight: 'Music and Drama', *New York Evening Post*, 7 Sep 1909, 7.

In the climax: 'Zangwill's New Play Has Thrills', *Chicago Daily Tribune*, 6 Oct 1908, 10.

Walker Whiteside was: 'Notes of Interest to Theatregoers', *New York Evening Telegram*, 7 Sep 1909, 6.

Mr. Whiteside is still: Matthew White, Jr., 'New York Scorns "The Melting Pot"', *Munsey's Magazine* 42, no. 2, Nov 1909, 258. *T-CLP (Melting Pot), Billy Rose Theatre Division, New York Public Library for the Performing Arts, Astor, Lenox and Tilden Foundations.

Out of nowhere: quoted in 'The Drama', *Rochester Democrat*, 17, November 15 1908, p. 17.

He has a resonant: 'The Day in the Playhouse World', *Christian Science Monitor*, 8 Feb 1910 , 7.

The heroine is: 'Zangwill's Play Here', *Baltimore Sun*, 13 Oct 1908, 9.

The fourth act: 'Dramatic Fare Highly Spiced', *San Francisco Chronicle*, 25 Sep 1910, 22.

His symphony: Caroline E. Clark, 'The Melting Pot', *Hartford Courant*, 13 Oct 1909, 6.

He realizes that: 'Playhouse World', *Christian Science Monitor*, 7.

David Quixano delivers: Adolph Klauber, 'The Week's Outlook', *NYT*, 12 Sep 1909, 66.

David and Vera are: 'Mr Zangwill's Play, The Melting Pot', *JC*, 30 Oct 1908, 22.

We hung in: 'Whiteside Tells', *Rome Daily Sentinel*, 2–3.

The audience was: V. Gilmore Iden, 'Roosevelt Is Pleased with Zangwill Play', *Show World*, 10 Oct 1908, 1.

The enthusiasm: 'The Theater', *Washington Evening Star*, 6 Oct 1908, 20.

Certain strong lines: 'Roosevelt Criticises Play', *NYT*, 10 Oct 1908, 9.

President Roosevelt was: 'Zangwill in Town', *Jewish Exponent*, 2.

Again and again: 'President Sees New Play', *Baltimore Sun*, 6 Oct 1908, 12.

Nearly every person: 'Playwright's Wife Lauds White House', *Washington Times*, 8 Oct 1908, 11.

The first night: Edith Zangwill to Mrs. Yorke, Oct 7 1908, Annie Russell Papers, Manuscripts and Archives Division, New York Public Library.

On the following day: 'The News-Harvest Gleaner', *American Hebrew*, 16 Oct 1908, 592.

Mr. Zangwill said: 'Jewish Review', *Brooklyn Daily Eagle*, 30 Oct 1908, 11.

I do not know: quoted in Taubenfeld, *Rough Writing*, 14.

"The Melting Pot" has led: 'Zangwill's New Dramatic Gospel', *Current Literature*, 672.

I have seen: quoted in 'News of the Playhouses', *Christian Science Monitor*, 6.

Has it remained: 'At the Local Playhouses', *Washington Post*, 11 Oct 1908, SM1.

The Melting Pot, written: quoted in Richard L. Bushman et al., eds, *Uprooted Americans: Essays to Honor Oscar Handlin*, Boston: Little, Brown, 1979, 304.

"The Melting Pot" has led: 'Zangwill's New Dramatic Gospel', *Current Literature* , 671–2.

Some persons think: 'Comedy and Drama', *New York Tribune*, 10 Oct 1909, 47.

New Zangwill: 'New Zangwill Play Cheap and Tawdry', *NYT*, 7 Sep 1909, 9.

Candidly, "The Melting Pot": Alan Dale, 'Supremacy of the American Stage', *Cosmopolitan* 48, no. 1, Dec 1909, 78.

What is this: 'Some New York Plays', *The Times*, 24 Nov 1909, 4.

Call it sentimental: 'Tragedy of Kishineff', *American Hebrew*, 467.

The emphasis upon: 'Mr Zangwill's Play', *JC*, 22.

Is it not strange: 'Editorial', *American Hebrew*, 3.

Nations, creeds: 'How a Washington Editor Views Zangwill's Play', *American Hebrew*, 558

We shall be melted: Bernard G. Richards, 'Notes', *American Hebrew*, 557.

It is hard to see: 'How a Washington Editor Views Zangwill's Play', *American Hebrew*, 558.

It is suggested: 'Mr Zangwill's Play', *JC*, 22.

Naturally enough: 'Some New York Plays', *The Times*, 4.

Chapter 17

By the late: Henry Berman, 'The Galveston Movement: A Resume', *American Hebrew*, 19 Jun 1914, 199.

Upon assuming: quoted in Best, 'Schiff's Galveston Movement', 60.

Jacob H. Schiff's: 'Jacob H. Schiff's Immigrants Held Up', *New York World*, 22 Aug 1910, 6.

These aliens: quoted in Best, *Schiff's Galveston Movement*, 62.

It was at a meeting: Waldman, 'Galveston Movement', 199.

Great and far-reaching: quoted in Szajkowski, 'Paul Nathan, Lucien Wolf, Jacob H. Schiff', 26.

Sir: The recent: Adler, ed., *Schiff*, 2:98–9.

It required: Berman, 'The Galveston Movement', *American Hebrew*, 199.

The Jewish Territorial: 'Israel Zangwill Sees a Great Future for the Drama', *NYT*, 4 Jun 1911, 60.

Chapter 18

Kieff, an important: 'Kieff Used as a Center of Emigration Society', *Brooklyn Daily Eagle*, 22 Oct 1909, 14.

The Emigration Regulation: 'Jewish Territorial Organisation: Striking Address by Mr. Zangwill', *JC*, 5 Jul 1912, 20.

Dr. Jochelmann, Vice-President: 'Jewish Territorial Organisation', *JC*, 11 Oct 1912, 38.

According to a cable: 'Jewish Territorial Organisation', *JC*, 25 Oct 1912, 34.

Dr. D. Jockelmann: 'Studying Immigration Laws', *Houston Post*, 7 Nov 1912, 9.

When the steamship: 'Jewish Colonization Planned For', *Brenham Daily Banner*, 8 Nov 1912, 6.

Dr Jochelmann, our Russian: quoted in Maurice Simon, *Speeches, Articles and Letters of Israel Zangwill*, 320.

It is precisely because: Zangwill, 'Territorialism as Practical Politics', *American Hebrew*, 18 Apr 1913, 693.

America is the land: Zangwill, 'Territorialism as Practical Politics', *American Hebrew*, 25 Apr 1913, 757.

Chapter 19

For some years: 'The Search of the Jews for a Land of Refuge', *Sheffield Evening Telegraph*, 22 Jun 1912, 4.

Angola is: 'Angola Is Offered for Zionist Colony', *NYT*, 28 Jun 1912, 8.

Portugal, it is: 'Editorial', *American Hebrew*, 24 May 1912, 99.

Die Welt of last Friday: 'Farther Statement by Senhor Lima on the Angola Project', *JC*, 6 Dec 1912, 36.

The official report: 'Among the Jews', *Hamilton Daily Times*, 18 Jul 1912, 12.

Where lies: 'Mr Zangwill on Territorialism and Zionism', *JC*, 20 Jan 1911, 28.

Chapter 20

Galveston Immigration Bureau: 'Galveston Immigration Bureau to Be Closed', *American Hebrew*, 29 May 1914, 117.

The announcement has: 'The Week', *JC*, 3 Jul 1914, 9.

As for the chief: 'The Galveston Immigration Bureau Discontinued on October 1st', *Jewish Voice*, 30 Oct 1914, 6.

A steerage voyage: 'Bureau to Be Closed', *American Hebrew*, 117.

If Baltimore: 'What Must Be Done about Immigrant Distribution?' *Reform Advocate*, 15 Aug 1914, 28.

This, coupled with: 'Bureau Discontinued', *Jewish Voice*, 6.

The bureau succumbed: quoted in Jack Glazier, *Dispersing the Ghetto*, Ithaca: Cornell University Press, 1998, 60.

From Corpus Christi: Berman, 'The Galveston Movement', *American Hebrew*, 199.

Towns which had: 'What Must Be Done about Immigrant Distribution?' *Reform Advocate*, 28,

The name Galveston: 'Bureau to Be Closed', *American Hebrew*, 117.

The "Galveston movement": 'Mr. Schiff on the Closing of the Bureau', *JC*, 17 Jul 1914, 14.

The Jewish Immigrants': 'Bureau Discontinued', *Jewish Voice*, 6.

It was my privilege: Adler, ed., *Schiff*, 2:111–13.

I have often thought: speech delivered by Edith Zangwill at Jochelman memorial meeting, 1941, A120\209, Central Zionist Archives.

Dr Jochelmann is lying: Zangwill to Schiff, Aug 1914, Central Zionist Archives, A12050-278.

He came over here: Zangwill to Schiff, 22 May1914, American Jewish Archives, MS-456 Schiff 2364/28, Zangwill, Israel, 1914.

It adds to the tragedy: Zangwill to Schiff, 11 Sep 1914, Jacob Schiff Papers, MS-456, American Jewish Archives.

Dear Jochelmann: Zangwill to Jochelmann, Zangwill Papers, A120/53, Central Zionist Archives.

PART TWO

Chapter 21

Young Playwright Who: 'Young Playwright Who Talks Much; Knows Little', *Variety*, 18 Nov 1925, 10.

"Adam Solitaire," a new: 'Exits and Entrances', *Oakland Tribune*, 5 Aug 1925, 8.

The Provincetown Playhouse: '"Adam Solitaire" at the Provincetown', *Brooklyn Standard Union*, 10 Nov 1925, 1925, 13.

The author is a: 'The Theater', *Messenger* 9, no. 5, May 1927, 157.

The author's name: Theophilus Lewis, 'They Call This Negro Drama', *Pittsburgh Courier*, 2 Apr 1927, M1.

The identity of Em Jo: 'Little Theaters', *Variety*, 26 Apr 1923, 14.

There is still: Walter M. Oestreicher, 'Lobby Gossip', *Brooklyn Daily Times*, 8 Nov 1925, 16.

When the final: 'The Play', *NYT*, 7 Nov 1925, 19.

To detail: R. Dana Skinner, 'Adam Solitaire', *Commonweal*, 18 Nov 1925, 51.

Adam is accused: 'Adam Solitaire', *Drama Calendar* 8, no. 15, Jan 1926, 3.

He suffered almost: Burns Mantle, ed., *The Best Plays of 1925–6*, New York: Dodd, Mead & Co., 1926, 489.

The settings form: 'Adam Solitaire', *Drama Calendar*, 3.

There is one: 'Broadway in Play Boom', *Freeport Daily Review*, 18 Nov 1925.

Here is a play: 'Adam Solitaire', *Drama Calendar*, 3.

The impression: Dixie Hines, 'Review of the Rialto', *Deseret News*, 21 Nov 1925, 19.

Personally, I found: R. Dana Skinner, 'Rumors of Better Things', *Independent*, 19 Dec 1925, 713.

"Adam Solitaire" will delight: 'Drama', *Brooklyn Standard Union*, 13.

The author is a man: Oestreicher, 'Lobby Gossip', *Brooklyn Daily Times*, 16.

The play is either: '"Adam Solitaire" at Provincetown Playhouse', *New York Herald Tribune*, Nov 7 1925, 12.

Whether Em Jo Basshe: 'New Plays on Broadway', *Billboard*, 14 Nov 1925, 10.

Now how far: 'Adam Solitaire', *Drama Calendar*, 3.

A happy experience: Mordecai Gorelik, *Toward a Larger Theatre*, Maryland: University Press of America, 1988, 6.

When I realized: H. L. Mencken, *The American Language*, New York: Alfred A. Knopf, 1937, 518.

I predict formally: H. L. Mencken to Em Jo Basshe, 17 Aug 1935, personal collection of Jo Atkinson.

Little of the work: Aben Kandel, 'Em Jo Basshe: A New Figure in the Drama of Contemporary America', publication unknown, personal collection of Jo Atkinson.

Em Jo Basshe told: Sender Garlin, "'The Centuries" Is a Play for Labor, says Em Jo Basshe', *New York Daily Worker*, 8 Dec 1927, 6.

One of the very: 'Em Jo Basshe: A Forceful Playwright', *JC*, 3 Aug 1928, 20–1.

That Em Jo Basshe: Kandel, 'Em Jo Basshe', personal collection.

Twenty years: 'Greenwich Village', *Variety*, 12 Oct 1927, 42.

Chapter 22

In 1925 Em's tragedy: Gorelik, *Toward a Larger Theatre*, 6.

Emjo was kept: Alexander King, 'Thanks to the Guggenheims!', *Brooklyn Daily Eagle*, 8 Apr 1934, 13.

Theirs was a: Bernard Smith, *A World Remembered, 1925–1950*, Atlantic Highlands, N.J.: Humanities Press, 1993, 16.

Em Jo has received: Gorelik Diaries 1926, Box 43, Folder 9, Mordecai Gorelik Papers, Southern Illinois University, Carbondale.

After the opening: Em Jo Basshe to Otto Kahn, 24 Nov 1926, Box 23, Folder 19, Otto H. Kahn Papers, Princeton University Library.

I have a medieval appreciation: quoted in Mary Jane Phillips-Matz, *The Many Lives of Otto Kahn*, New York: Pendragon Press, 1984, 272.

Otto Herman Kahn is: 'Personalities', *Jewish Criterion*, 27 Jan 1922, 38.

Mr. Kahn has his: quoted in Phillips-Matz, *The Many Lives of Otto Kahn*, 192.

Will you please ask: quoted in Lewis Brett Smiler, 'Was Thomas Edison anti-Semitic', https://edison.rutgers.edu/life-of-edison/essaying-edison accessed 02/03/2020.

Otto Kahn was my: Beverley Nichols, *All I Could Never Be*, London: Jonathan Cape, 1949, 111-2

I have met: Nichols, *The Star Spangled Manner*, London: Jonathan Cape, 1928, 171–2, 181.

I have never seen: Emil Ludwig, 'Ludwig Meets "New World Masters"', *Boston Advertiser*, 11 Mar 1928.

Artichokes, artichokes: Sergei Eisenstein, *Immoral Memories: An Autobiography*, Boston: Houghton Mifflin Co., 1983, 140-4.

Otto H. Kahn is known: Edgar Hay, 'Kahn Says Rich Owe Debt to Community', *Miami Herald*, 4 Mar 1928.

He looked more like: 'Personalities and Powers: Otto Kahn', *New Yorker*, 7 Apr 1922, 326.

On first impact: Alexander King, *Mine Enemy Grows Older*, New York: Simon and Schuster, 1958, 14–15.

"Ottokahn" so those: 'Our First Night Neighbors', *Theatre* 46, no. 319, Oct 1927.

There is about him: 'Portraits While You Wait', *New York Telegraph*, 24 Jun 1928.

By no means: 'Mr. Otto Kahn', *Daily Mail*, 25 May 1922.

German by birth: quoted in 'Life as a Boy Made Kahn Arts Patron', *NYT*, 18.

He is known: Clinton Gilbert, *The Mirrors of Wall Street*, New York: G. P. Putnam's Sons, 1933, 165.

Wall Street: Louis Levine, 'Otto H. Kahn's Views on the Vital Economic Problems Which the World at Large Faces', *New York World*, 22 Aug 1920.

Few Americans: quoted in 'Life as a Boy Made Kahn Arts Patron', *NYT*, 18.

He will drop: 'Otto Kahn', *New York World*, 27 Nov 1910.

He would far rather: 'Otto Kahn: A Paradox of Art Lover, Banker and Liberal', *Newsweek*, 1 Jul 1933, 17.

There can never: Alfred M. Frankfurter, 'A Tribute to Otto H. Kahn as Art Collector', *Art News*, 7 Apr 1934, 10.

Do not picture: quoted in 'Life as a Boy Made Kahn Arts Patron', *NYT*, 18.

Mr. Kahn's mind: Olin Downes, 'Kahn's Bold Fight Saved the Opera', *NYT*, 30 Mar 1934, 18.

There is another: Charles H. Joseph, 'Random Thoughts', *Detroit JC*, 4 Mar 1927, 7.

Coming away: 'Otto Kahn', *Newsweek*, 17.

He was a patron: Nichols, *All I Could Never Be*, 112.

There are millionaires: Harry Salpeter, 'Otto the Magnificent', *Outlook*, 4 Jul 1928.

Otto Kahn has done: Hay, 'Kahn Says Rich Owe Debt', *Miami Herald*.

For years, he has: Joseph, 'Random Thoughts', *Detroit JC*, 7.

Mr. Kahn may: 'A Financial Giant', *Huntington Long Islander*, 21 Apr 1922.

He is an actor: Herbert Knight Cruickshank, 'The Great Kahn', *Theatre*, Nov 1929, 26.

If the doctrine: 'Otto H. Kahn Wrote Plays When a Boy', *NYT*, 13 Feb 1922, 10.

I came to this country: Otto H. Kahn, *Of Many Things*, New York: Boni & Liveright, 1926, 23.

I was asked the other: Kahn, 'Leisure and Art', *Peabody Journal of Education* 6, no. 3, Nov. 1928, 133–4.

In the course: 'The Theatre's Hope in This Country', *NYT*, 14 Feb 1915, 5.

We all, rich and poor: Kahn, *Of Many Things*, 26.

What both men and women: 'The Theatre's Hope', *NYT*, 5.

In this vast country: Kahn, *Of Many Things*, 17, 97–103.

Chapter 23

In 1926 I received: Michael Gold, 'My Life' transcript, *T-CLP (Gold, Michael), Billy Rose Theatre Division, New York Public Library for the Performing Arts, Astor, Lenox and Tilden Foundations.

I think it was: Interview transcript, Aug–Nov 1966, Box 8, Mike Gold and Mike Folsom Papers, University of Michigan Library.

Dear Mr. Gold: Kahn to Gold, 14 Jan 1927, Correspondence, Box 2, Gold Papers, University of Michigan Library.

Mike Gold is a Hungarian: Carleton Beals, *Glass Houses*, New York: J. B. Lippincott Co., 1938, 35.

Mike was dark-eyed: quoted in Aaron Daniel, *Writers on the Left*, Oxford; New York: Oxford University Press, 1977, 86.

He affected dirty: ibid.

He was liked: Beals, *Glass Houses*, 35–6.

He had shaggy: Charles Shipman, *It Had to Be Revolution*, Ithaca: Cornell University Press, 1993, 42.

As a lad: Lewis Mumford, *Sketches from Life*, New York: Dial Press, 1982, 20.

I was eighteen: Dorothy Day, 'On Pilgrimage', *Catholic Worker*, Jan 1977, 6.

I was born: Michael Folsom, ed., *Mike Gold: A Literary Anthology*, New York: International Publishers, 1972, 64–5.

I can never forget: Gold, *Jews without Money*, New York: Horace Liveright, Inc, 1930, 13–14.

There was always somebody: Gold, 'Jews without Money', *New Masses*, Jun 1928, 11–12.

The Civil War was still: Gold, *The Mike Gold Reader*, New York: International Publishers of New York, 1954, 183.

I was born: Gold, 'Notes of the Month', *New Masses*, Jan 1930, 6.

In 1926, Mike Gold: John Howard Lawson, 'Rebellion in the Twenties', Parts VI–VII, John Howard Lawson Papers, Southern Illinois University, 306.

We stood nervously: ibid., 132–3.

Em Jo wore old: ibid., 307.

The awaited moment: ibid., 136.

Dos, writing from Europe: ibid., 313.

I like to remember: Malcolm Cowley, 'Dos Passos: The Learned Poggius', *Southern Review*, 1 Jan 1973, 3.

I met Dos Passos once: Sinclair Lewis, 'Manhattan at Last!', *Saturday Review*, 5 Dec 1925, 361, in Barry Maine, ed., *John Dos Passos: The Critical Heritage*, London & New York: Routledge, 2005, 65.

I met Dos Passos because: 'MacLeish Recalls Twenties, Lost Generation', *Bowdoin Orient*, 25 Oct 1974, 6.

Dos rarely recognized: Beals, *Glass Houses*, 24–6.

Dos is so shy: Max Eastman, *Love and Revolution: My Journey through an Epoch*, New York: Random House, 1964, 141.

Though still in his twenties: Cowley, 'Dos Passos', 3.

Often I wondered: Beals, *Glass Houses*, 247.

In *Manhattan Transfer*: Lewis, 'Manhattan at Last!', 361.

It is the best: D. H. Lawrence, 'Review', *Calendar of Modern Letters*, Apr 1927, 70–2, in Maine, ed., *Dos Passos*, 71.

I can still feel: Mary Ross, 'Review', *New York Herald Tribune Books*, 23 Feb 1930, 3–4, in Maine, ed., *Dos Passos*, 77.

This novel flies: Gold, 'Review', *New Masses*, Aug 1926, 25–6, in Maine, ed., *Dos Passos*, 69.

I had come back: John Dos Passos, *The Best Times: An Informal Memoir*, New York: The New American Library, 1966, 130.

I was fresh: quoted in George A. Knox, Herbert M. Stahl, *Dos Passos and 'The Revolting Playwrights'*, 25.

Four directors: Dos Passos, *The Best Times*, 164.

Chapter 24

Five rebellious young: 'The Young Radicals', *St Louis Daily Globe-Democrat*, 13 Mar 1927.

The organization: 'Broadway after Dark', *New York Sun*, 7 Feb 1927, 22.

They are Em Jo: Larry Barretto, 'The New Yorker', *Bookman*, May 1927, 332.

Most of our art theaters: Gold, 'White Hope of American Drama', *New York Sun*, 1 Mar 1927.

We have the theatre: John Howard Lawson, 'On "Processional"', *NYT*, 1 Feb 1925, 152.

The New Playwrights' Theater: Gold, 'Loud Speaker & Other Essays', *New Masses*, Mar 1927, 6.

It will insist: Emjo Basshe, 'Theatre, Mass and Machine', *Daily Worker*, 29 Mar 1927, M8.

The theatre is not: Francis Edwards Faragoh, 'The Peep-Show Is Doomed', *Chicago Daily Worker*, 12 Mar 1927.

Theories, iron, dynasties: Emjo Basshe, 'The Revolt in Fifty-Second Street', *NYT*, 27 Feb 1927, 145.

Emjo was the stormy: quoted in Knox, Stahl, *Dos Passos and 'The Revolting Playwrights'*, 59.

Well kid: quoted in Rena Sanderson, Sandra Spanier and Robert W. Trogdon, eds, *The Letters of Ernest Hemingway*, New York: Cambridge University Press, 3:491.

I'm in deeper: quoted in Townsend Ludington, ed., *The Fourteenth Chronicle: Letters and Diaries of John Dos Passos*, 368.

As soon as the drama: Sanderson et al., eds, *Letters of Hemingway*, 3:491.

The work that appealed: John Dos Passos, 'Looking Back on "U.S.A."', *NYT*, 25 Oct 1959, 431.

The group leased: Edward Eliscu and David Eliscu, *With or without a Song: A Memoir*, Lanham, Maryland, London: Scarecrow Press, 2001, 88.

Chapter 25

The enterprise started: quoted in Donald Pizer, ed., *John Dos Passos: The Major Nonfictional Prose*, Detroit: Wayne State University Press, 1988, 112.

Maybe I'm prejudiced: Gold, 'White Hope of American Drama', *New York Sun*.

The first production: John Howard Lawson, *Film: The Creative Process*, New York: Hill and Wang, 1964, 101.

I was numb: Lawson, 'Rebellion in the Twenties', Lawson Papers, SIU, 330.

"Loud Speaker" is a satirical: Harbor Allen, 'The Voodoo Orgy of Election', *Chicago Daily Worker*, 5 Mar 1927, 8.

The plot: quoted in Gerald Horne, *The Final Victim of the Blacklist*, Berkeley: University of California Press, 2006, 45.

It is a play: 'The Play', *Weekly People*, 16 Apr 1927.

"Loud Speaker" was staged: Alexander Woollcott, 'Second Thoughts on First Nights', *Hartford Courant*, 13 Mar 1927.

I designed: Mordecai Gorelik, 'Up from Burlesque', *New York Evening Post*, 8 Oct 1932.

The seats pitch: J. Brooks Atkinson, 'The Play', *NYT*, 20 Oct 1927, 33.

True, in "Loud Speaker": Barretto, 'The New Yorker', *Bookman*, 332.

It is beyond: Dixie Hines, 'Review of the Rialto', *Wilmington Morning News*, 11 Mar 1927.

It was fairly natural: Dos Passos, 'Did the New Playwrights Theatre Fail?', *New Masses*, Aug 1929, 13.

For the second: quoted in Pizer, ed., *Dos Passos*, 112.

New Playwrights: 'New Playwrights Theatre Find New Home in Greenwich Village', *Chicago Daily Worker*, 26 Aug 1927.

The tunnel-shaped: Dos Passos, 'Towards a Revolutionary Theatre', *New Masses*, Dec 1927, 20.

The New Playwrights was: Alan Reed and Ben Ohmart, *Yabba Dabba Doo!: The Alan Reed Story*, Albany: BearManor Media, 2009, 44.

Five New Playwrights: John Anderson, 'Putting the Authors to Work: Five New Playwrights Take Their Hammers in Hand and Do a Little Carpentry', *New York Evening Post*, 29 Oct 1927, 8.

Hem – I am busy: quoted in Ludington, ed., *Fourteenth Chronicle*, 372.

For God's sake: Quoted in Virginia Spencer-Carr, *Dos Passos: A Life*, Garden City, New York: Doubleday, 1984, 252.

Chapter 26

Variety is the spice: 'Basshe's Latest', *Brooklyn Daily Eagle*, 13 Nov 1927, 63.

Em Jo Basshe's play: 'The New Play', *Brooklyn Daily Times*, 30 Nov 1937.

It was rather: T. J. O'Flaherty, 'Current Events', *New York Daily Worker*, 22 Oct 1927, 10.

I saw him: John Anderson, 'Angels Rush In', *Town & Country*, Sep 1938, 42.

Smiles and whispers: 'Our First Night Neighbors', *Theatre* 46, no. 319, Oct 1927.

A cynical: 'New Playwrights Score a Hit: Em Jo Basshe's "The Centuries" Brings Laughs and Sobs', *New York Daily Worker*, 1 Dec 1927, 4.

The plight: 'The New Play', *Brooklyn Daily Times*.

The play portrays: 'The Play', *Weekly People*, 10 Dec 1927.

The dramatist has: Kelcey Allen, 'Amusements: 'The Centuries' Spans Jewish Life in Ghetto', *Women's Wear Daily*, 30 Nov 1927, 8.

One's interest: 'American Stage', *The Stage*, 22 Dec 1927, 22.

Characters come and go: 'News of Books', *Sacramento Bee*, 17 Jul 1928.

The set is built: 'The Play', *Weekly People*.

John Dos Passos shares: 'New Playwrights Score a Hit', *New York Daily Worker*, 4.

The steep, imaginative: Gilbert Gabriel, 'Last Night's First Night', *New York Sun*, 30 Nov 1927.

The actors even: 'The Play', *Weekly People*.

The author knows: 'The Tragedies of New York's East Side', *Detroit JC*, 25 Apr 1930, 11.

The stir: 'A Revolutionary Theatre', *New Masses*, Mar 1928, 22.

As for the name: 'The Play', *Weekly People*.

The hope is: Kelcey Allen, 'Amusements', *Women's Wear Daily*, 8.

One finds: 'American Stage', *Stage*, 22.

It has a massy: Gabriel, 'Last Night's First Night', *New York Sun*.

It is possible: 'News of Books', *Sacramento Bee*.

"The Centuries" is not: 'American Stage', *Stage*, 22.

For me, *The Centuries:* Lawson, 'Rebellion in the Twenties', Lawson Papers, SIU, 360.

It stirred my soul: quoted in Gary Carr, 'John Howard Lawson: Hollywood Craftsmanship and Censorship in the 1930s', *ICarbS* 3, no. 1, Jan 1976, 43.

As I watched: Lawson, 'Rebellion in the Twenties', Lawson Papers, SIU, 360.

Chapter 27

Down in: "'The International" Full of "Realism"', *NYT*, 16 Jan 1928, 24.

"The International" seemed: Alexander Woollcott, 'The Stage', *New York World*, 16 Jan 1928.

We would have: 'Two on the Aisle', *New York Evening Post*, 21 Jan 1928, 10.

The International may: Robert Benchley, 'Drama', *Life*, 2 Feb 1928, 21.

The International, I feel: quoted in Pizer, ed., *Dos Passos*, 112.

No one: Lawson, 'Rebellion in the Twenties', Lawson Papers, SIU, 368.

Otto Kahn was: Lawson, *Film: The Creative Process*, 101.

He understood: Lawson, 'Rebellion in the Twenties', Lawson Papers, SIU, 176–7.

One evening: Lawson, 'Rebellion in the Twenties', Lawson Papers, SIU, 370.

The "New Playwrights,": 'The Play', *Weekly People*, 19 Jan 1929.

Next season: quoted in Pizer, ed., *Dos Passos*, 112.

"Singing Jailbirds" dramatizes: Thomas H. Dickinson, *Playwrights of the New American Theater*, New York: Books for Libraries Press, 315.

The prisoner's delirious: Donald Mulhern, 'The New Play', *Brooklyn Standard Union*, 6 Dec 1928, 39.

Whether or not: 'Singing Jailbirds', *Brooklyn Daily Eagle*, 5 Dec 1928, 33.

The New Playwrights: 'In the Theatres on Broadway', *Brooklyn Daily Star*, 20 Feb 1929, 20.

It was the name: St. John Ervine, 'The New Play', *Brooklyn Daily Times*, 22 Feb 1929.

The critics guillotined: quoted in Ludington, *John Dos Passos: A Twentieth Century Odyssey*, New York: E. P. Dutton, 1980, 276.

By the end: Smith, *A World Remembered*, 16.

Considering the intellectual: J. Brooks Atkinson, 'Village Mumming', *NYT*, 26 Feb 1928, 105.

Smashing dramatic: Walter Pritchard Eaton, 'Here Are Plays', *New York Herald Tribune*, 5 Feb 1928.

The playwrights have: Stark Young, 'Playwrights and Causes', *New Republic*, 16 May 1928, 382.

The critics went: quoted in Pizer, ed., *Dos Passos*, 112.

We were submitted: Gold, 'Notes of the Month', *New Masses*, Jan 1930, 6.

This paragraph: 'Beyond the Bridge', *Brooklyn Daily Times*, 29 Apr 1929.

Chapter 28

The New Playwrights Give Up: Charles Vale Harrison, 'The New Playwrights Give Up the Struggle', *New York Evening Post*, 27 Apr 1929.

New Playwrights Abandon: 'New Playwrights Abandon Productions', *NYT*, 26 Apr 1929, 35.

Jo Basshe Quits: 'Jo Basshe Quits; Village Theatre Ends Existence', *New York Daily News*, 26 Apr 1929, 52.

Of the theatre's: 'New Playwrights Abandon Productions', *NYT*, 35.

Basshe and Faragoh: Lawson, 'Rebellion in the Twenties', Lawson Papers, SIU, 383.

It is a pity: Basshe to Kahn, 6 Mar 1929, Box 23, Folder 19, Kahn Papers, Princeton University Library.

The theatre didn't: David Sanders, 'John Dos Passos, The Art of Fiction no. 44', *Paris Review*, Spring 1969.

I was by nature: Dos Passos, 'Looking Back on "U.S.A."', *NYT*, 431.

I lived in: Sanders, 'Dos Passos', *Paris Review*.

The New Playwrights got: Dos Passos, *The Best Times*, 169.

I've forgotten: Dos Passos, 'Old Hem', *Sports Illustrated*, 29 Jun 1964, 60.

I arrived worn: Dos Passos, *The Best Times*, 197–201.

Am down here: quoted in Ludington, ed., *Fourteenth Chronicle*, 391.

Chapter 29

Miss Doris Troutman: 'Miss Doris Troutman Married in New York', *Marion Progress*, 29 Aug 1929, 1.

I got married: Basshe to Kahn, 27 Aug 1929, Kahn Papers, Princeton University Library.

In January a child: Basshe to Kahn, 17 Dec 1929, Kahn Papers, Princeton University Library.

Chapter 30

Wife of New York: 'Wife of New York Producer Visits Here', *Asheville Citizen-Times*, 17 Feb 1933, 6.

Chapter 31

Look how fat: Emjo Basshe, *Doomsday Circus: A Dramatic Chronicle*, New York: Contemporary Play Publishing, 1938, quoted in Irene Hoch, ed., *Day by Day with American Playwrights*, Modesto: Adobe Press, 1936, 59–60.

Chapter 34

Emjo Basshe, the playwright: 'Between Ourselves', *New Masses*, 31 Oct 1939, 4.

A week ago: 'Emjo Basshe', *New Masses*, 7 Nov 1939, 20.

Emjo Basshe, noted: 'Emjo Basshe Dead', *Hollywood Reporter*, 31 Oct 1939, 1.

Emjo Basshe Dead: 'Emjo Basshe Dead; Playwright Was 40', *NYT*, 29 Oct 1939, 40.

To the Editor: 'Letters', *Drama Review* 17, no. 1, Mar 1973, 150.

PART THREE

Chapter 35

Special branch: Nationality and Naturalisation: Jochelman, David Salomon, 1921, HO 144/1687/405772, National Archives, Kew.

Mr. Zangwill was the chief: 'Zangwill on Weizmann', *JC*, 27 Feb 1920, 18.

Chapter 36

London Jewry: '30,000 Jews March against Nazi Terror', *Daily Herald*, 20 Jul 1933, 4.

In Stepney: 'London Jews Big Protest', *Western Gazette*, 21 Jul 1933, 16.

Every shop: 'Nazi Arrests Reply to Jewish Parade', *Sheffield Independent*, 21 Jul 1933, 1.

Nearly every Jewish: 'Monster Jewish Protest Demonstration', *JC*, 11 Oct 1912, 38.

The ascension to power: David Jochelman, 'A Manifesto', London: United Jewish Protest Committee, 1933. Shapell Center, United States Holocaust Memorial Museum.

The main contingent: '30,000 Jews March against Nazi Terror', *Daily Herald*, 4.

London Jews Hold: 'London Jews Hold Anti-Nazi Parade', *NYT*, 21 Jul 1933, 4.

Immediately prior: 'Jewish Protest', *JC*, 38.

The long trek: 'The Great Protest Demonstration', *JC*, 28 Jul 1933, 20.

Bearded old men: 'London Jews Hold Anti-Nazi Parade', *NYT*, 4.

Huge crowds: 'Huge Protest Is Staged by London Jewry', *B'nai B'rith Messenger*, 28 Jul 1933, 1.

The leaders carried: 'Nazi Arrests Reply to Jewish Parade', *Sheffield Independent*, 1.

The British public: 'Great Protest', *JC*, 20.

The sun beat: 'Demonstration by Jews', *The Times*, 21 Jul 1933, 13.

The average: 'Jewish Protest Demonstration', *Scotsman*, 21 Jul 1933, 8.

Speakers addressed: 'Huge Protest', *B'nai B'rith Messenger*, 1.

Dr. Jochelman said: 'Great Protest', *JC*, 20.

The news of this: 'The Jews' March', *Daily Herald*, 21 Jul 1933, 6.

The procession: 'Great Protest', *JC*, 20.

Nazi Arrests: 'Nazi Arrests Reply to Jewish Parade', *Sheffield Independent*, 1.

This unhappy outbreak: Collinson Owen, 'It Happened', *Sunday Mirror*, 23 Jul 1933, 6.

Chapter 37

And the Stars: Charles Landstone, 'Some Recent Novels', *JC*, 29 Oct 1937, 7.

Fanny Jocelyn conceals: 'Theatre', *JC*, 12 Feb 1937, 51.

To David: Fanny Jocelyn, *And the Stars Laughed*, London: Fortune Press, 1937.

The book has: 'A Willesden Author', *Marylebone Mercury*, 21 Aug 1937, 5.

Gerald Doncastle: Phyllis Bentley, 'Books', *Yorkshire Post*, 18 Aug 1937, 6.

Fanny Jocelyn, known: 'A Willesden Author', *Marylebone Mercury*, 5.

Miss Jocelyn writes: Bentley, 'Books', *Yorkshire Post*, 6.

Chapter 38

No more gallant: Sir Ronald Storrs, *The Memoirs of Sir Ronald Storrs*, New York: G. P. Putnam's Sons, 1937, 440.

At this time: quoted in Joseph B. Schechtman, *The Vladimir Jabotinsky Story*, 2:259.

The whippy little: Edwin C. Hill, 'The Human Side of the News: Jabotinsky the Leader', *Peekskill Evening Star*, 13 Nov 1940, 4.

He was, when: Arthur Koestler, *Arrow in the Blue*, London: The Macmillan Company, 1952, 140.

Jabotinsky, the passionate: Weizmann, *Trial and Error*, 86.

There was in him: quoted in Schechtman, *The Jabotinsky Story*, 2:248.

Vladimir Jabotinsky came: Pierre van Paassen, 'As I Remember Him', in Vladimir Jabotinsky, *The War and the Jew*, New York: The Dial Press, 1942, 12.

I was captivated: van Paassen, 'Vladimir Jabosinky: A Reminiscence', in Shlomo Katz, ed., *The Midstream Reader*, New York: T. Yoseloff, 1960, 289.

I have heard: Arthur Koestler, *Arrow in the Blue*, 143.

Listening to him: Benzion Olsfanger, 'Memories of Ze'ev Jabotinsky', private collection of Sharon Klaff

He has a: quoted in Schechtman, *The Jabotinsky Story*, 2:42.

There was a kind: quoted in Alice S. Nakhimovsky, *Russian-Jewish Literature and Identity*, Baltimore: Johns Hopkins University Press, 1992, 45.

In the ghettos: William B. Ziff, *The Rape of Palestine*, New York: Longmans, Green & Co., 1938, 173–4.

I do not think: van Paassen, 'Jabosinky', in Katz, ed., *The Midstream Reader*, 279.

His speeches at: Weizmann, *Trial and Error*, 86.

The very term: Schechtman, *The Jabotinsky Story*, 2:178.

Zionism has lost: quoted in ibid., 2:149.

We Revisionists: ibid, 2:214–19.

It is for three: quoted in Benzion Netanyahu, *The Founding Fathers of Zionism*, Jerusalem: Balfour Books, 229–30.

Mass evacuation: Jabotinksy, *The War and the Jew*, 124.

Do not think: quoted in Schechtman, *The Jabotinsky Story*, 2:338–46.

We are facing: quoted in Rick Richman, *Racing against History*, New York: Encounter Books, 2017.

Destruction. Learn: quoted in Katz, *Lone Wolf*, 2:1718.

He never lived: Louis Lipsky, *Memoirs in Profile*, Philadelphia: Jewish Publication Society of America, 1975, 154.

Chapter 39

When the war broke: Hugh Cockerell, interview by Zoe Endacott, c. 1990, personal collection of Lolly Seager.

The Jew wants: Jabotinsky, 'Speech to Betar Formation', 31 Mar 1940, A-1 8/58, Jabotinsky Institute, Tel Aviv.

Our starting point: quoted in Amnon Rubinstein, *The Zionist Dream Revisited*, New York: Schocken Books, 1984, 4.

Seven months went by: interview by Endacott, collection of Lolly Seager.

Chapter 40

Immediately before this: 'Death of Dr. David Jochelman', *JC*, 11 Jul 1941, 4.

London, July 10: 'Dr. David Jochelman', *NYT*, 11 Jul 1931, 14.

Dr Jochelman, who: 'Death of Dr. David Jochelman', *JC*, 4.

Dr. Jochelman felt that: Speech delivered by Edith Zangwill at Jochelman memorial meeting, 1941, Zangwill Papers, A120\209, Central Zionist Archives.

Mrs. Zangwill recalled: 'Jochelman Trust Fund', *JC*, 15 Aug 1941, 8.

He had a fund: 'The Late Dr. Jochelman', *JC*, 25 Jul 1941, 20.

Because of my age: interview by Endacott, collection of Lolly Seager.

I went round: Joan Snow to Len Snow, 25 Dec 1945, personal collection of Sue Dorman.

Chapter 43

My dear: Annie Bach to Tamara Bach, 14 Oct 1944, personal collection of the author.

Chapter 47

It is quite impossible: Lillian Winstanley, 'Nationality and Palestine', *Welsh Gazette*, 4 Jul 1946, 4.

The Jews, the eleven: Wyndham Deedes, Maude Royden and Ronald Storrs, 'The Future of Palestine', *Listener*, 1 Nov 1945.

No one who: quoted in 'Gen. Morgan Asked to Resign', *Lancashire Daily Post*, 4 Jan 1946, 1.

The Jewish life: 'Life-Line of Judaism', *JC*, 9 Mar 1945, 10.

For the great: quoted in 'Morgan Not Coming to London', *Western Daily Press*, 7 Jan 1946, 1.

Is it fair: Thomas Horder, 'A Home for the Jews', *The Times*, 22 Sep 1945, 5.

There can scarcely: 'Palestine', *The Times*, 15 Aug 1945, 5.

The principal difficulty: Nevill Barbour, *Nisi Dominus*, London: George G. Harrap & Co., 1946, 149.

Had the situation: 'Palestine', *The Times*, 5.

No case: Carey Lord, 'Letters to the Editor: The Arab Case', *Clitheroe Advertiser and Times*, 9 Jul 1948, 2.

The strongest sentiment: 'Jerusalem', *Nottingham Journal*, 15 Feb 1949, 2.

If Hitler had: 'War of Aggression', *Truth*, 30 Apr 1948, 2.

It must: Henry Norman Smith, 'What Must Be Done Now in Palestine', *Nottingham Journal*, 30 Sep 1948, 2.

The Nazi empire: 'A Second Exodus', *Dundee Courier*, 4 Jan 1946, 2.

The most useful: 'Palestine Interval', *The Times*, 4 Oct 1946, 5.

No one can imagine: Winston Churchill, HC Deb, 1 Aug 1946, *Hansard*, vol. 425, col. 1252.

No power: John Squire, 'A Reasoned Summing-Up of the Palestine Problem', *Illustrated London News*, 7 Sep 1946, 21.

Is it too much: Thomas Comyn-Platt, 'Homes for the Jews', *Daily Telegraph*, 30 Oct 1945, 4.

If the United States: 'Conflict in Palestine', *The Times*, 19 Nov 1945, 5.

There is still: 'The First Step', *Daily Mail*, 1 Aug 1946.

Let us then: Maude Royden Shaw, 'A Home for the Jews: To the Editor of the Times', *The Times*, 5 Oct 1945, 5.

The Christian: Harold Reinhart, 'A Home for the Jews: To the Editor of the Times', *The Times*, 26 Oct 1945, 5.

We have to: Charles Graves, 'How the Arabs View the Palestine Problem', *Sphere*, 4 Oct 1947, 28.

There is little: 'Conflict in Palestine', *The Times*, 5.

Perhaps it is: 'The Jewish Outrages', *Aberdeen Press and Journal*, 2 Jul 1946, 2.

The most unquenchable: 'Verdict on the Mandate', *Scotsman*, 6 Aug 1947, 4.

British rule: John Hall, 'An Impossible Task', *Daily Mail*, 14 May 1948.

A whole generation: 'Palestine: The End of the Chapter', *Evening Standard*, 14 May 1948, 2.

The Mandate: 'Facing Realities in Palestine', *Sunday Mirror*, 21 Sep 1947, 8.

From that day: J. L. Garvin, 'Compromise or Chaos in Palestine', *Daily Telegraph*, 8 Aug 1946, 4.

If the Mandate: Quintin Hogg, 'Shall We Quit Palestine?', *Weekly Dispatch*, 14 Sep 1947, 4.

In 1939: 'Not Our Quarrel', *Daily Mail*, 1 Oct 1945.

Britain was attacked: 'Palestine', *Halifax Evening Courier*, 15 May 1948, 2.

Arabs and Jews: Hogg, 'Shall We Quit Palestine?', *Weekly Dispatch*, 4.

When we undertook: Edward Spears, 'Crux of Palestine Problem', *Daily Telegraph*, 8 Oct 1945, 4.

The two sides: 'Not Our Quarrel', *Daily Mail*.

Above all: Garvin, 'Compromise or Chaos in Palestine', *Daily Telegraph*, 4.

A question larger: 'Not Our Quarrel', *Daily Mail*.

What right: Hogg, 'Shall We Quite Palestine?' *Weekly Dispatch*, 4.

British Military: 'British Military H.Q. Blown Up', *Gloucester Citizen*, 22 Jul 1946, 1.

The limit: 'Danger Ahead', *Daily Telegraph*, 11 Mar 1948, 4.

Mr. Churchill came: 'The Task of Britain in Palestine', *The Times*, 2 Aug 1946, 4.

Mr. Winston Churchill: 'Britain May Abandon Her Task in Palestine', *Daily Mail*, 2 Aug 1946.

The handling: Winston Churchill, HC Deb, 1 Aug 1946, *Hansard*, vol. 425, col. 1252.

Three decades: Henry Brandon, 'Onus Now on United States', *Sunday Times*, 28 Sep 1947, 1.

Britain, as a: 'Palestine: The End of the Chapter', *Evening Standard*, 2.

For those who: Leonard J. Stein, 'The End of a Chapter', *JC*, 14 May 1948, 11.

After 27 years: 'End of a Chapter', *Hull Daily Mail*, 15 May 1948, 3.

History will call: 'The Holy Places', *Sunday Times*, 27 Mar 1948, 4.

Farewell to Zion: 'Farewell to Zion', *Truth*, 21 May 1948, 7.

The Jews: 'The Palestine Exodus', *Coventry Evening Telegraph*, 12 May 1948, 4.

What will happen: 'New Crusade Needed to Save the Holy Land', *Belfast Telegraph*, 3 May 1948, 4.

There is now: 'Crisis in Palestine', *The Times*, 28 Apr 1948, 5.

When British: 'New Plan for Palestine', *Sunday Times*, 21 Mar 1948, 4.

Many Jews now: 'Jews Confident in Palestine', *The Times*, 6 May 1948, 4.

In a few: L. S. Amery, 'British Policy in Palestine', *The Times*, 14 May 1948, 5.

As the Union: J. L. Hays, 'Palestine', *Sunday Sun*, 16 May 1948, 2.

Jews Proclaim: 'Jews Proclaim "New Israel" As We Quit Today', *Shields Daily News*, 14 May 1948, 2.

Jews in Tel Aviv: 'Jews Proclaim the New State', *Yorkshire Evening Post*, 14 May 1948, 1.

The simple ceremony: 'The Jewish State Born', *Manchester Guardian*, 15 May 1948, 5.

The hall was packed: Zeev Sharef, *Three Days*, trans. Julian Louis Meltzer, Garden City, New York: Doubleday, 1962, 281–8.

Jews all over: 'Salute to the New Israel', *JC*, 21 May 1948, 10.

American Jews: 'Palestine: Mr. Truman Surprises U.N.', *Leicester Evening Mail*, 15 May 1948, 4.

Tomorrow, a new: 'May 15', *JC*, 14 May 1948, 10.

Immigration begins: 'Immigration Begins', *Sunderland Daily Echo*, 15 May 1948, 1.

The Jewish people: quoted in 'Dream Comes True', *Belfast News-Letter*, 15 May 1948, 5.

Can it be true: Shlomo Z. Shragai, 'For Jews a Dream Becomes Reality', *Daily Mail*, 15 May 1948.

While the founding: Gordon Waterfield, 'Progress in the Middle East', *Civil & Military Gazette*, 20 Oct 1949, 2.

For six months: 'Arab Refugees', *Manchester Evening News*, 25 Mar 1949, 2.

Arab women: 'Palestine Picture one of Chaos', *Civil & Military Gazette*, 20 Apr 1948, 8.

They came: Andrew Hurst, 'A Million Arabs are Facing Extinction', *Coventry Evening Telegraph*, 5 Aug 1949, 6.

In most: Richard Crossman, 'My Report on the State of Israel', *Sunday Mirror*, 9 Jan 1949, 6.

The problem: 'Plight of Arab Refugees', *The Scotsman*, 22 Sep 1948, 5.

The once: J. L. Hays, 'Arab D.P.s – Whose Problem Are They?' *Aberdeen Press and Journal*, 24 Mar 1949, 2.

It is one: 'Appeal', *London Daily News*, 22 Mar 1949, 2.

Jews should: Victor Gollancz, 'Arab Refugees', *The Times*, 13 Aug 1948, 5.

Bewildered: Hays, 'Arab D.P.s', *Aberdeen Press and Journal*, 2.

Afterword

Five minutes spent: 'Zangwill on Dreyfus', *Washington Times*, 11 Sep 1899, 2.

He strays about: 'Zangwill's Personality', *American Hebrew*, 1 Feb 1895, 381.

In my family: Olia Hercules interviewed by Davide G. Martins, *Turning Chickens and Breaking Dishes* (podcast), 31 Jul 2020.

Was he one: Frederick Whyte, 'A Bachelor's London: Memories of the Day before Yesterday, 1889–1914', London: G. Richards, 1931, 179.

If Zangwill had: Robert Lynd, 'Novelist of the Ghetto', *London Daily News*, 2 Aug 1926, 6.

He confessed: Jerome K. Jerome, *My Life and Times*, London: Hodder and Stoughton, 1926, 118.